GOVERNING
WASHINGTON

GOVERNING WASHINGTON

Politics and Government in the Evergreen State

Edited by
Cornell W. Clayton
and
Nicholas P. Lovrich

Washington State University Press
Pullman, Washington

Washington State University Press
PO Box 645910
Pullman, Washington 99164-5910
Phone: 800-354-7360
Fax: 509-335-8568
Email: wsupress@wsu.edu
Website: wsupress.wsu.edu

Library of Congress Cataloging-in-Publication Data

Governing Washington : politics and government in the Evergreen State / edited by Cornell W. Clayton and Nicholas P. Lovrich.
    p. cm.
  Includes bibliographical references.
  ISBN 978-0-87422-308-8 (alk. paper)
1. Washington (State)--Politics and government--1951-   I. Clayton, Cornell W., 1960- II. Lovrich, Nicholas P.
  JK9216.G66 2011
  320.4797--dc23

                                                        2011038635

Fine Quality Books from the Pacific Northwest

Table of Contents

Foley Institute Sponsorship

F OR MANY YEARS the spotlight of American politics has been on Washington, D.C., but in recent years American states have reemerged as powerful centers of political change and policy innovation. Understanding the institutions and dynamics of state politics has never been more critical.

Governing Washington offers a rich and absorbing look into the continuing experiment with self-government in the Evergreen State—the 'other' Washington. From its Populist and Progressive era roots through today's shifting demographic trends, vast interest group system, and changing media coverage of state political leaders, the chapters in this volume provide insightful portraits of the state's most important political institutions and processes. It will be of interest to students of government and casual readers alike, and is a must-read for anyone wishing to understand political life in the Evergreen State.

Governing Washington is the fifth volume in a series of books dedicated to Washington government and politics published by the WSU Press. The four predecessors include *Washington State Government and Politics* (2004), edited by Cornell W. Clayton, Lance T. LeLoup, and Nicholas P. Lovrich; *Government and Politics in the Evergreen State* (1992), edited by David C. Nice, John C. Pierce, and Charles H. Sheldon; *Political Life in Washington: Governing the Evergreen State* (1985), edited by Thor Swanson, William F. Mullen, John C. Pierce, and Charles H. Sheldon; and *The Government and Politics of Washington State* (1978), edited by William F. Mullen, John C. Pierce, Charles H. Sheldon, and Thor Swanson. This new volume provides fresh and updated information and analysis from top political authorities and commentators.

The Thomas S. Foley Institute for Public Policy and Public Service is a proud sponsor of this volume. The Foley Institute at Washington State University honors the service of Thomas S. Foley, former Speaker of the U.S. House of Representatives and U.S. Ambassador to Japan. The institute promotes public service, supports public policy research, and fosters education on public affairs. As part of its mission, it is pleased to be part of publishing this important volume.

Foreword

Washington State's story is a rich, sometimes quirky work in progress, always evolving with a restlessness and a creative urge that has characterized our history in the Northwest corner of the nation. Our story is deeply personal, reflecting our sense of place, influenced by our political and tribal heritage, our melting-pot and egalitarian roots, our conflicted notions about the role of government and limits on power, and our Old West sense that "ordinary" citizens must always have a central role in the drama of self-government.

This complex and nuanced view is fitting, given the state's traditions of self-reliance and rugged individualism on the one hand, and our profound instinct that we are called to collaborate and run the government for the common good on the other. We bring to the task a spunky pioneer spirit, zeal for innovation and invention, and mindfulness of our obligations to this place and to each other. Many of the issues we confront, such as environmental protection, economic development, the proper role of government, and equality and access to opportunity, as this volume notes, are ongoing; solutions can sometimes be elusive as each new generation deals with its own unique challenges and opportunities.

But even in our failures, we are fun to watch.

We are an optimistic, but realistic, people capable of learning from the mistakes and soaring achievements of our forebears—and at the same time, always looking for that "better mousetrap." We regularly reform our elections process, for example, and look for ways to improve oversight of campaign finances and the power elites, tackle issues of diversity and race, and improve the core functions of government. (And like taxpayers everywhere, we struggle with champagne appetites for spending on ever-expanding public services—on a beer budget.)

At its root, you can see the impact of the Populist and Progressive movements rippling through our institutions, our constitution, our distrust of concentrations of power in government or the private sector, and our continuing interest in citizen engagement in "direct democracy" to help guide our government and shape our public policy.

And, yes, there is something distinctly "Washington" that can inspire—or puzzle—observers in other parts of the country with a different political heritage. In elections, for example, our lack of party registration for voters, voting exclusively by mail, and a wide-open Top 2 Primary system reflect our unique Populist heritage, as does our veritable love affair with the initiative process (that celebrates its centennial year in 2012).

What will the new trends and plot twists look like in the coming years? We can hardly wait to see. As a 40-year veteran of watching Washington's politics, elections, and government from a front-row seat as an AP political reporter, TVW host, and senior official with the Secretary of State, I find our individual and collective stories endlessly fascinating. We're predictable—except when we're not!

As one who retains an optimistic view of self-government and the potential for continuous improvement, I welcome this volume. It offers us an insider's guide to Olympia and Washington State with a minimum of jargon. Civics education, coupled with civic engagement and a respectful civil discourse, have never been more important, if frequently in short supply.

The authors, drawn from academe, media, government, and political consulting, explore various facets of the political and governmental world here in Washington. Although the chapters were each written independently, some common themes emerge. One recurrent comment is the notion that many citizens are conflicted about government and how well the political/governmental processes work for them. Even when an institution such as our legislature is highly rated by any number of measures, many retain an arched eyebrow. As we will read, that is a modern-day reminder that the framers of our constitution showed a similar wariness about government and powerful interests. We shattered the executive branch into a bureaucracy answerable to no fewer than nine separately elected statewide officials, not to mention college trustees and autonomous boards and commissions. We put the legislature on a short leash with an easily accessed initiative and referendum process. We put constitutional limits on corporations and other interest groups in our society. We require our judges to be subject to popular election. We minimized the role and influence of the political parties and made our state a haven for independents and ticket-splitters.

In the opening chapter, John Pierce, Nicholas Lovrich, and Stuart Elway set the stage by exploring our "moralistic" political culture and how that plays out. This culture invites high expectations of government, the authors say, adding, "This political culture was brought to Washington by its early settlers, and this perspective on politics was reflected in—and received reinforcement from—the Populist and Progressive reform movements that swept across the American West at the turn of the century." Within that framework, various parts of Washington differ in their "social capital, their creative vitality, and their support for public policies that reflect either trust or cynicism toward public institutions."

Todd Donovan's chapter on elections explores many of the ways Washington follows its own drummer—the Top 2 Primary, vote-by-mail, not providing for party registration, redistricting by citizen commission, voter-imposed campaign finance reporting and limits, and the ubiquitous initiative process—"direct democracy." Although in recent years the state has voted Democratic for governor, legislature, and most statewide and congressional offices, the pendulum can swing quickly as the political winds blow. On several occasions Washington voters have elected a state house where partisan membership is exactly tied at 49-49, and divided government is not uncommon in our political history. We are indeed an independent lot.

In their chapter on political parties, Andrew Appleton and Reneé Edwards note that our parties have "evolved in a particular, if not peculiar, context... characterized in political terms by [our] own brand of 'western populism,' a sometimes volatile mix of progressivism, individualism, and conservatism." In recent years, they note, religious conservatism and anti-establishment politics have "spiced the stew." The chapter provides a useful primer of how our primary process has evolved over the past decade. It also gives a backstage look at intraparty dynamics, party finance, and the state's campaign finance limits.

A chapter on interest groups, written by Clive S. Thomas and Richard Elgar, describes the key role that powerful interests have always played in Washington, through lobbying, campaign contributions, and by helping set the agenda. Thomas and Elgar also note that although most of us belong to a number of advocacy groups and special interests, we also are suspicious of interest groups as a general proposition, always looking for new ways to regulate and rein them in.

The chapter recounts how interest groups evolved since statehood, including the early railroad and timber barons, public–private power battles, Boeing and other heavy hitters, transformation through initiative and regulation, and growing sophistication and professionalization.

The writers trace the role of the Public Disclosure Commission and tracking lobbyists, their expenses, and campaign gifts. As of 2011, they note, 893 lobbyists representing 1,265 employers are reporting and have posted a six-fold increase in spending since 1980. They note that the PDC is rated the best watchdog agency in the country and assert that Washington is "very clean" by national standards, probably in the top 10 states.

We are a state that values diversity, and have a burgeoning minority population—and yet Washington has had trouble translating that into a "place at the table" for some. An excellent chapter by Luis Ricardo Fraga and María Chávez tells the story.

For the past 16 years, Washington has been governed by Gary Locke, the state's first Chinese-American chief executive, and Chris Gregoire, the state's second female governor. Blacks have risen to preeminent roles, and a number of Native Americans, Asian Americans, and Latinos have distinguished themselves. The legislature, judiciary, and bureaucracy have high percentages of women, and the state was early to approve women's suffrage and to enshrine an Equal Rights Amendment in its constitution.

The 2010 census numbers show our state is becoming less white, with "profound shifts" led by the Hispanic population. The authors note that Washington's political culture is "dominated by a sense of the 'common good'" and that the state has "a unique opportunity to not only actively incorporate communities of color politically, but also to empower local communities of all classes, races, and backgrounds by the way it decides to adapt to demographic changes."

But the authors poignantly note that minority communities are not represented in state and most local governments commensurate with their numbers. They add, "Washington is perhaps at a tipping point regarding which direction it will go. Washington State political leaders can broaden their conception of the moralistic political culture, or it can turn toward a more stratified and segregated style of political life."

As the longest-serving statehouse reporter before departing in 2008, I have a special interest in the chapter on the amazing shrinking Capitol Press Corps, and concur with the comment that government and our public officials must be monitored and that a well-educated electorate needs independent sources of information—both unfiltered and value-added reporting by professionals "without a dog in the fight."

Kathleen Searles and Austin Jenkins summarize the implosion of large chunks of American political journalism as the economic model that once sustained it no longer works. Newspapers and radio and television broadcasters, buttressed by web-based news sites, remain a central source of political information, but they are trying to survive in the new economic and technological world. Bloggers from across the spectrum, often without journalism training, and sites such as *Crosscut*, *PubliCola*, and *Washington State Wire* add to the mix of media keeping watch over Washington's politicos.

The chapter describes how the Capitol Press Corps, already a small cadre with a huge task, has been shrinking even as the job of keeping tabs on government and informing citizens has become more complicated and layered. One happy note, though, is the emergence of TVW, which airs gavel-to-gavel coverage of the legislature and its committees, major news conferences, Supreme Court oral arguments, meetings of important boards and commissions, and many public affairs events.

Chapters on our state constitution and the judiciary provide an excellent primer on a little-understood, and crucial, side of state government.

In their chapter on the politics of state constitutional interpretation, Cornell W. Clayton and Lucas McMillan explain how the framers pieced together our main governing document to reflect the values of the late 1880s, borrowing liberally from other states and the impulses of Populism and Progressivism.

The constitution dispersed executive power, placed limits on corporations, empowered voters as central players, and restricted the legislature in key ways. The document, unlike the federal constitution, stated positively many individual rights rather than focusing on restrictions. It is much longer—about 40,000 words versus 6,000—and has been amended over 100 times.

An interesting backstory is how the state became an early leader in developing an independent constitutional jurisprudence and the many challenges that continue to shape that process.

The chapter on the judiciary likewise is an excellent primer on our court system, which the writers describe as "a unique blend of decentralization, responsiveness, and judicial independence." The authors, Simon Zschirnt, J. Mitchell Pickerill, and Carl McCurley, conclude that the Washington judiciary "has responded to a range of challenges and adopted a number of important reforms with deftness."

The chapter explains the four levels of courts. It might surprise the casual reader to learn that district and municipal courts are the true workhorses of the system, with 2.5 million filings in one recent year, compared with 300,000 in the Superior Courts. Most of the judges in Washington serve at the trial court level. The two appellate courts have only 31 jurists—22 on the Court of Appeals and 9 on the Supreme Court. In addition, the entire judiciary gets only 17 percent of its budget from the state treasury—amounting to three-tenths of 1 percent of the state budget.

The writers discuss the continuing conversation about whether judges should be elected or appointed, the role of campaign contributions and attack ads, and more. The chapter also notes that the state has successfully innovated with "problem-solving courts," such as drug courts.

A chapter on the executive branch illuminates the work of over 110,000 state employees in the bureaucracy of state government. Authors Steven D. Stehr and Michael J. Gaffney note that most of those employees "educate, medicate, and incarcerate."

The writers note the strong federal presence in Washington, and high expectations of state and local government for schools, roads, parks, and other services—and also ambivalence about the size and scope of government.

David Nice and Jacob Day, in a chapter on statewide elected officials, describe how the duties of administering Washington State government are divided among nine independently elected leaders. The high-profile office of governor is explored, as is the significant influence of the other statewide officers. Shared governance and considerable checks and balances are built into the system.

The legislature, note authors Francis Benjamin and Nicholas Lovrich, operates in the crosshairs of the public's "undeniably cynical" view of state government. Using survey data, they explore the declining level of civility and other challenges of serving in a milieu where bipartisan collaboration often seems out of fashion.

Related issues are also covered, including the citizen redistricting process, big technological changes over time, the initiative process that often circumscribes lawmakers' efforts, the increasingly expensive campaigns, and the huge role of special interests and lobbyists.

The concluding chapter, by Jenny L. Holland and Steve Lundin, gives a helpful grounding in how public services are financed and how the operating, construction, and transportation budgets are written. Again, the heavy role of voter-approved mandates and revenue limits are highlighted, as are some of the big budget-drivers, including funding of basic education and public pensions.

In all, the volume provides a handy "armchair guide" for both the veteran Olympia-watcher and the newcomer to the subject matter. But keep in mind that Washington and its institutions and practices continue to evolve—our story continues to be written.

—David Ammons
Olympia, Washington

Section I

CHAPTER ONE

The Political Culture of Washington State

John Pierce, Nicholas Lovrich, and H. Stuart Elway

Political Culture

NEARLY EVERYONE is familiar with the term "culture shock." When moving to a new area of our country, Americans typically experience a period of adjustment to the norms and values that predominate in their new surroundings. This chapter sets forth a description of the culture of Washington from the perspective of the political life of the state. The term *political culture* is used to describe that political ambience. A political culture is the mix of shared attitudes, values, behaviors, and institutions that reflects a particular history and approach to politics. Such political cultures are characteristic of people within a particular geographic boundary (e.g., the political culture of Washington State), within an ethnic group (e.g., Latino political culture), or within a specific demographic category (e.g., youth political culture) as well as other clearly bounded geographic or social groupings. In this chapter we present some evidence about the political culture of Washington State and suggest how that mix of shared perspectives on society compares to the political cultures of other places in the United States. We also show evidence of the presence of differences in political culture in different parts of Washington State and discuss how those differences may influence localized political behavior, such as voting outcomes on significant initiatives. In each of the previous WSU Press books covering Washington State government (Mullen, Pierce, Sheldon, and Swanson 1978; Swanson, Mullen, Pierce, and Sheldon 1985; Nice, Pierce, and Sheldon 1992; Clayton, LeLoup, and Lovrich 2004) some attention has been devoted to these two aspects of the political culture of the Evergreen State, an enduring aspect of politics and governance in Washington.

Most of the major political science research into questions of political culture in the United States has focused on comparison at the state and city level. In

Washington State, the largest cities on either side of the Cascade Mountains—
Spokane and Seattle—are most often characterized as areas featuring quite different political cultures. Political cultures are important to our understanding
of politics because they provide a kind of distinctive funnel or filter through
which leaders and citizens interpret and seek to understand both historical
and contemporary events and political issues. Political cultures provide the
framework upon which many attributes of government and societal practices
are built. Thus, *democratic* political cultures—ones in which individuals are
tolerant of differences, norms of civility prevail, and citizens participate actively
in elections and are informed about important issues—might be expected to be
more likely to have governmental structures and processes that are open to and
provide opportunities for influence and access by their citizens.

To date, among the most influential classifications of American cities and
states into types of political culture was developed by Daniel Elazar. In his work,
The American Mosaic (1994), Elazar suggested that there are three major types
of political cultures in the United States: the *individualistic*, the *moralistic*, and
the *traditionalistic*. He argues that any particular place holds a mix of those three
culture types, but that nearly always one of these three cultures is predominant,
and often a second cultural strain is also present to a noteworthy degree. Why an
area exhibits a particular type of political culture reflects "the streams and currents of migration that have carried people of different origins and backgrounds
across the continent in more or less orderly patterns" (229).

The *individualistic* political culture features a view of politics in democracies
as constituting a "free marketplace," and the role of government is to be held to
the very minimum required in order to "encourage private initiative and widespread access to the marketplace" (230). In this individualistic political culture,
politics are dedicated to enhancing the success of individual and group needs.
The *moralistic* political culture, in contrast, emphasizes the "positive potential"
of politics and sees the goal of political activity as "centered on some notion of
the public good and properly devoted to the advancement of the public interest" (232). Citizens are expected to participate in political affairs, and there is
an obligation on the part of government to intervene in the activities of individuals if it is necessary to promote the public or common good. Finally, the
traditionalistic political culture "is rooted in an ambivalent attitude toward the
marketplace coupled with a paternalistic and elitist conception of the common-
wealth" (234). This political culture is dominated by elites whose primary goal
is to maintain existing social and political arrangements.

Where do the two largest cities of Washington stand on the question of political culture when compared to other cities around the country? Table 1 presents
Elazar's rating of Spokane and Seattle on each of the three highlighted political
culture dimensions, as well as the ratings he assigned to a group of other cities
from around the country for comparison. Neither Seattle nor Spokane have any

elements of the traditionalistic political culture, suggesting that there is a virtual absence of any dominant force committed entirely to sustaining the historical class structure status quo through political activity. Both Seattle and Spokane differ, for example, from Atlanta, where traditional political values are the major theme of the culture. According to Elazar, the historical record of Seattle's formative period of settlement features a minor strain of individualistic political culture, while the Spokane area has no such element in its formative phase.

Table 1

Elazar Political Culture Types for Seattle and Spokane
and Selected Other American Cities

| City | Political Culture Types | | |
	Traditionalistic	Individualistic	Moralistic
SEATTLE	None	Minor	Major
SPOKANE	None	None	Sole
Atlanta	Major	Minor	None
Boston	None	None	Sole
Chicago	None	Major	Minor
Denver	None	None	Sole
Houston	Sole	None	None
Kansas City	None	Sole	None
Los Angeles	None	Minor	Major
Miami	None	Sole	None
Minneapolis	None	None	Sole
Sacramento	None	Minor	Major
Salt Lake City	None	None	Sole
San Diego	Minor	None	Major
San Francisco	None	Minor	Major
St. Louis	None	Sole	None

Source: Elazar 1994, 242–43.

This observation may seem unexpected in light of the reputation of Spokane as a more conservative city than Seattle, both in terms of contemporary issues and historical events. But recall, however, that Elazar is writing about the relative emphasis on the individual as opposed to the common good, and also that Seattle and Spokane really are quite similar in one important respect. The shared distinctiveness of Seattle and Spokane may be best expressed in their respective ratings on the dimension of *moralistic political culture*. The moralistic political culture is seen as the sole strain in Spokane and as the major strain in Seattle. Recall that the term moralistic in this context does not refer to how "moral" the politics of the city are; rather, the term refers to the relative emphasis placed on the common good as opposed to private interest. On this dimension, both Seattle and Spokane are more like the other Western cities of San Francisco, San Diego, Sacramento, and Salt Lake City than they are like other cities across the country. For example, Seattle and Spokane differ greatly from Atlanta, Houston, Kansas City, and Miami.

Overall, then, the state's two major cities seem similar in their dominant political cultures, as well as similar to other cities of the American West—and to Minneapolis, a city that lies along the same immigrant stream that moved across the northern reaches of the country. But the political cultures of Washington's two major cities differ from many U.S. cities, especially those in the lower Midwest and the South.

Social Capital

One of the most important concepts in understanding the culture and politics of a place is its level of *social capital*. Social capital is based on the behaviors, attitudes, and values held by citizens and constitutes a significant part of its political culture (Coleman 1990; Putnam 2000; Halpern 2005). Social capital is a resource based on the degree to which individuals trust each other and assume good intentions on the part of others. If people trust each other they are more willing to join in social networks, and the resulting experience of interpersonal interaction may increase those trust levels. Those social networks can be used to influence the character and the quality of their social and political environment. This trust/network-based social capital is often described as having three forms. *Bonding social capital* is based on individuals' trust of other people who are like themselves, as in a church congregation or a neighborhood comprised of residents similar in ethnicity or social class. *Bridging social capital* reflects trust and networks that span across "natural" groups of people. Bridging social capital exists when citizens trust and form networks from one neighborhood to another, from one religious organization to another, or from one ethnic group to another. *Linking social capital* is imbedded in trust and networks that link individuals at different levels together in the political and social structures, such as lower and higher socioeconomic groups, or neighborhood organizations and citywide political leaders.

Individuals who trust other people, especially those in groups other than their own, are inclined to invest in interpersonal networks (bridging social capital) that benefit others because they have faith that those others can be trusted to reciprocate when needed (Uslaner 2004). This mutual trust binds people together in ways that allow them to exert greater collective influence than they would have individually (Walker and Ostrom 2009). Many scholars argue that social capital is required to ensure the sustainability of democratic political practices featuring broad-based public involvement (see discussion of the connection between social capital and civil society in Simon, Steel, and Lovrich 2010, 66–8).

Some highly regarded observers of contemporary American society have argued that social capital is on the decline in America (Putnam 2000). Evidence of this decline is seen in a decrease in public involvement in political (e.g., voting) and social (e.g., civic organizations) activities, even those that are not explicitly political in form (Putnam 2000). Even such long-lived and highly revered organizations as the PTA have declined substantially in level of membership and range of activity. While some scholars dispute the claim that social capital is in decline (e.g., Ladd 1999; Compaine 2001; Katz and Rice 2002; Dalton 2009, 161–78), this possible adverse social trend is an important subject of study because major U.S. cities featuring higher levels of social capital tend to have higher quality city government services (Pierce, Lovrich, and Moon 2002) and feature higher quality health care services (Hendryx et al. 2002; Kim and Kawachi 2007). Despite a good deal of disagreement as to the precise meaning, degree of presence, and societal effects of social capital, the concept of social capital has attained nearly ubiquitous presence in political science and has a growing presence in the literature of other disciplines (Woolcock 2010).

Table 2 displays scores for a number of U.S. cities on a measure of political and social trust expressed by their citizens in large scale surveys conducted in major media markets across the country over the course of the past decade. The higher the score, the higher the level of trust in others and the reserve of social capital; some scholars refer to this as "diffuse trust" (Rothstein and Uslaner 2005). Seattle's social capital score is among the highest of the cities listed, surpassed only by that of Minneapolis. Spokane's score, in contrast, is much lower than that of Seattle—although higher than a number of other major U.S. cities, including Miami, Atlanta, and St. Louis. Hence, while Spokane and Seattle share a moralistic political culture, Seattle enjoys a substantially higher level of social capital—and the concomitant higher levels of civic engagement, voluntary section action, and political participation.

Another recent study of social capital in the United States has looked not at the trust levels of citizens, but at the relative presence of the interpersonal networks that are the result of both the trust and the source of building the trust (Rupasingha, Goetz, and Freshwater 2006). This study, conducted by a team of economists interested in studying the effects of social capital at the level of U.S. counties, generated social capital scores for the more than 3,000 counties in the nation. In their work they identified contributing factors for the production of social capital using an array of individual-level and community-level traits that are theoretically important determinants of social capital. They made use of data derived from the Bureau of the Census, County Business Patterns, USA Counties on CD, National Center for Charitable Statistics, and Regional Economic Information System for two time periods. They found that ethnic

Table 2

Political and Social Trust Levels in Seattle and Spokane
Compared to Selected Other American Cities for 1990–2003

City	Trust Score	City	Trust Score
Seattle	**205.75**	Los Angeles	178.94
Spokane	**195.39**	Miami	189.13
Atlanta	192.36	Minneapolis	210.08
Boston	197.92	Sacramento	190.90
Chicago	199.01	Salt Lake City	205.16
Denver	200.86	San Diego	198.30
Houston	176.06	San Francisco	199.64
Kansas City	184.66	St. Louis	190.26

Source: Data for the calculation of political and social trust scores provided by the Leigh Stowell and Company market research firm in Seattle, Washington. Digital archives containing these data can be accessed through the Division of Governmental Studies and Services at Washington State University and Dataverse at the Institute for Quantitative Social Science at Harvard University.

homogeneity, income inequality, attachment to place, education, age, and female labor force participation are strongly associated with levels of social capital across U.S. counties as measured by the richness of group and associational networks.

Rupasingha and his colleagues reported the results in the form of two types of scores. First, detailed data are reported on the relative presence of a number of different kinds of networks (recreational, civic, religious, etc.) in each county; second, a composite social capital score is reported that combines the network data with several other indicators of trust-based civic behavior such as county voting turnout in presidential elections, the number of tax-exempt nonprofit organizations, and the percentage of households participating in the decennial census household survey process. Table 3 shows the average county network-based social capital score for each state; the table entry is the average score of all the counties in the state.

The Rupasingha scores are reported such that a score near zero for a state on the network-based measure indicates that the state is about average in social capital. Positive scores for a state suggest social capital levels higher than average, while negative scores indicate a below-average level of social capital. The Rupasingha scores displayed in Table 3 indicate that, when compared to other states around the country, Washington State (-.039) is about average in network-based social capital scores as compiled by Rupasingha and his associates. On the other hand, when compared to other states in the American West, Washington fares somewhat better. Both Montana and Oregon have higher social capital scores than does Washington, but the Evergreen State's score is clearly higher than those of Alaska, Arizona, California, Idaho, Nevada, and Utah.

Table 3

Network-Based Social Capital Scores for All States[1]

State	Mean	No. of counties	Std. Deviation
Alabama	-.94247	67	.556098
Alaska	-.96884	5	3.794293
Arizona	-1.52058	15	.658047
Arkansas	-.62678	75	.545148
California	-.42708	58	.958702
Colorado	.57464	63	1.429155
Connecticut	.54323	8	.274711
Delaware	-.42612	3	.682014
Florida	-.89265	66	.666627
Georgia	-1.41987	159	.723298
Idaho	-.38394	44	.795577
Illinois	.70643	102	.658287
Indiana	.12158	92	.607761
Iowa	1.31521	99	.685099
Kansas	1.46926	105	1.193805
Kentucky	-.81245	120	.895225
Louisiana	-.54046	64	.511963
Maine	.86926	16	.842663
Maryland	-.35804	24	.791415
Massachusetts	1.43155	14	2.059092
Michigan	.11274	83	.664636
Minnesota	1.76876	87	.956941
Mississippi	-.88720	82	.628029
Missouri	.18553	115	.858414
Montana	.99747	56	1.122337
Nebraska	1.17583	93	1.195256
Nevada	-.98276	17	.880402
New Hampshire	.69617	10	.653093
New Jersey	-.26846	21	.672152
New Mexico	-.65453	33	1.050285
New York	.17646	62	1.021397
North Carolina	-.58625	100	.844646
North Dakota	2.01996	53	1.286553
Ohio	.42476	88	.616840
Oklahoma	-.23200	77	.883111
Oregon	.22675	36	.577781
Pennsylvania	.17083	67	.548604

(continued, next page)

(Table 3 continued)

State	Mean	No. of counties	Std. Deviation
Rhode Island	.32939	5	.351762
South Carolina	-1.17862	46	.542920
South Dakota	1.79545	66	1.342920
Tennessee	-.93035	95	.729238
Texas	-.75784	254	1.068475
Utah	-1.03514	29	.757348
Vermont	.79796	14	1.017412
Virginia	.14845	134	1.440951
Washington	**-.03869**	**39**	**.876053**
West Virginia	-.56166	55	.753112
Wisconsin	.51446	72	.718667
Wyoming	1.50388	23	1.234301
Total	.00000	3,111	1.298174

[1]Hawaii data unavailable.
Source: Rupasingha, Goetz, and Freshwater 2006.

Now we turn to the question of whether those state-level differences are reflected in all kinds of networks or whether Washington is higher in some types of networks when compared to other states. The answer to this question lies in the data analysis displayed in Table 4. In regard to civic organizations, such as Kiwanis, Rotary, or the Lions Club, Washington has more per capita network social capital than any other western state with the sole exception of Montana. Washington is below the national average for the per capita presence of religious organizations. This finding fits with the fact that Washington is often said to be one of the "least churched" states in the country (Killen and Silk 2004); most of the American West falls in that category as well. A little more perspective is offered by a comparison to a state such as Kansas that has twice as many religious organizations per capita as does Washington. Washington stands out in the relative presence of political organizations compared to the other western states. That is no surprise, of course, given Washington's history of significant citizen involvement in state and local politics (see discussion of this history in relation to city and county government home rule in Newman and Lovrich 2001 and Lundin 2009, 60–71, 142–45). The widespread use of the initiative and referendum and longtime use of the open primary system for partisan elections are key features of the state's Progressive and Populist political heritage. (See chapter two, Elections in Washington, for a more detailed discussion of primary elections and initiatives; see also Lundin 2009, 757, for initiative and referendum procedures.)

Table 4

Per Capita State Scores on Specific Networks/Associations[1]

| State[2] | Type of Interpersonal Networks/Associations Present | | | | | |
	Civic	Religious	Political	Professional	Business	Labor
Alabama	.51	9.07	.04	.10	.41	.61
Alaska	1.39	7.50	.01	.06	.67	1.79
Arizona	.55	4.15	.01	.13	.54	.23
Arkansas	.77	8.44	.02	.08	.58	.46
California	1.41	3.66	.05	.22	.72	.34
Colorado	2.37	7.57	.03	.43	1.18	.23
Connecticut	1.68	4.86	.04	.33	.38	.88
Delaware	2.00	5.46	.07	.43	.70	.83
Florida	1.21	6.18	.04	.16	.57	.32
Georgia	.54	7.53	.02	.11	.74	.26
Idaho	1.14	4.00	.01	.07	.57	.37
Illinois	2.14	11.12	.04	.16	.47	1.22
Indiana	2.50	8.93	.03	.13	.47	.97
Iowa	1.70	12.78	.03	.17	.66	.54
Kansas	2.25	14.65	.01	.18	1.23	.30
Kentucky	.50	8.85	.02	.14	.37	.63
Louisiana	.53	7.35	.02	.10	.35	.40
Maine	1.71	6.33	.05	.27	.81	.62
Maryland	1.87	6.25	.06	.34	.46	.46
Massachusetts	2.04	5.15	.05	.26	.62	.68
Michigan	1.79	7.55	.02	.14	.63	1.18
Minnesota	4.20	12.72	.04	.14	.85	.54
Mississippi	.50	8.92	.01	.08	.45	.38
Missouri	1.40	10.48	.03	.13	.57	.50
Montana	2.70	7.35	.03	.20	.72	.33
Nebraska	2.52	11.88	.01	.14	.86	.18
Nevada	1.22	2.29	.03	.14	.99	.30
New Hampshire	2.34	5.77	.03	.24	.97	.37
New Jersey	.90	4.89	.06	.36	.41	.87
New Mexico	1.82	6.10	.02	.14	.71	.22
New York	1.76	5.98	.03	.18	.44	.77
North Carolina	.86	10.45	.02	.15	.49	.20
North Dakota	4.52	13.46	.06	.35	1.06	.37
Ohio	2.14	8.09	.02	.14	.39	1.29
Oklahoma	1.15	11.54	.03	.13	.61	.18
Oregon	1.86	6.56	.05	.15	.83	.54

(continued, next page)

(Table 4 continued)

| State[2] | Type of Interpersonal Networks/Associations Present | | | | | |
	Civic	Religious	Political	Professional	Business	Labor
Pennsylvania	3.15	9.08	.09	.16	.45	.94
Rhode Island	2.00	4.61	.13	.25	.45	.73
South Carolina	.82	9.26	.03	.21	.41	.22
South Dakota	2.51	13.14	.04	.36	.74	.16
Tennessee	.69	8.75	.02	.09	.33	.44
Texas	1.12	9.70	.03	.10	.84	.16
Utah	.76	.94	.01	.06	.67	.41
Vermont	2.63	5.78	.04	.43	.87	.49
Virginia	1.14	10.10	.06	.37	.74	.50
Washington	**2.24**	**7.23**	**.06**	**.22**	**.70**	**.54**
West Virginia	1.95	8.11	.02	.08	.29	1.30
Wisconsin	1.17	8.52	.02	.11	.65	1.18
Wyoming	3.51	7.83	.05	.28	1.28	.86
Nation	1.72	7.90	.04	.19	.65	.58

[1]The scores are the result of multiplying the per capita results by a constant (10,000) for all states so that differences are more readily observable.
[2]Hawaii data unavailable.

Added insight into Washington's social networks is shown in regard to civic and political organizations, where the state is above the national average in per capita participation rates. Thus, the overall network-based social capital score for the state is near the country's average, but is near the top in the West, as are the scores for particular types of political- and community-based networks such as civic, political, professional, and business organizations.

The next question to be answered to better understand the social capital aspects of Washington's political culture is whether there are significant differences within Washington State in terms of network-based social capital. In order to answer that question we turn to the county-level results shown in Table 5, which contains the summary social capital scores for each of the state's 39 counties. Where is social capital most likely to be found in Washington State? The answer is that all parts of the state have some counties with high levels of social capital. The two highest network-based social capital scores are on opposite sides of the natural dividing line of the Cascade Mountains—San Juan County (2.68) and Lincoln County (2.43), and in densely populated counties (e.g., King County .80) and less densely populated counties (Garfield County .93). Similarly, the counties with low social capital scores are found spread around the state—Okanagan (-1.05), Mason (-1.24), Ferry (-1.38), Yakima (-.95), Grant (-.83), and Pierce (-.77).

Table 5

Washington County Social Capital Scores

County	Mean	County	Mean
Adams	-.22	Lewis	-.38
Asotin	-.35	Lincoln	2.43
Benton	.19	Mason	-1.24
Chelan	.34	Okanogan	-1.05
Clallam	.22	Pacific	-.26
Clark	-.59	Pend Oreille	-.69
Columbia	.55	Pierce	-.77
Cowlitz	.01	San Juan	2.68
Douglas	-1.29	Skagit	.16
Ferry	-1.38	Skamania	-.74
Franklin	-.69	Snohomish	-.34
Garfield	.93	Spokane	.27
Grant	-.83	Stevens	-.49
Grays Harbor	-.18	Thurston	.36
Island	-.49	Wahkiakum	.63
Jefferson	1.14	Walla Walla	.37
King	.80	Whatcom	.44
Kitsap	-.36	Whitman	.61
Kittitas	.06	Yakima	-.95
Klickitat	.41		
State of Washington	**-.04**		

Washington Counties

The next question to explore is whether the state's counties differ in terms of the per capita presence of the specific types of networks and organizations. Table 6 provides a glimpse into the answer. The same six types of networks/associations displayed in Table 4 are also used here—namely, civic, political, religious, professional, business, and labor. While all of these networks at least occasionally enter into the public arena, we will limit the discussion to the presence of the civic, religious, and political organizations present at the county level at the time of the Rupasingha et al. study (using data from the 2000 census and other sources collected at approximately the same time). Civic organizations, in relationship to the population size of the county, tend to be present most frequently in smaller counties such as Pacific, San Juan, Grays Harbor, Grant, and Garfield. The same pattern tends to characterize the presence of religious

organizations, where Lincoln, Garfield, Adams, and Wahkiakum rank at the top of the category. A different pattern is seen in regard to political organizations. Perhaps not surprising, political organizations per capita are more densely concentrated in the counties with the largest population (King County) and with the state capital (Thurston County).

In summary, social capital is a potential resource based in the networks and associational connections existing among people, and the networks and associations themselves tend to rely on the prevalence of the interpersonal trust they build among people. Those trust-based networks provide a way for citizens to organize and to press claims on governments at all levels. Overall, Washington State is at about the national average in terms of social capital, although it clearly rests near the top of its state neighbors in the American West. Within Washington State there is considerable variation in county-level social capital, with the highest ranking counties spread around the state geographically and differing in terms of population size. When looking at the presence of specific types of networks, some clear cross-county patterns emerge. Civic and religious networks are more likely to be present in counties with smaller populations, perhaps as the result of some need to compensate for the greater difficulty in establishing informal relationships. But political networks are right where one would expect to find them, in the state's largest county where political activity would be most efficient in terms of mobilizing support, and in the county housing the state capital, where political activity is most likely to be directed.

Table 6

Washington County Networks/Associations as Per Capita Presence

| County | Type of Interpersonal Networks/Associations Present | | | | | |
	Civic	Religious	Political	Professional	Business	Labor
Adams	2.57	12.87	.00	.64	1.29	.64
Asotin	.94	9.14	.00	.00	.94	.00
Benton	1.77	5.16	.00	.22	.44	.96
Chelan	2.85	8.04	.00	.50	1.67	.17
Clallam	2.98	5.32	.00	.16	.78	.63
Clark	.79	4.58	.09	.25	.32	.95
Columbia	2.34	11.69	.00	.00	.00	.00
Cowlitz	1.76	6.83	.00	.22	.22	1.65
Douglas	.30	5.67	.00	.00	.30	1.19
Ferry	1.38	2.76	.00	.00	.00	.00
Franklin	1.49	6.80	.00	.43	.85	2.98
Garfield	4.39	17.56	.00	.00	.00	.00
Grant	3.15	6.88	.14	.14	.71	.00
Grays Harbor	4.27	7.36	.00	.00	1.18	1.47
Island	2.12	4.81	.00	.28	.42	.14
Jefferson	2.70	7.32	.00	.39	1.54	.39
King	1.60	5.16	.29	.54	.77	.89
Kitsap	.98	5.54	.04	.26	.34	.60
Kittitas	1.91	6.37	.00	.32	.96	.00
Klickitat	2.10	6.82	.00	.00	1.05	.52
Lewis	1.78	7.10	.00	.00	.30	.30
Lincoln	2.04	21.42	.00	1.02	1.02	.00
Mason	2.83	3.44	.00	.00	.40	.20
Okanogan	2.59	6.21	.00	.00	1.03	.26
Pacific	6.16	9.00	.00	.00	.95	.47
Pend Oreille	2.66	6.21	.89	.00	.89	.00
Pierce	1.13	5.10	.05	.23	.33	.84
San Juan	6.52	7.34	.00	.00	.82	.00
Skagit	1.84	6.45	.10	.31	.72	.51
Skamania	3.11	3.11	.00	.00	1.04	.00
Snohomish	1.42	4.60	.05	.30	.28	.58
Spokane	1.53	6.33	.10	.42	.62	1.16
Stevens	1.53	6.33	.00	.25	.51	.25
Thurston	1.55	5.61	.30	.85	1.60	1.05
Wahkiakum	.00	12.84	.00	.00	.00	.00
Walla Walla	2.99	6.92	.00	.00	.56	.94
Whatcom	2.07	7.91	.06	.45	.71	1.04
Whitman	2.03	8.65	.25	.25	1.02	.00
Yakima	1.24	6.09	.05	.23	.64	.46
State of Washington	2.24	7.37	**.06**	**.22**	**.70**	**.54**

Creative Culture and Vitality

At this point we move beyond the more traditional notion of political culture to what one might call "culture-culture." This culture-culture has to do with the mix of attitudes, behaviors, and activities relating to culture (as in the arts, for example) and creativity. Arts and creative culture activities may not seem to have major political culture implications at first, but in recent years the boundaries between the creative arts and economic vitality have become much less rigid. Richard Florida (2002), for example, has identified and measured creative life-styles in American cities and has argued that those places with a large "creative class" are economically better off and politically distinct in terms of tolerance and innovation. Other scholars have suggested that a vital and creative arts culture is important to the development of a community's social capital (Greenwood and Holt 2010, 42–3). Thus, it becomes both interesting and important to understand how Washington State stacks up on creative vitality and how the various counties in the state differ in that regard.

The most exhaustive and detailed investigation into the creative vitality of American counties done to date has been conducted by WESTAF—the Western States Arts Federation, a Denver, Colorado-based nonprofit organization that consults with and provides information to state and local arts organizations around the country. WESTAF has developed a measure called the Creative Vitality Index (CVI). The CVI is a composite score based on three distinct sets of data: 1) creative industry data, which reflect the volume of the goods and services related to creative arts activity, such as store sales, gallery revenues, and performing arts participation; 2) creative occupation data, which represent employment in occupations reflecting "creative thinking, originality, and fine arts knowledge"; and 3) nonprofit arts data, which reveal the "total number of non-profit organizations and arts-active organizations" (WESTAF 2011). The CVI is constructed so that the national average score is set at 1.0. States or counties can then be compared to each other and to the national average by the amount they are above or below the universal average.

Table 7 shows how Washington compares to the other western states on the CVI. The results displayed in that table are in line with our prior analyses; as in the case of social capital, Washington is near the national average on the Creative Vitality Index with a score of 1.03. Of the other western states, California is clearly the highest in creative vitality, while Idaho is the lowest. Washington has the same CVI score as Oregon.

The question that clearly follows this cross-state comparison is whether there are noteworthy variations in the CVI among Washington State's counties. Table 8 contains findings that address that question. The findings indicate there is indeed noteworthy variation; Washington's counties do vary significantly in their creative vitality as measured by the Western States Arts Federation. Only three

Table 7

Creative Vitality Index Scores for Six Western States

State	Creative Vitality Score
California	1.39
Idaho	.70
Montana	.93
Oregon	1.03
Utah	.83
Washington	**1.03**
United States	1.00

Source: Western States Arts Federation.

of the state's counties (Jefferson, King, and San Juan) are above the national average of 1.0 on the CVI measure. The three counties with the lowest CVI scores (Douglas, Adams, and Garfield) are found in eastern Washington, areas generally not very densely populated and perhaps without the critical mass required to support much creative activity.

In summary, then, two major political culture patterns are present in Washington. The first is that on the whole, Washington's political culture is heavily influenced by moralistic, communitarian values and (as indicated by social capital and creative vitality) is near the average for the entire country. The second pattern is that significant differences are found within Washington State in social capital and creative vitality. It should come as no surprise that Washingtonians who live in central or eastern Washington experience very different political lives than do citizens who live in King County. Those different political lives are at least in part a reflection of the distinctive political cultures present in those areas.

The Public Agenda

It would be fair to ask what these particular measures of political culture have to do with political outcomes in Washington. Is there any evidence of the impact of political culture differences on citizen views of important questions about how government ought to operate in Washington? The answer to this question is yes. In the 2010 general election, the state's citizens were faced with voting on two important ballot measures that clearly reflected central dimensions of political culture. As noted in many places in this book, the state's initiative process plays a large role in the state's political life, greatly affecting the legislative, executive, and judicial branches and the electoral process discussed in the following chapters. The first ballot measure of particular interest to us is Initiative 1053. This measure reinstated a legislative "supermajority" requirement (two-thirds

Table 8

Creative Vitality in Washington Counties as Measured by the
Creative Vitality Index

County	Mean	County	Mean
Adams	.168	Klickitat	.605
Asotin	.353	Lewis	.334
Benton	.662	Lincoln	.293
Chelan	.891	Mason	.363
Clallam	.622	Okanogan	.423
Clark	.645	Pacific	.344
Columbia	.566	Pend Oreille	.244
Cowlitz	.341	Pierce	.647
Douglas	.130	San Juan	2.137
Ferry	.296	Skagit	.559
Franklin	.189	Skamania	.245
Garfield	.182	Snohomish	.550
Grant	.207	Spokane	.756
Grays Harbor	.358	Stevens	.273
Island	.734	Thurston	.786
Jefferson	1.403	Wahkiakum	.268
King	2.080	Walla Walla	.590
Kitsap	.656	Whatcom	.758
Kittitas	.432	Whitman	.695
		Yakima	.396
State of Washington	**1.026**		

Source: Western States Arts Federation.

approval in both chambers) for any increases in taxes or fees. A prior supermajority requirement established by initiative was suspended by legislative action in 2010; the legislature can suspend initiatives after a two-year period by simple majority vote (suspension before the end of the two-year period requires a two-thirds majority in both chambers). The advocates for controls on government revenue generation were successful in placing Initiative 1053 on the ballot in the next election following the suspension of the tax-limiting initiative. Initiative 1053 passed with 63.75 percent of the statewide vote.

It is reasonable to interpret the strong support for that measure as an expression of public distrust of and cynicism toward government and politics. The second ballot measure of similar interest as a surrogate for public trust/cynicism is Initiative 1098. That initiative would have imposed a flat rate income tax on "the wealthy" (individuals with an adjusted gross annual income of $200,000 or more, or $400,000 or more for joint filers) and reduced other taxes in proportion to revenue generated. Initiative 1098 received support from only 35.85 percent of the voters, despite its promotion by Bill Gates Sr. and his many tax equity reform associates. This vote too can be seen as representing a cynical or mistrustful view of government activity in the economic sphere; opponents of the measure were persuasive with voters in arguing that the legislature could not be trusted to keep the income tax restricted to only "wealthy" Washingtonians.

Even with the clear majorities supporting Initiative 1053 and opposing Initiative 1098 statewide, there was substantial variation among the counties with respect to voting outcomes. The supermajority measure received more than 75 percent support from voters in Columbia, Douglas, Ferry, Garfield, Grant, Lewis, Lincoln, Pend Oreille, and Stevens counties. Less than 60 percent of the citizens supported that measure in King, Jefferson, San Juan, and Thurston counties. The income tax on the wealthy measure received more than 40 percent support in Jefferson, King, San Juan, and Whatcom counties, and less than 25 percent support in Adams, Benton, Columbia, Douglas, Franklin, Grant, Lewis, and Yakima counties. On both measures, statistically significant differences were found between the counties on the west side of the Cascades (mean 66.8 on the supermajority measure and 35.5 on the tax measure) and those on the east side of the mountains (mean 73.84 on the supermajority measure and 26.7 on the tax measures). Moreover, differences in county levels of support for those measures are clearly rooted in the social capital levels of the counties themselves. Counties with high social capital levels were significantly less likely to support the supermajority measure ($r=-.45$, $p=.002$), and were significantly more likely to support the tax measure ($r=.38$, $p=.008$).

Conclusion

The citizens of Washington are inclined to have high expectations for their state government and their political leaders. The state's moralistic political culture invites these high expectations. This political culture was brought to Washington by its early settlers, and this perspective on politics was reflected in—and received reinforcement from—the Populist and Progressive reform movements that swept across the American West at the turn of the century. This same moralistic political culture continues in strong force today. As the following chapters will reveal, the moralistic political culture is reflected in the way that political parties operate in the state, how interest groups have been both accommodated and regulated, how the initiative process has come to occupy a major role in the policy process, and how the major political institutions of state and local government have taken shape and tend to operate and interact. Even within that common cultural umbrella, though, significant contrasts are present in different parts of the state in terms of their levels of social capital, their creative vitality, and their support for public policies that reflect either trust in or cynicism toward public institutions.

References

Clayton, Cornell W., Lance T. LeLoup, and Nicholas P. Lovrich, eds. 2004. *Washington State Government and Politics*. Pullman: Washington State University Press.

Coleman, James S. 1990. *Foundations of Social Theory*. Cambridge, MA: Belknap Press.

Compaine, Benjamin M. 2001. *The Digital Divide: Facing a Crisis or Creating a Myth?* Cambridge, Mass.: MIT Press.

Dalton, Russell J. 2009. *The Good Citizen: How a Younger Generation is Reshaping American Politics*, rev. ed. Washington, D.C.: CQ Press.

Elazar, Daniel J. 1994. *The American Mosaic: The Impact of Space, Time, and Culture on American Politics*. Boulder, CO: Westview Press.

Florida, Richard. 2002. *The Rise of the Creative Class: And How It's Transforming Work, Leisure, Community, and Everyday Life*. New York: Basic Books.

Greenwood, Daphne T., and Richard P.F. Holt. 2010. *Local Economic Development in the 21st Century: Quality of Life and Sustainability*. Armonk, NY: M.E. Sharpe.

Halpern, David. 2005. *Social Capital*. Malden, MA: Polity Press.

Hendryx, Michael S., Melissa M. Ahern, Nicholas P. Lovrich, and Arthur H. McCurdy. 2002. "Access to Health Care and Community Social Capital." *Health Services Research* 35(1): 87–103.

Katz, James E., and Ronald E. Rice. 2002. *Social Consequences of Internet Use: Access, Involvement, and Interaction*. Cambridge, MA: MIT Press.

Killen, Patricia O'Connell, and Mark Silk. 2004. *Religion and Public Life in the Pacific Northwest: The None Zone*. Walnut Creek, CA: Altamira Press.

Kim, Daniel, and Ichiro Kawachi. 2007. "U.S. State-Level Social Capital and Health-Related Quality of Life: Multilevel Evidence of Main, Mediating, and Modifying Effects." Annals of Epidemiology 17(4): 258–69.

Ladd, Everett Carll. 1999. *The Ladd Report*. New York: The Free Press.

Lundin, Steve. 2007. *The Closest Governments to the People: A Complete Reference Guide to Local Government in Washington State*. Pullman: Washington State University Division of Governmental Studies and Services.

Mullen, William F., John C. Pierce, Charles H. Sheldon, and Thor Swanson. 1978. *The Government and Politics of Washington State*. Pullman: Washington State University Press.

Newman, Meredith A., and Nicholas P. Lovrich. 2001. "Washington." In *Home Rule in America: A Fifty-State Handbook*, edited by Dale Krane, Platon N. Rigos and Melvin B. Hill Jr. Washington, D.C.: CQ Press.

Nice, David C., John C. Pierce, and Charles H. Sheldon, eds. 1992. *Government and Politics in the Evergreen State*. Pullman: Washington State University Press.

Pierce, John C., Nicholas P. Lovrich Jr., and C. David Moon. 2002. "Social Capital and Government Performance: An Analysis of 20 American Cities." *Public Performance and Management Review* 25(4): 381–97.

Putnam, Robert. 2000. *Bowling Alone: The Collapse and Revival of American Community*. New York: Simon and Schuster.

Rothstein, Bo, and Eric Uslaner. 2005. "All for All: Equality, Corruption, and Social Trust." *World Politics* 58(1): 41–72.

Rupasingha, Anil, Stephen J. Goetz, and David Freshwater. 2006. "The Production of Social Capital in U.S. Counties." *Journal of Socio-Economics* 35(1): 83–101.

Simon, Christopher, Brent Steel, and Nicholas P. Lovrich. 2011. *State and Local Government: Sustainability in the 21st Century*. New York: Oxford University Press.

Swanson, Thor, William F. Mullen, John C. Pierce, and Charles H. Sheldon. 1985. *Political Life in Washington: Governing the Evergreen State*. Pullman: Washington State University Press.

Uslaner, Eric. 2004. "Trust as a Moral Value." In *Handbook of Social Capital*, edited by Dario Castiglione, Jan W. Van Deth, and Guglielmo Wolleb. Oxford: Oxford University Press.

Walker, James, and Elinor Ostrom. 2009. "Trust and Reciprocity as Foundations for Co-operation." In *Whom Can We Trust? How Groups, Networks, and Institutions Make Trust Possible*, edited by Karen S. Cook, Margaret Levi, and Russell Hardin. New York: Russell Sage Foundation.

WESTAF (Western States Arts Federation). 2011. *Creative Vitality Index*. cvi.westaf.org.

Woolcock, Michael. 2010. "The Rise and Routinization of Social Capital, 1988–2008." *Annual Review of Political Science* 13: 469–87.

CHAPTER TWO

Elections in Washington

Todd Donovan

E LECTIONS ARE ONE MECHANISM for gauging what voters think about their government. They act as a barometer that measures public sentiments on a regular basis. Most of all, elections are the primary method for holding government accountable. This chapter demonstrates that elections are conducted differently in Washington than in other states. How does this affect elections, and what do election results say about Washington?

Unique Aspects of Washington Elections

The United States Supreme Court sets basic parameters states follow when conducting elections. Within bounds established by the court, states set qualifications about who is allowed to vote, determine how voter registration is managed, establish criteria for drawing electoral districts, and set rules about who appears on the ballot. States also have some discretion in defining how (or if) campaign finances are regulated. States thus have substantial discretion in how they conduct elections and Washington has adopted a number of rules that are rather unique. These rules have consequences for who participates in elections, and for who wins or loses.

Voter Registration

One unique aspect of Washington's elections is voter registration. All states but North Dakota require that residents register prior to voting so the state may validate that a person is eligible to vote. States differ in terms of how far in advance of an election new voters must register, and in terms of how voters register.[1] Voter registration in Washington differs from other states on both of these features. Most states have traditionally required registration 30 days before an election; however eight states[2] allow registration on election day. Washington does not provide election day registration (EDR), but it does have one of the nation's more liberal rules for registration since it allows new voters to register within eight days of an election.

Shorter advance registration requirements correspond with higher voter turnout (Rosenstone and Hansen 2003). One study suggests that EDR may have a modest effect on promoting turnout in some states (a 4% increase), but that the effect is absent in other states (Hanmer 2009). EDR has been proposed for Washington. A 2007 EDR bill passed in the state senate but did not pass in the house. It was opposed by Secretary of State Sam Reed and county auditors. Reed (2007) argued EDR would make it more difficult to identify people voting illegally and auditors feared they lacked resources needed to process registrations on election day.

Registration without Parties

Registration in Washington differs from many other states in a more fundamental manner. Many states require that voters declare a party affiliation when registering. This record of the voter's party affiliation can then be used to determine how (or if) a person can participate in primary elections. Primaries determine which candidates appear on general election ballots in November. In most other states, voters receive a primary ballot listing candidates from a single party. For example, Republican voters receive a ballot that only lists Republican primary candidates. Partisan registration is one mechanism that insures only Democratic voters pick Democratic nominees for offices elected in November. The Washington legislature adopted partisan registration in 1921, but voters repealed it by popular referendum in 1922. This means that primary elections are conducted without information about voters' partisan affiliations.

Primary Elections in Washington

Most states can be classified as having closed or open primaries. In 28 states, Republican primaries are closed to Democrats, and Democratic primaries are closed to Republicans. In some closed primary states, independent voters are allowed to pick one party's ballot and vote. Twenty other states open their primaries so any voter can pick one party's ballot, regardless of whether or not they are registered with a party (Donovan, Mooney, and Smith 2011, 158). In these 48 states "closed" or "open" primary ballots list candidates from just one party.

Washington and Louisiana do not fit easily into either the closed or open categories. In 1934, an initiative from the Washington Grange directed the legislature to adopt a primary where candidates from all parties appeared on a single ballot. With no record of voters' partisan affiliation, all voters received the same primary ballot. This meant a voter could support a Republican as the nominee for Governor and then cross over and support a Democrat as nominee for U.S. Representative, and so on. The Democratic candidate for each office with the most votes (regardless of their overall place of finish) would appear on the November ballot. Likewise, the top Republican would win a spot on the November ballot.

The Blanket Primary: 1935–2002

Washington used this "blanket primary" system from 1935 to 2002. Alaska used it briefly, and California did in one election (1998). In 2000, the U.S. Supreme Court ruled that the blanket primary unconstitutionally forced the Democratic Party to let independents and Republicans pick their nominees, and forced Republicans to let non-Republicans pick Republican nominees (*California Democratic Party et al. v. Jones* 530 U.S. 567, 2000). The court nullified Washington's blanket primary when ruling a political party had a First Amendment right to determine who nominated its candidates.

The "Pick a Party" Primary: 2004–2006

Since 2000 the state has used two different primary election systems. In 2004 the legislature passed a "pick a party" open primary law. This system allowed any voter to select a party's ballot, and participate only in that party's primary. Under this system, a voter could not select nominees from different parties for different offices. The 'pick a party' system was used again in 2006, but it was short-lived.

The Top 2 Primary: 2008–Present

Voters approved another Grange initiative in November 2004 that established a "Top 2 Primary." This sent the first and second place candidates for each office to the November ballot regardless of their party. The top-two ballot places all candidates on one ballot and allows any voter to participate. Candidates can list a party they "prefer," but the ballot states that a candidate's party preference does not imply that a party nominated, endorsed, or approved the candidate. In addition to stating they prefer "Democrat" and "Republican," candidates have said they prefer the "Lower Taxes Party," the "R Problem Fixer Party," the "Reluctant Republican Party," the "Constitution Party," and the "Independent Democratic Party." A candidate who said he preferred the latter won office in 2010. The "top-two" aspect means that two Democrats (or two Republicans) can end up facing each other in the general election if two candidates from the same party placed first and second in a primary.

As of 2010, Top 2 primaries for statewide offices produced general election contests between candidates who said they preferred the Democratic Party and candidates who said they preferred the Republican Party. Most state legislative contests in November were also between a Democrat and a Republican. However, some legislative primaries in eastern Washington produced general election contests between two Republicans, and some primaries in western Washington produced contests in November between two Democrats.

Some argue that electoral competition between two parties is important because it may increase the likelihood that elected officials will be responsive to

Table 1

Percent WA State House Seats Contested in General Elections

	% seats D vs. R	% Seats Two Major Party Candidates
1968–1995	87%*	87%
1996	83*	83
1998	70*	70
2000	77*	77
2002	66*	66
2004	84+	84
2006	73+	73
2008	66^	73
2010	66^	73

*Blanket Primary
+Pick a Party Primary
^Top 2 Primary

the public (e.g., Key 1949). Others note that electoral competition can dampen public corruption (Meier and Holbrook 1992; Hill 2003), increase public attention to local campaign news (Bowler and Donovan 2011), and increase voter turnout (Cox and Munger 1989).

Electoral competition in state elections has been declining for decades (Ansolabehere et al. 2007; Neimi et al. 2006). Reduced competition may reflect higher costs of campaigns, increased incumbent advantages, types of primaries used, or the way districts are drawn. Under the blanket primary, Washington's legislative elections were among the most competitive in the nation (Hamm and Moncrief 1999). Washington still ranks among the states with more contested elections (McGlennon 2009), but as Table 1 illustrates, electoral competition declined in Washington while the blanket primary was still in use. Under the Top 2 Primary some of the remaining competition reflects intra-party contests (D vs. D or R vs. R), rather than Democrats running against Republicans. It is too early to tell if intra-party contests have the same effects on politics as two-party competition.

The Effects of Primary Election Rules

Washington has a long tradition of primary rules that open participation to all voters. This conflicts with efforts by parties to assert more control over who participates. But what difference does it make if participation in primaries is open to everyone?

Proponents of open and top-two systems suggest that if primaries shut out independent voters, "hard core" partisans may elect candidates who appeal to only a narrow portion of the electorate. Closed partisan primaries could leave general election voters facing choices between Democrats from the far left competing against Republicans from the far right. Washington-style primaries, by encouraging independent and moderate voters to participate, may help "moderate" candidates win elections (Fiorina et al. 2005, 107; also see Cain and Gerber 2002).

Moderates, Mavericks, and the Median Voter

The state's primary rules are cited as one reason Washington occasionally elects people who do not fit standard partisan categories. In legal proceedings the parties cited anecdotes of candidates winning nominations despite not being preferred by voters from the party. The Democrats' 1976 gubernatorial candidate, Dixy Lee Ray, is one example. Ray had limited formal interaction with the party prior to the primary, but she defeated three other Democrats in a close race with 24 percent of the vote.[3] There is no survey data to test who supported Ray in the primary, but the fact that she was elected governor by a large margin in November suggests she had wide appeal among voters in both parties. Observers also point out other moderates elected in Washington, such as former Republican Governor Daniel Evans (1965–1977) and former Democratic Senator Henry "Scoop" Jackson. Jackson is cited as a classic "maverick" who was not easy to pigeonhole as a partisan (Borger 2002). Yet the blanket primary system also produced many candidates who might be seen as highly predictable partisans (e.g., former Democratic Governor Mike Lowry or U.S. Representative Jim McDermott), and others so ideologically extreme that they were unelectable statewide (e.g., 1996 Republican gubernatorial candidate Ellen Craswell).

One study of the effect of different primary rules found that members of Congress from states with closed primaries cast votes that were further from the policy preferences of the median voter in their district. Representatives from Washington and other states with more open rules cast votes more in line with the typical voter (Gerber and Morton 1998, 321). This suggests that open primaries and top-two systems do produce different candidates than closed primaries. It also suggests that candidates who win in closed primaries have a greater incentive to cast votes that appeal to their narrow partisan base.

Presidential Primaries and Caucuses

Presidential primaries are governed by different rules. The state and national committees from each party determine when and how delegates are selected for their party's national convention. Candidates who win the most delegates nationally win their party's presidential nomination. Most states use primaries to award these delegates. Washington has used a mix of precinct caucuses and primary elections. A citizen initiative led to the use of presidential primaries from 1992 to 2008. The parties have been reluctant to award many of Washington's delegates based on primaries that were open to all voters, and the state's major parties have long relied on using precinct caucuses to select most delegates. As a result, Washington's presidential primary, particularly for Democrats, has been little more than a beauty contest.[4] Secretary Reed and Governor Gregoire proposed suspending the presidential primary in 2012 in order to save $10 million, then resuming it in 2016.

Voting by Mail: 'Election Day' Can Go for Weeks

Nationally, a growing proportion of votes are now cast well in advance of election day. Scholars estimate that between 28 and 35 percent of votes nationally in the 2010 midterm congressional election were cast early, either sent through the mail or cast at early voting stations (Gronke 2011). In nearly all states, however, most votes are still cast at traditional polling places on election day.

Oregon and Washington are the only states where elections are conducted exclusively by mail. Oregon conducted the nation's first statewide all-mail election in 1996 (Southwell 2004). The transition to elections by mail in Washington was gradual. In 2000, just over 50 percent of votes were cast by mail, yet most counties continued to staff polling places on election day. In 2005 legislation was passed that allowed counties to close polling places and conduct elections exclusively by mail. By 2007, 36 of 39 counties had switched to all-mail elections. Kittitas went vote by mail in 2008, and King County switched in 2009. As of 2011, only Pierce County had yet to adopt full vote by mail, although 89 percent of ballots cast there in 2010 were sent through the mail by voters using permanent absentee status.

This means that 98 percent of votes statewide were cast by mail in 2010. Ballots are mailed two weeks prior to an election. Unlike Oregon—where votes are counted only if they arrive back by election day—Washington will count a ballot that bears an election day postmark. Ballots dropped in the mail on election day (or just before election day) can take days to meander through the postal system. This, combined with the fact that a substantial proportion of voters wait until election day to vote, means that it can take several days (or longer) to know the winner of close elections.

In 2010, officials were able to count just 73 percent of votes on election night. By comparison, 96 percent of Oregon's votes were counted on election night. It is not uncommon for candidates who had a lead on election night to end up losing after several days of counting. Given King County's large population and the heavy concentration of Democratic voters there, late arriving ballots in statewide races can tilt toward liberal and Democratic candidates. In 2010, conservative incumbent Supreme Court Judge Richard Sanders led 51 percent to 49 percent on election night, but Sanders was eventually defeated by Charlie Wiggins after several days of post-election ballot counting. Wiggins, a candidate backed by interests that support Democratic candidates, took the lead as King County ballots added to the total.

The trend is not always so clear cut, and vote counts can drag even longer as provisional ballots and mailed ballots with signature problems are added to the mix. In 2004, Republican gubernatorial candidate Dino Rossi came out on election night, November 2, with a 1,000 vote lead over Democrat Christine Gregoire. Yet 800,000 votes remained to be counted. Gregoire opened a 14,000 vote lead the next day as a block of late votes from King County were counted. Her lead expanded to 18,000 by Thursday, November 4, but Rossi narrowed the gap over the following days as late votes came in from other counties. By November 9, Rossi re-took the lead with a 3,000 vote margin. On November 12, with 40,000 ballots still to count, Rossi held a 1,900 vote lead (Gilmore et al. 2004). After court battles about which provisional ballots should be counted and whether Democrats could track down people in King County whose mailed ballots were rejected because election officials could not confirm their signatures, Gregoire posted a 158 vote lead on November 15, with 6,000 votes still to count. A "final" tally on November 16—two weeks after election night—had Rossi with a 261 vote lead out of 2.8 million votes cast. After two recounts, however, Gregoire was eventually declared the winner.[5] This long count resulted from an extremely close race and from accepting mailed ballots that arrived after election day.

The Effects of Voting by Mail

What are the effects of voting by mail? Regardless of when votes are finally totaled, mail elections change campaigns. Early voting requires campaigns to target events and advertising differently. Mail elections may also increases turnout while not necessarily changing who participates. Turnout increases because mail ballots make voting more convenient. Studies suggest that participation increases among older, wealthier, well-educated, white people—people who already vote at the highest rates (Karp and Banducci 2000; Berinsky 2005). In Oregon, the increase in turnout appeared to be most pronounced in local races that generate limited interest. Turnout in vote by mail presidential elections, in contrast, was just 2 percent greater than in presidential elections conducted at polling places (Karp and Banducci 2000, 228). After five years of use in Oregon, voting by mail was widely popular—over 75 percent of voters approved of it (Southwell 2004). Attitudes may still be crystallizing in Washington. Surveys conducted in King County in 2006 (before the change to vote by mail) found voters were split when asked if they supported the change. Republicans were less supportive than Democrats, in part because of lingering suspicions about the contentious recount of the 2004 governor's race.

Campaign Finance

Campaign finance regulations also affect how elections are conducted. Washington has some of the nation's most detailed rules for disclosure of campaign revenue and spending. Voters approved initiative 276 in 1972 to establish the state's Public Disclosure Commission (PDC). Candidates for state and local contests must file detailed weekly reports to the PDC of contributions received and monthly reports of how money is spent. Reports must be filed more frequently immediately prior to the general election. Another initiative (I-134 of 1992) established some contribution limits. In 2011 contributions to judicial candidates and candidates for state office from individuals, interest groups, unions, and corporations were limited to $1,600 per primary and general election. Contributions to legislative candidates and local candidates were limited to $800 per election.[6]

The limits do not really constrain what can be given to parties, nor what parties can spend. Each party's state central committee can collect unlimited contributions and then contribute up to $58,000 per state legislative contest and $2.9 million per contest for a statewide office. In addition, each house and senate party caucus committee can collect unlimited contributions and contribute another $58,000 per legislative contest. Each party's county party committees can also collect unlimited contributions and spend another $29,000 per legislative contest. Thus, each party can funnel close to $150,000 to each legislative contest and millions into each statewide race.

Parties have not come close to collecting enough funds to direct the maximum amount of cash to every race—and as noted above, many races are uncompetitive and require little expenditure. However, in 2008 the Democratic Central Committee and other Democratic Party funds bundled at least $1.5 million for Christine Gregoire's reelection campaign—about 10 percent of her total spending. In some hot legislative elections, party funding provided around $100,000 per candidate, almost half of a candidate's total funds.[7] Candidates raise the balance of their funds in the form of contributions from individuals and PACs, which are subject to contribution limits.

Effects of Campaign Finance Rules

One effect of these rules is that parties play a more significant role in financing elections in Washington than they do in many other states. Another is that citizens and media have more access to information about the sources and uses of campaign money. But it is not always easy to track campaign cash. Millions of dollars of Political Action Committee (PAC) funding ends up in a few legislative races after first being donated to different candidates' personal campaign accounts. That money is then laundered through party caucus accounts, and then perhaps transferred again to a different state party fund, before finally being bundled into large gifts to a candidate in a close race.

U.S. Supreme Court decisions make it difficult (if not impossible) to limit how much additional money a group or PAC may spend on elections as long as these "independent expenditures" are not formally coordinated with a campaign.[8] Big spending groups sympathetic to the major parties often use generic names to mask their identity while running ads. In the 2008 election, "Its Time for a Change PAC" used over $7 million in independent expenditures to attack Governor Gregoire. PDC records show It's Time for a Change PAC received all of its funds from "ChangePAC", and that ChangePAC was an arm of the Building Industry Association of Washington. Likewise, the "Evergreen Progress PAC" spent $6 million attacking Republican Dino Rossi. Evergreen Progress PAC accepted $3 million from the Democratic Governors' Association, and over $1 million from the Service Employees International Union and other unions. State law requires these independent groups to reveal who their donors are, but there are no limits on what someone can contribute and no limits on what the groups spend. The PDC does not track who funds all the groups that spend heavily on independent expenditures.[9] Some independent groups have challenged the states' disclosure rules and have refused to identify their donors during the campaigns (Broder 2000, 182).

Washington's disclosure rules have generally made the sources of campaign spending more transparent, but regulations do not limit total spending. In 2008 over $140 million was spent on state and local elections in Washington. The 2010 total matched this when the U.S. Senate race is included. Figure 1 illustrates that

Figure 1. Campaign Spending in Washington Election

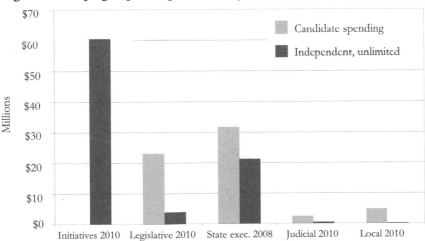

Sources: PDC 2008 Election Fact Book, 2010 reports.

Figure 2. Trends in Spending per Legislative Candidate 1992–2008, Inflation-adjusted Dollars

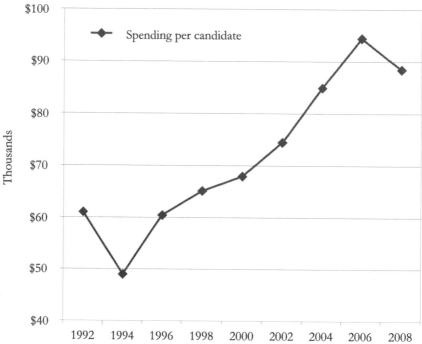

Source: *Washington Public Disclosure Commission.*

recently, most spending went to initiative campaigns and a gubernatorial race. Initiative spending in 2010 was three times greater than the previous record year (2005), and 2008 set a record for spending on a state executive contest. Figure 1 also illustrates that most money spent in state elections is not subject to contribution limits. The figure understates spending not subject to limits since a large portion of direct "candidate" spending in legislative races (perhaps 42%)[10] and executive races are large, (nearly) unlimited contributions to parties redirected to candidates. Spending on legislative races also hit a new high in 2010 at $23 million. However, when inflation adjusted dollars are considered, total spending by candidates in legislative races has been relatively stable since 1992. Figure 2 demonstrates that spending per candidate has increased substantially as fewer candidates seek legislative office.

Redistricting

Within bounds set by federal courts, states also determine how state legislative and U.S. Congressional districts are drawn. In most states, maps that define districts must be approved by the legislature then signed by the governor.

As a result of population growth and mobility, the number of people in existing districts changes. Washington added more than 800,000 residents over the decade ending in 2010. Districts in the state's fastest growing areas such as Benton, Clark, Cowlitz, and Walla Walla Counties and east King County ended up with as many as 30,000–45,000 more people than districts in slower growing places like Pacific County and Spokane. The population of congressional districts also became unbalanced. Without redistricting, people in heavily populated districts would end up with less representation per person than people in sparsely populated areas.

This is why states redraw district maps at least once every ten years after new census data are available. The last redistricting was done in 2011. Much was at stake. For example, some of the fastest growth in Washington has been in eastern and southern King County districts with competitive elections (e.g., the 41st, 45th, and 47th legislative districts circa 2010) and in safe Republican areas (e.g., the 5th legislative district) by 2010. Some neighboring districts that were heavily Democratic grew much slower (e.g., Seattle area 11th, 37th, and 46th legislative districts and the 32nd legislative district in Shoreline). If "surplus" Republican voters from the over-populated, safely Republican 5th legislative district were transferred to neighboring, competitive districts, Republicans could win more seats. Conversely, if new districts placed parts of fast growing Republican strongholds into solidly Democratic Seattle districts, Democrats would have the advantage. The stakes were even greater in 2011 because Washington gained a new 10th congressional district.

Given such stakes, redistricting tends to be a highly politicized process. But redistricting in Washington differs from the national norm. In most states, laws that define district maps are adopted through the normal legislative process. A party with majorities in both houses that also controls the governor's office can take advantage of the minority party by gerrymandering districts to maximize the number of safe seats for themselves. The U.S. Supreme Court simply requires that districts must be drawn such that they are "contiguous" and equal in population. This leaves room for a good deal of strategic cartography.

Washington is one of a dozen states where redistricting is largely out of the legislature's hands. Voters approved a constitutional amendment in 1983 to have districts drawn by a five member commission composed of two members appointed by Democrats, two appointed by Republicans, and a fifth member chosen by the other four. The commission must agree on a plan for congressional and state legislative district boundaries by January 1, 2012. The plan can only be amended by a 2/3 vote by both houses of the legislature, and it cannot be vetoed by the governor. If the commission fails to produce a plan, the State Supreme Court does so.

Effects of Redistricting Practices

Given incentives to gerrymander, and given that people move where they are near people like themselves, it is difficult to produce many districts that have the same number of Democratic and Republican voters. However, states with bipartisan redistricting commissions (such as Washington) are slightly more likely to adopt plans that produce districts that are two-party competitive than states that rely on redistricting by the state legislature. Districting done by legislators tends to produces more districts that are safe for incumbents (Krebs and Winburn 2011).

The Electoral Landscape

The previous section details how Washington's electoral practices are unique when compared to other states. But what do the election results in Washington tell us about the state?

Well before the 2008 presidential election, Washington was seen as a safe Democratic state. Many expect it to remain solidly Democratic in 2012, if not for years to come. Consider the evidence that Washington voters have made this a solidly "blue" state. Democrat John Kerry carried Washington in 2004 by 7 percent over George W. Bush, while Bush won a national vote majority. Democrat Al Gore won Washington handily in 2000, despite Green candidate Ralph Nader capturing 4 percent of the state's presidential vote. Bill Clinton put up double-digit victory margins in the 1990s. The last Republican presidential candidate to win Washington was Ronald Reagan in 1984. Barack Obama won Washington with 57 percent—posting the largest victory margin for a Democratic presidential candidate in the state since 1940 (when Franklin D. Roosevelt defeated Wendell Willkie).

More daunting for Republicans is the fact that support for Democrats in Washington appears to be deep and enduring. Going into 2012, Democrats have won every gubernatorial election since 1984. At every state election since 1992, Democrats won at least five, and usually six, of the eight statewide partisan executive offices. Democrats have won all four U.S. Senate contests since 1998, and controlled majorities of the state's U.S. House delegation in every election since 1994. While the 2010 midterm election produced massive gains for Republicans in other states, Democrats reelected a U.S. Senator and maintained their majorities in both chambers of the state legislature.[11]

Given all of this, we might categorize Washington as one of the nation's most solidly Democratic states. Scholars have categorized Washington as one of the nation's 12 most Democratic-dominant states. Indeed, among the 12 states where

Democrats were dominant from 2003 to 2006, only Illinois, New Jersey, and New Mexico had gains for Democrats during this period that exceeded those in Washington (Holbrook and La Raja 2008).[12]

However, categorizing Washington as safe for the Democrats is problematic, since a number of elections demonstrate that Washington is a microcosm of the larger, highly competitive national electoral landscape. The geography and demography of voting in Washington mirrors what is often seen nationally. Republicans dominate elections in Washington's rural areas and are competitive in the state's suburban regions—just as they are nationally. Likewise, just as Democrats run well in larger cities and on the coasts, voters west of the Cascades provide large margins for Democratic candidates in Washington. In many contests this political geography produces very competitive state races.

Obama dominated in Washington in 2008 for the same reason he won nationally: voters in Washington,[13] and nationally,[14] reported that the economy and jobs were their top issue concerns that year. Republican John McCain, who was popular in the state when he sought his party's nomination in 2000, fared badly in 2008 for several reasons—the main one being that he was the candidate of the party in control of the White House when the national economy spiraled into crisis. Evaluations of economic conditions typically have a major effect on vote choice (Fiorina 1978; Markus 1988). Any Republican presidential candidate would have likely lost in Washington in 2008 as a result of voters punishing the Republican Party for controlling the White House as the economy declined (Erickson and Wlezien 2009).

Given this, the 2008 election may have been a high-water mark for Democrats in Washington. Many other elections illustrate that, statewide, Washington remains competitive. Democrat Maria Cantwell won her first senate race in 2000 by a narrow 0.09 percent margin. The 2004 governor's race between Rossi and Gregoire was decided by just 133 votes. Republicans Sam Reed and Rob McKenna were reelected to statewide executive offices with large margins in 2008. Patty Murray's reelection for a fourth term in 2010 was one of the most competitive and expensive U.S. Senate contests of 2010. Under different circumstances than those facing McCain in 2008, a Republican presidential candidate could potentially win Washington in 2012 or 2016. Republicans who appeal to independent voters west of the Cascades do win state races. However, as documented below, some trends appear to continue to favor Democrats.

Trends in Voting and Attitudes

There are a number of ways we can illustrate trends in Washington elections over time. Figure 3 uses decades of election results to illustrate the balance of power in the legislature. Since 1994, Democrats made steady gains in winning state legislative seats and flirted with supermajority status in 2008. But Washington's statewide electoral competitiveness is also reflected here. Since

1980, partisan control of at least one chamber has often been narrow, and every election from 1992 to 2002 altered party control of at least one chamber. However, Democrats won legislative majorities in both chambers from 2004 to 2010. Figure 4 illustrates trends in electoral competition using popular vote totals from U.S. House elections. Again, we see high points for Republicans in 1994 and 2010 but an overall trend that has advantaged Democrats. Since 1990 the combined statewide vote for Republican house candidates reached a majority just once (1994).

Figure 3. Democratic Seat Shares in Washington State Legislature After Elections: 1974–2010

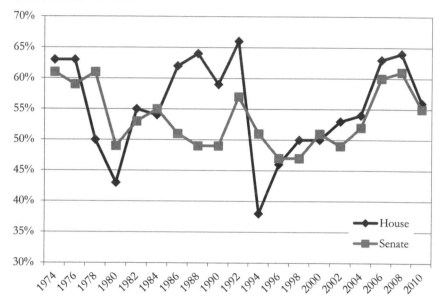

A voter's partisan identification is usually a good predictor of their voting behavior (e.g., Campbell et al. 1960; Bartels 2000). Overall levels of party identification may thus describe each party's long-term electoral base. Figure 5 shows trends in response to the question, "Generally speaking, do you consider yourself a Democrat, Republican, independent, or what?" From 1999 to 2010, more Washingtonians identified themselves as Democrats than Republicans. As Table 2 illustrates, a large plurality of "independents" usually said they leaned toward Democrats.[15] Yet by 2009 independents split rather evenly between Democrats and Republicans. As for the future, in 2009 voters under 35 were three times as likely to see themselves as Democrats than as Republicans. Self-described independents under 35 were also more likely to see themselves as Democrats. If party identification remains stable as a person ages, as some suspect (Flanigan

Figure 4. Trends in Statewide Popular Vote for U.S. House Candidates: 1990–2010

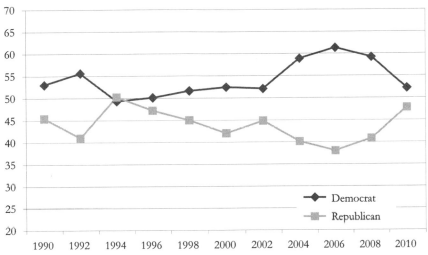

Source: Washington Secretary of State's Office.

Figure 5. Partisan Identification, Washington Voters: 1999–2010

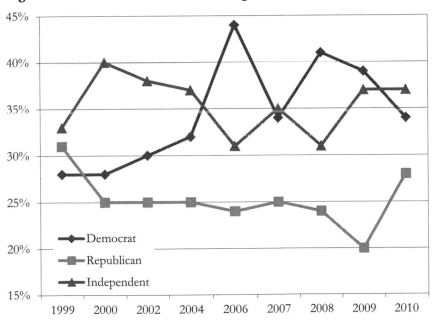

Sources: Washington Poll (2006–2010); Author's polls (1999–2002).

and Zingale 2010, 105; Jennings and Neimi 1984) this may give Washington Democrats an advantage in future elections. That said, more voters identified themselves as Republican in 2010 than in 2009.

Table 2

Washington Independent Voters' Party Preferences

	2006	2007	2008	2009	2010
Democrat	47%	41%	42%	37%	37%
Republican	29	35	30	39	40
Total Other	24	23	28	25	23
other	6	7	11	12	7
none/neither	11	11	11	9	13
don't know	2	3	3	2	2
refused	5	2	3	2	1

Source: Washington Poll, various years.

Conclusion

This chapter illustrates that elections in Washington are somewhat unique when compared to other states. Washington's unique election rules reflect popular preferences for elections that are transparent and open to full voter participation. Surveys asking about the voter's role in elections find enduring strands of populism in Washington. Polls show Washington voters think they are just as good at making important policy decisions—or more capable—as elected representatives. Very few voters think their representatives are better qualified than they are. Polls also find that Washingtonians want the ability to use elections as a check on their representatives and judges. Large majorities of Washingtonians oppose proposals that would limit their ability to hold the state's judges accountable via elections (Bowler, Donovan, and Parry 2009). Year after year, Washington voters express high levels of support for the citizens' initiative process, and they resist proposals to limit it (Bowler et al. 2001). Indeed, many of the election rules discussed in this chapter—nonpartisan voter registration, wide-open primary elections, campaign finance disclosure rules, and contribution limits—were adopted through direct democracy.

Endnotes

1. Federal law (the Help America Vote Act) has created some national standards for these practices.
2. As of February 2011, these included Idaho, Iowa, Maine, Minnesota, Montana, New Hampshire, Wisconsin, and Wyoming.
3. The second place Democrat had 23%. The first place Republican had 22%.
4. All Democratic delegates, and half of Republican delegates, were selected through caucuses in 2008.
5. In June of 2005, a judge ruled the official vote total gave Gregoire a 133 vote margin.
6. Local limits were added by the legislature in 2010.
7. Tim Knue ($52K party cash + $50K party in-kind mailings out of a total $246,200 spent); Roger Goodman ($52K cash + $52K in-kind of $287K total); Fred Finn ($45K cash + $52K in-kind of $293K); Mary Margaret Haugen ($32K cash, $36K in-kind of $335K total).
8. See *Buckley v. Valeo*, 424 U.S. 1 (1976) and *Citizen's United v. Federal Communications Commission*, 558 U.S. 08-205 (2010).
9. Groups such as the DGA are tax-exempt political groups incorporated through section 527 of the federal tax code. The IRS had released information on donors to these 527s in 2008. After *Citizens United*, groups have been able to raise and spend unlimited funds for independent expenditures in federal races without disclosure requirements.
10. Legislative party organizations and legislative party-linked PACs spent $9 million in 2008. The total spent on legislative races that year was $21.3 million.
11. Republicans picked up one U.S. House seat in 2010 after retiring Democrat Brian Baird was replaced by Republican Jamie Herrera in the 3rd Congressional District.
12. Democrats posted larger electoral gains in Colorado and Iowa than in Washington by 2006, but Democrats were not the dominant party in those states prior to this period.
13. 2008 Washington Poll.
14. 2008 National Exit Poll. CNN.
15. From 2006 to 2008, more independents said they felt closer to Democrats than Republicans. In 2009, more independents said they felt closer to Republicans.

References

Ansolabehere, Stephen, John Mark Hansen, Shigeo Hirano, and James M. Snyder Jr. 2007. "The Incumbency Advantage in U.S. Primary Elections." *Electoral Studies* 26(3): 660–68.

Bartels, Larry. 2000. "Partisanship and Voting Behavior: 1952–1996." *American Journal of Political Science* 44(1): 35–50.

Berinsky, Adam J. 2005. "The Perverse Consequences of Electoral Reform in the United States." *American Politics Research* 33(4): 471–91.

Borger, Julian. December 6, 2002. "Democrat Hawk Whose Ghost Guides Bush." *The Guardian*. guardian.co.uk/world/2002/dec/06/usa.julianborger.

Bowler, Shaun, and Todd Donovan. 2011. "Electoral Competition and the Voter." *Public Opinion Quarterly* 75(1): 151–64.

Bowler, Shaun, Todd Donovan, Max Neiman, and Johnny Peel. 2001. "Institutional Threat and Partisan Outcomes: Legislative Candidates' Attitudes toward Direct Democracy." *State Politics and Policy Quarterly* 1(4): 364–79.

Bowler, Shaun, Todd Donovan, and Janine Parry. March 18–20, 2009. "Public Reasoning about Judicial Selection Methods." Paper presented at the Annual Meeting of the Western Political Science Association, Vancouver, British Columbia.

Broder, David S. 2000. *Democracy Derailed: The Initiative Movement and the Power of Money.* New York: Harcourt.

Cain, Bruce E., and Elisabeth R. Gerber. 2002. *Voting at the Political Fault Line: California's Experiment with the Blanket Primary.* Berkeley: University of California Press.

Campbell, Angus, Philip E. Converse, Warren E. Miller, and Donald E. Stokes. 1960. *The American Voter.* Chicago: University of Chicago Press.

Cox, Gary W., and Michael C. Munger. 1989. "Closeness, Expenditures and Turnout in the 1982 U.S. House Elections." *American Political Science Review* 83(1): 217–31

Donovan, Todd, Christopher Z. Mooney, and Daniel A. Smith. 2011. *State and Local Politics: Institutions and Reforms.* Boston: Wadsworth Cengage Learning.

Erickson, Robert, and Christopher Wlezien. 2009. "The Economy and the Presidential Vote in 2008." *PS: Political Science and Politics* 42(1):22.

Fiorina, Morris P. 1978. "Economic Retrospective Voting in American National Elections: A Micro-Analysis." *American Journal of Political Science* 22(2): 426–43.

Fiorina, Morris P., Samuel J. Abrams, and Jeremy C. Pope. 2005. *Culture War? The Myth of a Polarized America.* New York: Pearson Longman.

Flanigan, William H., and Nancy H. Zingale. 2010. *Political Behavior of the American Electorate* 12th edition. Washington, D.C.: CQ Press.

Gerber, Elisabeth R., and Rebecca B. Morton. 1998. "Primary Election Systems and Representation." *Journal of Law, Economics and Organizations* 14(2): 304–24.

Gilmore, Susan, Andrew Garber, and Ralph Thomas. November 12, 2004. "Rossi Leading; Gregoire Allies Win in Court." *Seattle Times.*

Gronke, Paul. 2011. The Early Voting Information Center. earlyvoting.net.

Hamm, Keith E., and Gary F. Moncrief. 1999. "Legislative Politics in the States." In *Politics in the American States: A Comparative Analysis* 7th edition, edited by Virginia Gray, Russell L. Hanson, and Herbert Jacob. Washington, D.C.: CQ Press.

Hanmer, Michael J. 2009. *Discount Voting: Voter Registration Reforms and Their Effects.* Cambridge: Cambridge University Press.

Hill, Kim Quaile. 2003. "Democratization and Corruption" *American Politics Research* 31(6):613–31.

Holbrook, Thomas M., and Raymond J. La Raja. 2008. "Parties and Elections." In *Politics in the American States: A Comparative Analysis* 9th edition, edited by Virginia Gray, Russell L. Hanson, and Herbert Jacob. Washington, D.C.: CQ Press.

Jennings, M. Kent, and Richard G. Neimi. 1984. *Youth Parent Socialization Panel Study 1965–1973.* Ann Arbor, MI: Inter-university Consortium for Political and Social Research.

Karp, Jeffrey A., and Susan A. Banducci. 2000. "Going Postal: How All-Mail Elections Influence Turnout." *Political Behavior* 22(3):223–39.

Key, V.O. [1949] 1984. *Southern Politics in State and Nation.* Knoxville: University of Tennessee Press.

Krebs, Timothy B., and Jonathan Winburn. 2011. "State and Local Elections: The Unique Character of Sub-National Contests." In *New Directions in Campaigns and Elections,* edited by Stephen K. Medvic. New York: Routledge.

Markus, Gregory B. 1988. "The Impact of Personal and National Economic Conditions on the Presidential Vote: A Pooled Cross-sectional Analysis." *American Journal of Political Science* 32(1): 137–54.

McGlennon, John. 2009. "The Competition Gap: How Candidate Recruitment in State Legislative Elections Foreshadows Party Change." Report for the Thomas Jefferson Program in Public Policy. College of William and Mary.

Meier, Kenneth J., and Thomas M. Holbrook. 1992. "'I Seen My Opportunities and I Took 'Em': Political Corruption in the American States." *Journal of Politics* 54(1):135–55.

Neimi, Richard G., Lydia W. Powell, William D. Berry, Thomas M. Carsey, and James M. Snyder Jr. 2006. "Competition in State Legislative Elections: 1992–2002." In *The Marketplace of Democracy: Electoral Competition and American Politics*, edited by Michael McDonald and John Curtis Samples. Washington, D.C.: Brookings Institution Press.

Reed, Sam. April 10, 2007. "Voter Registration Change Would be a Costly Step Backward." *Tacoma News Tribune*.

Rosenstone, Steven J., and John Mark Hansen. 2003. *Mobilization, Participation, and Democracy in America*. New York: Longman.

Southwell, Priscilla. 2004. "Five Years Later, A Re-Assessment of Oregon's Vote by Mail Electoral Process." *PS: Political Science and Politics* 37(1): 89–93.

CHAPTER THREE

Political Parties in Washington

Andrew Appleton and Reneé Edwards

Introduction

POLITICAL PARTIES IN THE EVERGREEN STATE have, in many respects, been subject to the same forces and trends that have marked parties at the national level and in other state arenas. Among these forces and trends—not necessarily in any particular order—we might cite the decrease in classic partisan affiliation among the electorate, the increase in partisanship in legislative politics, the increasing professionalization of party organizations (especially in the area of fundraising and candidate support), and the increase in competition from environmental rivals (such as candidate-centered campaign organizations and Political Action Committees). Before the rise of candidate-centered campaign politics, party organizations were largely masters of the state political landscape; now they exist in a complex and shifting political environment. Washington State is no different from any other in that regard.

On the other hand, Washington State political parties have evolved in a particular, if not peculiar, context (Appleton and Grosse 2004). The state has long been characterized in political terms by its own brand of "western populism," a sometimes volatile mix of progressivism, individualism, and conservatism. In recent years, the revitalization of the political right has added a mix of Christian conservatism and anti-establishment politics to spice up the stew. Because Washington State has an open set of procedures for initiatives and referenda, state parties have had to adapt to these special circumstances. In some respects, that adaptation has taken the form of an accommodation with new forces and actors. At other times, parties—especially the major ones—have attempted to seize the advantage and wrest control from voters and state institutions.

In this chapter, we will look at the ongoing process of party adaptation in Washington State. We will begin by laying out the changes in the legal framework that governs party competition in the state. Here, the bulk of our analysis will be devoted to the controversy about primary elections, which has dominated the world of political parties in the state. The predominance of this issue has promoted strange alliances and produced odd bedfellows; even after several years, the issue has not been completely settled. However, the change in the primary system will arguably shape electoral and party politics in the state, more than any other recent development, for years to come. Next, we will turn to a discussion on the internal dynamics of the major parties, with a view to assessing the nature of the political coalitions that lie behind the state party organizations. Finally, we will evaluate the degree to which state political parties have evolved since the last edition of this book, *Washington State Government and Politics*, was published in 2004.

The Legal and Institutional Environment: Major and Minor Parties

Political parties in the Evergreen State are regulated under the Revised Code of Washington (RCW). This is not uncommon, since most states have, to varying degrees, specified how political parties may organize and select representatives. Indeed, observers have noted that the legal restrictions placed by states on parties and party organizations were an effective obstacle to the renewal and modernization of political parties in America (e.g., Bennett 2009). But many of the provisions governing the regulation and functioning of state level parties have been examined by the nation's highest court. It has been argued that, in recent years, the Supreme Court has tended toward freeing major political parties from some of the dictates of state control, leaving them more able to control their own internal processes; on the other—and perhaps in apparent contradiction—the court has opted to not intervene to open up the political space to minor parties and new entrants (Salka 2011; Black 1996).

A political party in Washington State is, prima facie, free to "(a) Make its own rules and regulations; and (b) Perform all functions inherent in such an organization" (RCW 29A.80.011). However, the state makes a (not uncommon) distinction between major and minor parties, each of which is treated differently in regard to candidate selection, organizational, and financial procedures. Under state law (RCW 29A.04.086), a political party in Washington State is considered a major party if its nominees for president, U.S. Senate, or a statewide office received a minimum of 5 percent of the total votes cast in the state during the previous election in an even-numbered year; the party retains this status until the next even-numbered year election when there are qualifying offices up for election. Major parties are mandated to nominate candidates through primary elections, are the only organizations permitted to form political caucuses in the legislature, and must hold internal organizational elections according to state law.

The system is supposed to ensure that major party status is a direct reflection of voters' political ideologies, rather than simply a reflection of national trends. Currently Washington State has only two major parties—the Republican and

Democratic parties. In the past, however, the Libertarian Party has also enjoyed status as a major party within the state and continues to flirt with that designation following recent elections. Indeed, as we will discuss below, the aspirations of the Libertarian Party to regain and hold major party status has been one of the drivers behind its collusion with the Democratic and Republican parties in the ongoing battle over primary elections. Aside from the Libertarian Party, other minor parties within the state include the American Heritage Party, the Constitution Party, the Green Party, and the Progressive Party.

One of the principal distinctions between major and minor parties is that the latter are free to designate candidates through conventions, whilst the former are bound to hold primary elections in accordance with state law.[1] However, the primary election system in Washington State has been the subject of intense scrutiny and conflict in recent years, and has pitted the three major parties (Democratic, Republican, and Libertarian) against the state—and, arguably, against public opinion. As outlined in previous work (Appleton and Grosse 2004), the Washington primary had, for much of its history, been relatively unique. It was a product of the "western populism" of the Depression era, and it gave a peculiar character to the internal organization and operations of political parties in the state.[2] However, the intrusion of national-level influences (via the mechanism of the Supreme Court) has forced a recasting of the system and has engendered a long period of uncertainty and confusion about the future of the system.

Primary Elections

One of the classic functions of political parties, ascribed to them by political scientists, remains the selection of candidates for office. Since the Progressive era and the accompanying political reforms adopted across states and municipalities, the ability of parties to select candidates has been largely circumscribed by legal restraints. Party organizations have been constrained to operate within the culture of the primary election process, although how that process works varies from state to state. For many years, Washington State was quite distinct in the design of its primary process; however, from the perspective of the major party organizations, the primary process has been an unwarranted intrusion on the right to free association guaranteed in the Constitution of the United States.

Figure 1. Timeline of Washington State Primary Changes

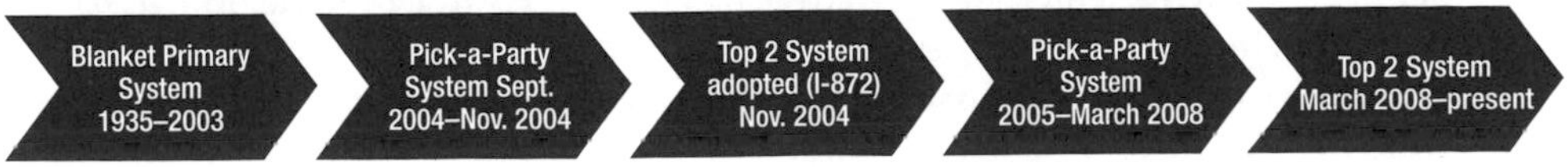

| Blanket Primary System 1935–2003 | Pick-a-Party System Sept. 2004–Nov. 2004 | Top 2 System adopted (I-872) Nov. 2004 | Pick-a-Party System 2005–March 2008 | Top 2 System March 2008–present |

Non-Presidential Primaries

Since its induction in 1935, the "blanket primary" system both enjoyed immense public popularity and endured strong disproval by the state's major political parties. Because the system allowed citizens to vote for a candidate of one party for one office, and another party candidate for a different office, voters were able to engage in cross-over voting or "ticket splitting." The state's majority parties were staunchly opposed to the system, claiming it unconstitutionally violated the parties' right of free association; at its core, the claim of the party organizations was that it strips them of the possibility of nominating their own candidates. Since its inception there have been multiple attempts to replace the blanket system by the state's major parties, claiming the primary was unconstitutional; however, it continued to pass constitutional muster over time.[3] Despite sporadic attempts by both the Republican and Democratic parties to force the issue back onto the political agenda, the system seemed immune to challenge from within.

The "blanket primary" was, in large part, the brainchild of the Washington State Grange, an offshoot of the national fraternal order. Established in 1889, just months before Washington Territory achieved statehood, the nonprofit, nonpartisan organization has lived up to its self-proclaimed role as "the people's voice of Washington." Designed to allow rural communities and agricultural families a voice in state politics, the Grange is a fraternal organization that started its existence in 1867 as the "Order of Patrons of Husbandry." The organization participates in a variety of activities, ranging from community-based fundraisers, children's camps, and talent contests to state-level political lobbying and participation in politically motivated lawsuits. The Grange was one of two organizations directly responsible for the implementation of the blanket primary in the state and was involved in the establishment of the additional two types of primaries the state has had since the blanket system was ruled unconstitutional. In addition, the Grange maintains direct involvement with legislative affairs and public policies within the state. It is part of the organization's mission to create a forum in which "men, women and young people assemble for fellowship, discussion and formulation of policies on current issues" (wa-grange.org). Because Washington State is comprised of many rural areas, small communities, and farming towns, the organization attempts to bridge the urban-rural divide and provide a voice for these smaller areas and rural citizens. The group states that "political powers from heavily populated urban areas push their agendas and the Grange is frequently the only voice the rural residents have to express their needs." The organization has been extremely active within the state and has definitely proved a vehicle for legislative change. As the battle over the primary system has intensified in the last few years, the Grange has been one of the most active and involved nonpartisan organizations, allying with the state against the concerted efforts of the party organizations.

The blanket primary was one of the truly unique political institutions in Washington State for a long period, although it gained some notoriety when both Alaska and Louisiana adopted similar systems. Ironically, it was this increasing visibility that would spell its eventual demise. In March 1996, California voters adopted an initiative, similar to that of Washington's, that initiated a blanket primary system in that state (SOSa "History"). Similar to Washington's system, the California primary was beset with multiple lawsuits concerning its constitutionality. In 2000, following a case in which the California Democratic Party challenged the California State blanket system, the U.S. Supreme Court ruled California's primary unconstitutional because it violated the political parties' right to free association (*California Democratic Party*). Following the ruling by the Supreme Court, Washington's three major political parties at the time once again challenged the system in the United States District Court for the Western District of Washington. After a week of negotiations by attorneys for both the state and the political parties, the blanket primary system in Washington was left unchanged for the 2000 elections. During the ongoing court battles by the states' major parties, the attitude of the general public toward the primary system stayed largely unchanged and the blanket primary maintained its popularity, despite its legacy of legal troubles.

In fact, in 2001 the new secretary of state, Sam Reed, released a report which overwhelmingly found that voters still preferred the blanket system and were strongly in favor of retaining it. After conducting 11 hearings in various areas of the state, the report summarized the findings, stating that "most of the voters (in Washington) are independent and want to continue to participate in the primary without having to affiliate with a political party and without being restricted to the candidates of only one party in the primary" (SOSb "History"). Also evident from the hearings was the general objection voters had to being required to publicly declare party affiliation by registration or at polls, even if given the potential to change party affiliation in future elections. The Federal District Court upheld the blanket system as constitutional again in 2002 (*Democratic Party of Washington State*), although immediately the majority political parties appealed the decision. On September 15, 2003, the Ninth Circuit Court of Appeals found Washington's blanket primary unconstitutional on grounds that it violates the parties' right to free association. In particular, the court invalidated the system because it found it to be "materially indistinguishable" from the California system, which had already been found unconstitutional (Faulkner and McCall "Commentary").[4] Although the state and the Washington State Grange asked the U.S. Supreme Court to review the Court of Appeals decision, the request was denied and the decision was left unchanged, ending the blanket primary system in the state.

Two systems were then considered to replace the blanket primary, the "Top 2" primary and the "pick-a-party" primary. The Top 2 Primary was considered by the

Grange to be a better choice, as it was assumed it would be more popular with the general public than the pick-a-party would be. In January 2004, the Grange filed Initiative 872, which proposed a Top 2 Primary system; it would be placed on the ballot in the November elections. The system would grant the voter the "right to cast a vote for any candidate for each office without any limitation based on party preference or affiliation of either the voter or the candidate." The two candidates with the most votes advance to the general election, and the voter does not declare party affiliation. In this type of system it is possible that the top two candidates receiving the most votes and therefore advancing to the general election may be members of the same political party (Oldham 2009). Because the state had historically enjoyed a primary system in which voters could cross party lines, proponents of the Top 2 system were content with it as a potential replacement for the blanket primary. In response to I-872, the legislature passed a bill that would allow the executive branch to essentially choose between two alternatives: the Top 2 system favored by the Grange or the pick-a-party system favored by the party organizations. In April 2004, Governor Gary Locke chose to veto the portions of the bill that would have mandated the Top 2 system, in a move that was widely seen as motivated by partisan concerns (Sam Reed, the secretary of state and a moderate Republican, opposed the veto). The governor's veto left Washington State forced to provisionally adopt the alternative version of the primary to that proposed in I-872.

Also referred to as a "Montana-style primary," the pick-a-party system asks voters to choose a political party to affiliate with once they have entered the voting booth and then constrains them to vote for candidates of that party only. Affiliation remains confidential, with the intention that the voter would still maintain a feeling of party independence during the election. (This issue of affiliation was to become central to the subsequent court case.) The pick-a-party system was used in the September 2004 primaries. It was wildly unpopular among the voting public, and according to the Office of the Secretary of State, more than 14,000 calls and letters were received by voters in opposition to the system (SOSb "History"). Following the September primary, surveys revealed that only 21 percent of Washington State voters were in support of the pick-a-party primary system.

The pick-a-party system stood out in stark contrast to the largely popular blanket primary. A public accustomed to party independence was suddenly forced to choose party affiliation on a ballot—something that had not occurred since 1934. While party affiliation was kept confidential, it was quickly apparent that the voting public did not care to associate with a party at the polls, confidential or not.

Due to the overwhelming dissatisfaction of the public regarding the pick-a-party primary system, Initiative 872, which would instate the Top 2 Primary, found its way onto the general election ballot in November 2004 and was approved by nearly 60 percent.[5] Despite the popularity of the Top 2 Primary with the public, once again the state's primary was in court. The Washington State Republican Party immediately filed suit in the United States District Court for the Western District of Washington, claiming that Initiative 872 violates the political parties' right to free association.[6] The pick-a-party primary was reestablished while the court reviewed the primary system in regard to constitutionality.

In this case, it was argued that the parties' right to free association was violated because candidates were allowed to identify their personal party preference without input from that party (Faulkner and McCall "Commentary"). In other words, the political party did not have the right to control who would become affiliated with the party. This occurred because under Initiative 872 any candidate could print a political party of their choice next to their name on the ballot. The right to free association derives from the First Amendment to the Constitution which states that "Congress shall make no law respecting…the right of the people to peaceably assemble." Because the Top 2 system would allow candidates to be associated with a particular party without that party's consent, the Washington State Republican Party asserted the system was unconstitutional.

The Top 2 system underwent much scrutiny by the court. The primary simultaneously held great benefit for both the candidates and the voters, but it allowed limited involvement by political parties. It allowed voters to vote for any candidate, regardless of party affiliation, and also gave uninformed voters the ability to cast their vote based solely on political party affiliation. The candidate, then, could appeal to voters based on individual beliefs and campaign promises, but also on the grounds of party affiliation. The voter, likewise, could choose a candidate based on their campaign goals and personal beliefs, or on the party platform that most appealed to them. The Republican Party's desire to remove party preference information would eliminate the ability of the voter to vote a "straight ticket" or choose a candidate based solely on party affiliation. Straight ticket voting is not well regarded nationally, however, and many states have taken measures to discourage it. By allowing candidates to list their own personal party preference on the ballot, the Republican Party asserted that it would not have control over who claimed to represent a party's platform simply for the chance to be elected. For instance, a candidate whose political ideals aligned more closely with another party could claim to affiliate with the Republican Party on the ballot, thus potentially securing votes based on that affiliation and not on actual ideologies, resulting in voter confusion. The Republican Party claimed that this would create a situation in which majority parties would be forced to affiliate with someone who would otherwise be a rival, which would ultimately remove a party's value and ability to stand for particular beliefs and ideologies over time (Faulkner and McCall "Commentary").

Heeding the arguments of the Republican Party, the court struck down Initiative 872 on August 22, 2006, ruling it unconstitutional. Immediately,

Washington State and the Grange filed petitions for a writ of certiorari to the United States Supreme Court and oral arguments were held in October 2007. On March 18, 2008, a divided Supreme Court (on a 7 to 2 vote) overturned the Ninth Circuit Court of Appeals decision, and upheld Initiative 872 as constitutional. The court's majority ruled that the initiative did not impose a "severe burden" on the political parties' right to free association and that the parties' claims that voters would be confused could not be evaluated until after the primary was implemented (Faulkner and McCall "Commentary"). The Top 2 Primary was reestablished as Washington's primary system, and in August 2008 the first complete Top 2 Primary in the country was conducted. After the election, surveys revealed that 76 percent of voters approved of the system.

The Presidential Primary

Since 1989 Washington State has had a presidential primary system in addition to the state primary. The presidential primary was instated in order to give Washington residents the ability to participate in the presidential selection process, and to create a more open system that represented the average voters' will, indicating that the caucus system by nature eliminates some voters from the process. The law (RCW 29A.56) states:

> The…presidential nominating caucus system in Washington State is unnecessarily restrictive of voter participation in that it discriminates against the elderly, the infirm, women, the disabled, evening workers, and others who are unable to attend caucuses and therefore unable to fully participate in this most important quadrennial event that occurs in our democratic system of government.

Over 200,000 voters signed the initiative to the legislature in 1988 proposing a presidential primary system. The presidential primary has been widely popular with voters since its inception. Secretary of State Sam Reed stated that voter turnout for the caucuses in 2008 was 1/10th of the turnout for the primary, indicating that the primary system was overwhelmingly favored by voters.

There are two ways a candidate may appear on a presidential primary ballot—the Secretary of State compiles a ballot of the candidates most popular nationally, and by petition signed by over 1,000 voters. The primary allows every Washington voter to participate, not just those who are part of the caucuses. A voter may participate in both the primary and the caucus as long as they sign an oath to cast their vote for the same political party. A voter cannot, therefore, vote for a candidate representing one party in the primary and a candidate representing a different party in the caucus. Voters feel the primary system has allowed them to directly participate in who is chosen to run in the general election, and that it also tends to encourage presidential candidates to visit and campaign on issues directly affecting Washington State. The presidential primary is not always used by political parties in choosing the candidate that will represent the party in the general election, however. Each political party may choose whether or not they will use the results from the primary, the caucus, or a combination of both. The Democratic Party has never used primary results to allocate delegates to their presidential nominating convention. The Republican Party has historically used a combination of both caucus and primary results. For example, in 2008, 37 Republican delegates were chosen; of these 51 percent were selected by primary and 49 percent were selected by caucus (Berg-Andersson "Green Papers"). No party has ever solely used the presidential primary to choose its candidates.

The presidential primary race in Washington has not occurred at every presidential election since it was instated. In 2004 the election was canceled to save the state the roughly $6 million estimated cost. In April 2010 it was again canceled for the same reasons. Due to economic hardships the presidential primary for 2012, which was estimated to cost roughly $10 million, was canceled. In lieu of the presidential primary system, political parties will use the caucuses to determine their candidates for the general election. Interestingly, the cancelation of the presidential primary came at a time when the Democratic Party says it is considering moving away from the caucus system for choosing candidates and was considering at least partially using the primary system for determining candidacy. Both the Democratic and Republican parties lobbied for lawmakers to at least delay canceling the primary; the Republican Party in particular opposed the move as it uses the primary to select some of its delegates to the convention. The bill, however, recommended by the House Ways and Means Committee and introduced by the governor and the secretary of state, passed both the house and senate in spring 2011. The bill (SB 5119) will only temporarily suspend the primary; it will be reestablished as of January 1, 2013, which means there will be a presidential primary in 2016 (unless it is canceled again).

Critics of the presidential primary believe it should be canceled permanently, mostly due to the economic burden on the state for something that has not historically been used by political parties to choose candidates. In addition, critics claim that because the primaries are held so late in the year, other states have already chosen the nominees and there is little purpose in holding a presidential primary.

Ongoing Controversies with the Primary System

The reaction to the Top 2 Primary system has been mixed, at best. While the nonpartisan nature of the individual vote remains popular with the voters themselves, the system cannot be said to increase the likelihood that minor party candidates will (a) be represented on the ballot at the general election or (b) get elected. For example, in the most recent primary election, held on August 17, 2010, only one minor party or independent candidate made it on the ballot in contests for any partisan offices at the state or national level in races where both major parties were represented. And, that one candidate (Bob Jeffers-Schroder, Independent) polled under 7 percent of the vote against 79 percent for the incumbent, Jim McDermott, who was opposed by three Democrats and two independents.[7] Furthermore, following the November 2010 election, Washington State is one of only five states in the country where all statewide offices are held by either Democrats or Republicans.[8] Even proponents of the system conceded that it might diminish access to minor party or independent candidates, but the most vigorous arguments in favor of the Top 2 Primary emphasized the probability that it would lead to stronger competition between parties—and, as a corollary, weaken the position of strong incumbents.

In the first general election held after the transition to the Top 2 system, in November 2008, all nine members of the Washington State delegation to the House of Representatives ran for reelection and all were elected. All statewide offices remained in the control of the same party (with the exception of public lands commissioner, where Peter Goldmark, a Democrat, defeated the Republican incumbent, Doug Southerland, by a 31,000 vote margin). At the state level, only four incumbents were defeated out of a total of 124 races—of those four, one was defeated in the primary that had been held in August. While it is hard to prove that using any of the previous primary election systems would, in fact, have changed this outcome, it is clear that two rounds of the Top 2 system have not diminished the ability of incumbents to be reelected and parties to retain control over offices and districts. Critics have even seen an acceleration of that control in the moving of the primary from late-August to the first Tuesday of August (passed by the legislature in April 2011), which means that independent and non-major party candidates have to file for the ballot in early May, nearly six months before the general election.

Perhaps the biggest question about the Top 2 system is whether it will survive yet another court challenge. In January 2011, the Western District Court upheld the constitutionality of I-872 and dismissed the case filed by the Washington State Republican Party (in which both the Democratic and Libertarian parties had intervened as plaintiffs). Central to the dismissal was whether "reasonable, well-informed voters" would be misled by party labels on the primary ballots; specifically, the parties themselves assert that their logo (which they equate to a trademark) should be in their control, rather than controlled by candidates. The district court echoed the position of the Supreme Court, which had found (in its 2008 decision) that there was no compelling evidence to show that this would, in fact, be the case.[9]

As of this writing, the case is on appeal before the Ninth Circuit Court of Appeals. Briefs have been filed by the two major parties and the Libertarian Party, asking for the constitutionality of I-872 and the primary system that it embodied to be once more reviewed. In its brief, the Libertarian Party encapsulates the broad arguments advanced against the system by all three parties; first, it infringes upon the right to free association; second, it distorts access to the ballot (including inhibiting minor parties from gaining major party status); and third, it removes control of its trademark from the party organization.[10] Washington State and the Grange are due to be filing their own briefs defending the system with the court; it appears that the recent turmoil over the primary system in the Evergreen State is not over.

Party Organization

The Party Organizational Framework

As we noted at the beginning of the chapter, Washington State law lays out the framework within which major parties organize. That framework specifies four distinct levels of organization: precinct, county, legislative district, and state. RCW 29A.80.020 calls for major parties to have a state committee composed of two members from each county committee. (Interestingly, Washington has a gender-equality provision that states that the county delegation should be of opposite sexes, and that the chair and vice chair of the state committee are also of opposite sexes.) The state committees are enjoined to meet every two years—in January of odd-numbered years—to elect new officers and to adopt rules and bylaws. State law requires a minimum notification time to all new committee members of the time and place of the meeting. In addition to these specifications, the RCW lists the functions of the state parties as (but not limited to) organizing state party conventions, selecting delegates to national party conventions, selecting nominees for state and federal office, and nominating presidential electors.

In practice, there is minimal variation in the formal organization of the major parties from the precinct level up. County central committees are composed of all precinct officers within that county, and have a requirement to elect a chair and vice chair of opposite sexes. County committees are required to meet under similar conditions to state committees (once every two years in even-numbered years). County chairs are responsible for convening a meeting of precinct officers from each legislative district to elect legislative district officers. At the base of the pyramid, then, are the precinct committee officers (PCO); RCW 29A.80.51 allows any candidate for the position of precinct officer to declare themselves on the ballot in the primary election (as long as they conform to the general standards for candidacy prescribed in election law); the top vote getter for each party is declared elected following the primary election.

The election of the precinct committee officers through the primary process did not escape the controversies described above, and it has been thrown into doubt in the wake of the January 2011 federal district court decision upholding the constitutionality of the Top 2 Primary. While Judge John Coughenour sided with the state and the Grange over the major electoral provisions of I-872, he found that its application to the election of PCOs does not pass constitutional muster. Crucially, he found no merit in the contention that I-872, in and of itself, does not specify the conditions for the election of PCOs, which is a matter of existing state law. Coughenour ruled that I-872 serves, in the case of the partisan public office, not to "determine the nominees of a political party but serves to winnow the number of candidates to a final list of two for the general election"—just as the Grange had argued in its brief. Yet, he wrote, this standard cannot be applied to the selection of PCOs through the primary itself. Furthermore, he found that there is a critical distinction between selecting public officials and selecting individuals to serve as members of political parties. And finally, he noted, the application of I-872 inevitably violates the "ten percent" rule embedded in the relevant state law.[11]

In ruling thus, Judge Coughenour relied, in part, upon the influential 1989 *Eu vs. San Francisco Democratic Central Committee* ruling by the U.S. Supreme Court, in which the court asserted the right to freedom of association of political parties, and acknowledged the public interest in parties being able to select their own leaders and shape the party message. The *Eu* decision strikes at one of the acknowledged weaknesses of the party system in the United States, namely the formalization—or lack thereof—of the relationship between political parties and their "members." Since political parties in the United States, in general, have no formalized system of memberships and dues, such as exists in most European countries, the question of who is and who is not a member is hazy at best and relies, to a great degree, on self-identification. However, Judge Coughenour agreed with the plaintiffs in the case that "personal 'consideration' of party association is insufficient to withstand constitutional scrutiny." Or, further in the opinion, "Washington's PCO election similarly infringes on the political parties' freedom to identify the people who constitute their association" (*Washington State Republican Party v. Washington State Grange* 2011). Crucially, Coughenour's ruling was also seen as applying to the possibility of electing PCOs through the general as opposed to the primary election process.

One solution to the problem that has been suggested in the Washington State Legislature is to move the election of party PCOs to the presidential primaries (which, necessarily, restrict voter participation to one of the parties holding primaries). In March 2011, the house passed a bill to do this, but it did not advance in the senate. Whether such a move would go unchallenged by the state political parties (especially the Republicans and the Libertarians; the former had expressed deep opposition in the legislative hearings) and survive another court challenge is uncertain. However, the issue is moot in the short term because the presidential primaries scheduled for 2012 have been canceled. This would appear to leave the state with no constitutionally acceptable vehicle by which to fulfill the legal requirement for the election of party PCOs. In all likelihood the selection of PCOs may well be removed from state jurisdiction and returned to party organizational control.

The Washington State Democratic Party explicitly limits the authority of the State Committee (which it labels "the Statutory State Committee") to the duties ascribed to it under RCW 29A.42.020, as discussed above. The party has chosen to vest authority in the State Convention and in its executive branch—the Washington State Democratic Central Committee (SCC). As the SCC is selected by the State Convention essentially free of any mandates of state law, it serves as the real locus of power and authority within the party. The bylaws specify that the Statutory State Committee will make bylaws (as it is required to do by law) that delegate its duties to the SCC.[12] The Republican Party, in contrast, has established a State Executive Board composed of two members (of opposite sex) from each legislative committee. The executive board is the principle alternative power structure to the mandatory state central committee. In contrast to the Democrats and Republicans, the Washington State Libertarian Party—unconstrained by the laws applying to major parties—is comprised of a State Executive Committee of four or five at-large representatives, a vice chair, and a chair. The Libertarian Party selects all candidates by endorsement from their state convention. In order to be considered as a candidate, a person must attend the state convention and "gain the support of [LPWA] membership" (www.lp.org).

Intraparty Dynamics

In recent years, much of the attention of those who focus on state level parties in the state of Washington has been focused on the factional struggles for control of the Washington State Republican Party. In previous editions of this book, we have described how the party organization responded to the growth of conservative Christian activism through the 1980s and 1990s. To a certain extent, the splits inside the Washington State Republican party during that time mirrored trends at the national level and in other states. Today, that dynamic is not much different. Following the 2008 Democratic landslide, Republican Party organizations and grassroots conservative movements have been reassessing their strategies, and the outcome has been far from consensual.

In the Evergreen State, the influence of the Tea Party insurgency made itself felt in the 2010 election cycle. The most prominent example was provided by the contest between Dino Rossi and Clint Didier for the nomination as Republican candidate for the U.S. Senate. Patty Murray, the three-term Democratic senator, was up for reelection and her seat was beginning to look, even to outside observers, potentially vulnerable. Clint Didier, a former NFL player and alfalfa farmer in Eltopia, Washington (near Pasco), and a Tea Party activist, declared his candidacy early, only to be joined in the race by Dino Rossi, a real estate developer and former candidate for governor who lost to Christine Gregoire by a margin of only 133 votes in 2004. The two candidates could not have been more opposite; Rossi, from Seattle, with prior experience as a state senator and a reputation as a consensus-seeker, versus Didier, the plain-spoken NFL player-turned-farmer, given to analyzing politics in terms of the game he had spent much of his life playing.

Rossi ran with strong encouragement and backing from the Republican National Campaign Committee and the state Republican establishment. It was widely reported that Karl Rove was providing strategic support and fundraising capabilities to the Rossi campaign. On the other hand, Didier courted conservative, grassroots organizations, and received endorsements from Ron Paul and Sarah Palin—even if the latter backed away from a personal appearance in support of him (although she did lend her voice to a recorded "robocall" advertisement). In a highly visible test of Tea Party strength in Washington State, Didier ran his campaign as a challenge not only to the Democrats but also to moderate Republicans.

As most analysts had predicted, the Top 2 Primary worked against Didier; anecdotal evidence showed that even voters who leaned toward views closer to the Tea Party agenda were likely to vote for Rossi, given that polls showed him more likely to beat incumbent Senator Murray.[13] Didier polled just under 13 percent of the vote, compared to 46 percent for Murray and 33 percent for Rossi. However, vote tallies suggested that Rossi had a potentially winning margin in the general election; in all, the Republican candidates in the primary totaled 49.88 percent of the vote, versus 48.54 percent for the declared Democrats. What would be crucial in determining the outcome would be Rossi's ability to pull together the more segmented Republican electorate, and especially to garner the bloc of voters who had supported Didier in the primary. The most immediate post-election polls showed Rossi with a projected lead over Murray (Rasmussen Reports 2010).

Demonstrating the gulf between mainstream Republicans and Tea Party supporters in the state, Didier called a Seattle press conference and announced that he would refuse to endorse Rossi unless the latter acceded to three demands (in a public statement): first, to sign a pledge against abortion, second, to oppose all tax hikes, and third, to commit to reducing the size of the federal government. The Rossi campaign responded with a statement that they would not let the message of the campaign be dictated by any person or group. Didier's intent was made clear in an interview that he gave to local news media, when he stated that Rossi "doesn't have a chance of winning right now. I'm trying to help him win" (Associated Press 2010). Three weeks later, Didier sent an open letter to Republicans in the state explaining his position. "To all those who are saying I owe Mr. Rossi an open endorsement I say: it's time to ask Dino Rossi—or any Republican—to either honor these simple platform planks or get out of the way for those who will," he wrote (Toeplitz 2010). Didier did not change his position; with just a few days before the election, he announced that he would be voting for Rossi but would still not offer him an endorsement. In the end, Rossi lost the general election to Murray by a four point margin.

Republicans had harbored hopes of performing well in Washington State in the 2010 election, particularly given the national mood. Furthermore, the historical experience of 1994—when the Republican landslide was highly visible in the state—had raised expectations. However, the modest gains of the party in the state legislative elections (4.72%) coupled with the failure to make breakthroughs in any of the major nationwide or statewide races (compared to the dramatic swing in U.S. Congressional elections and in other states), set off a period of soul-searching within the party organization. Two competing narratives of the shortcomings of the party in 2010 emerged. Moderate Republicans highlighted the increasingly liberal nature of the Washington electorate, and the damage caused by infighting in the Republican Party between moderates, conservatives, and libertarians.[14] The Tea Party version emphasized weak leadership in the state party, a lack of organizational coordination, and the inability of the party to connect with angry and disillusioned voters (Isackson 2011). This narrative questions why voters who supported three anti-tax initiatives could also reject the Republican candidate for the U.S. Senate. A common theme in both narratives is the hurdle of the new primary system, with its potential to fatally fragment the Republican vote.

The fallout from the 2010 election was to make itself felt at the State Republican Committee meeting in January, held in Tukwila. In a surprise move, the county representatives rejected the reappointment of then-party chair Luke Esser and replaced him with conservative former talk-show host and Tea Party supporter Kirby Wilbur.[15] Wilbur's impeccable conservative credentials and friendships with prominent national right-wing figures certainly fuelled suspicions that his election represented a swing to the right for the state Republican Party. However, Wilbur himself has tried to downplay this aspect of his chairmanship and has attempted to portray his leadership as the start of a new 'big tent' era for the state party (Smith 2011). His ability to do so will be put to the test in the 2012 gubernatorial election, for which Rob McKenna, the popular (and moderate) Republican attorney general has announced his candidacy. McKenna is a leader of the Mainstream Republicans of Washington (washingtonmainstream.org), an organization dedicated to anchoring the state party organization in the political center-right.

Just as its lackluster election performance sparked upheaval in the Republican Party, the better-than-predicted showing of the state Democratic Party—retaining both U.S. Senate seats, the governor's office, and five U.S. House seats out of nine, plus majorities in both chambers of the state legislature—has largely exempted the party of post-election infighting. At the state central committee meeting in January 2011, the incumbent chair, Dwight Pelz, who has been in the position since 2006, was reelected without a serious challenge. While the party has lost its toehold in the eastern part of the state, where former Speaker of the House Thomas S. Foley represented the Fifth Congressional District for

30 years, King County has become steadily more liberal and Democratic in its political complexion. While Washington State's electorate cannot be qualified as uniformly Progressive, the electoral terrain remains promising for Democrats for the immediate future.

Party Finance

Party finance in the state of Washington is tightly controlled by state law. The principal regulatory mechanism is the Public Disclosure Commission, created by voter initiative in 1972. Subject to an early challenge in the state court system, where it was upheld in a 7-2 vote by the State Supreme Court, the immediate impact of the Public Disclosure Act was to prompt a flurry of resignations from elected officials rather than disclose their personal finances (*Spokesman-Review* 1974). The act was significantly amended in 1975, when the controversial "bounty hunter" provision (under which a citizen could receive half of any money recovered by the state in enforcing the act, if the citizen were to bring the case to the attention of the commission) was removed, and provisions were adopted restricting the ability of unions to enforce mandatory political dues on members. Thirty years after its creation, Washington State and the PDC were ranked top in the nation on campaign finance and lobbying disclosures by the Center for Public Integrity (*Moscow-Pullman Daily News* 2003).

The obverse of the drive to more tightly regulate campaign spending at the federal level in the 1990s and 2000s was the potential for it to magnify the role that state party organizations might play in funneling money—both from within state and out of state—to candidates. In fact, recent literature has convincingly shown that the cumulative effect of federal campaign finance regulation has been to provide disincentives to national, state, and local party organizations to move money through the party conduit; national and state party spending has become increasingly disaggregated (La Raja 2008). Operating in this context, the public disclosure laws in Washington State have played a huge role in tracking the flow of political money in and through state elections. For example, in the 2000 election cycle, the PDC determined that both major parties were guilty of failing to disclose out-of-state gifts; it ordered the Republican Party to return $6 million and the Democratic Party to return $1 million (Galloway 2002).

In 1992, the voters passed Initiative 134, which was intended to cap the amount of money that individuals, PACs, and political parties could donate to state legislative campaigns. While the regulation of political money in state elections was a trend across states, the Washington law was particularly restrictive in the allowable amounts: $500 for an individual or a PAC and approximately $22,500 for political parties in house races and $42,500 in senate races. (Those limits currently stand at $800 for individuals and PACs, and $0.80 per registered voter for political parties).[16] In general, the voter-approved regulations have had the effect of limiting the amount of money spent on state legislative races; one analysis shows an average decrease of $1.64 million in the four election cycles following the implementation of I-134. The decrease in overall spending was accompanied by a decrease in political competitiveness (measured by fewer incumbents losing); the causal relationship between these two observations is hotly contested by opponents and advocates of campaign spending limits. While it is beyond the scope of this study to settle such a question, it is clear that I-134 has had a profound impact on state party organizations and their ability to act as conduits for money to coordinated campaigns.

Despite these stringent laws and campaign spending limits, the PDC has been criticized for being less active in seeking punitive redress than it is in promoting transparency, and being slow to close continuing loopholes in existing legislation. Two recent cases illustrate the problems that face the PDC in the application of the law. In the first, a Seattle based consulting company, Moxie Media, was accused of creating a web of PACs that funneled money from labor unions and education associations into primary races in support of moderate Democrats (Smith 2010). Under pressure from two key business interest groups and members of his own party, Attorney General Rob McKenna announced that he would bring suit on behalf of the state against Moxie. In the other high profile case, the state Democratic Party and the Sierra Club alleged that the Washington chapter of Americans for Prosperity (then headed by Kirby Wilbur), violated PDC rules in not disclosing its role in financing non-candidate political advertisements against vulnerable Democrats.[17]

What these cases highlight is that, despite the tight net that the campaign finance and disclosure laws in Washington State draws around political money, loopholes still exist, and the PDC, with only 25 full-time staff members, has a hard time tracking all of the money that is flowing into those elections. Defenders of the system point out that in both of the above cases, the alleged violations of campaign finance laws were in fact revealed by the comprehensive disclosure requirements and that without them, they might never have come to light. Critics suggest, however, that these sorts of practices are a routine occurrence and that further strengthening of the finance laws needs to take place. Currently, there are pending efforts to do so in the state legislature; targets of the new legislation include more clearly identifying and defining campaign coordination and looking at the role of money in non-individual campaigns (such as initiatives, referenda, and recall efforts). Notwithstanding, Washington State political parties continue to find their fundraising and spending activities subject to stringent reporting requirements, defined limits, and intense media scrutiny.

Conclusion

In conclusion, state parties are alive and well in Washington. We have described how the legal requirements for parties condition the environment within which they operate, from elections to organization to campaign finance. Furthermore, in a state that has a historical culture of persistent western populism, and institutional devices that reflect that legacy (such as initiatives, referenda, and the nonpartisan primary), the political parties of the state do not necessarily find great sympathy when in the media spotlight. As we have noted, these challenging environmental conditions have frequently pushed the state's major parties to cooperate in defending their terrain, and to pool their resources in protecting the rules that structure and foster party competition. It is a matter of great interest to party scholars to note that in the state of Washington, many of the so-called 'anti-party' initiatives have come from the electorate (e.g., I-134, I-276, and I-872), while the state parties themselves have been frequent interveners on the same side in litigation stemming from those initiatives.

So, if the state parties find themselves constrained in their ability to raise and spend money on campaigns, in their ability to control candidacies for public office, and in their ability to control the political agenda, what do they do? More than anything else, political parties at the state level—and especially so in Washington—have become the most effective vehicles for coordination across a variety of arenas. No other institution or political entity is able to connect such a wide and diverse array of actors—voters, interest groups, PACs, lobbyists—to and across the political process; no other institutions or political entities are able to exert such an influence on the interaction between national forces and ideological constructs and individual mobilization as the political party. Paradoxically, the very same state laws that serve to regulate and define the scope of party activity also serve to bolster their presence in the public eye. That presence may be poorly understood, but it is far from irrelevant, and, for the foreseeable future, political parties will continue to be active in the heart of the Washington political system.

Appendix

Washington State Political Finance Limits

RECIPIENTS	CONTRIBUTORS					
	State Party	County or LD Party Committee	Caucus Political Committee (House or Senate)	Candidate Committees	PACs, Unions, Corps and other entities	Individuals
State Party	Not Applicable	No Limit	No Limit	Only from Surplus Funds No Limit	$4,000/calendar year (non-exempt) / No Limit (exempt)	No Limit
County or LD Committees	No Limit	No Limit	No Limit	Only from Surplus Funds No Limit	$4,000/calendar year (non-exempt) / No Limit (exempt)	No Limit
Caucus Political Committee	No Limit	No Limit	No Limit	Only from Surplus Funds No Limit	$800/calendar year	No Limit
Statewide Executive Candidate Committee	$0.80/voter/cycle (Joint Limit)	$0.40/voter/cycle (Joint Limit)	$0.80/voter/cycle	Prohibited	$1,600/election	$1,600/election
Legislative Candidate Committee	$0.80/voter/cycle (Joint Limit)	$0.40/voter/cycle (Joint Limit)	$0.80/voter/cycle	Prohibited	$800/election	$800/election
Judicial Candidate	$1,600/election	$1,600/election	$1,600/election	Prohibited	$1,600/election	$1,600/election
County Office Candidate Committee	$0.80/voter/cycle	$0.40/voter/cycle (Joint Limit)	$0.80/voter/cycle	Prohibited	$800/election	$800/election
City Council or Mayor Candidate Committee	$0.80/voter/cycle	$0.40/voter/cycle (Joint Limit)	$0.80/voter/cycle	Prohibited	$800/election	$800/election
Port of Seattle or Tacoma Commissioner Candidate Committee	$0.80/voter/cycle	$0.40/voter/cycle (Joint Limit)	$0.80/voter/cycle	Prohibited	$1,600/election	$1,600/election
PACs	No Limit	No Limit	No Limit	Prohibited	No Limit	No Limit

Source: PDC 2010.

Endnotes

1. This provision was first adopted by the state legislature in 1907 as a response to general concerns, which were part of Progressive-era critiques of the American political system, about the power of party committees to determine nominations.
2. The main objection to the "open primary" in use prior to 1935 was that it forced voters to publicly 'declare' party affiliation by accepting ballots for only one party before entering the voting booth. This stands in contrast to the "Montana-style primary," in which voters make that same choice inside the voting booth; see below.
3. The first of those challenges occurred in 1936, when the court upheld the blanket primary in *Anderson v. Milliken*; the state's case was argued by future-Senator Warren G. Magnuson; the constitutionality of the primary system was reaffirmed in 1980 in *Heavy v. Chapman*.
4. This was also the opinion of the Ninth Circuit Court, 460 F.3d 1108 (9th Cir. 2006).
5. The vote tallies were 1,632,225 for and 1,095,190 against.
6. This challenge reflects the stated motivations of Governor Locke for preferring the Montana-style system in 2004; he argued that the parties would challenge the Top 2 system in court if it was implemented.
7. Jeffers-Schroder polled 17% of the vote in the general election in November 2010.
8. The others were Alabama, Kentucky, New Mexico, and Pennsylvania.
9. Students of voting behavior might take issue with the court's declaration that the "unreasonable, uninformed voter" is irrelevant to consideration of electoral rules.
10. The "unreasonable, uninformed" voter controversy formed a substantial part of the case against I-872; the Libertarian Party brief argued that the state's expert (Dr. Todd Donovan, a contributor to this volume) was misrepresented in the state's own brief in the earlier District Court hearing.
11. This rule requires winning candidates in PCO elections to garner at least 10 percent of the votes for the winning candidate of their party. However, since I-872 eliminates party primaries, this provision is necessarily null and void.
12. Whether, in the case of intraparty conflict, such an explicitly tautological provision could be enforced is doubtful; nonetheless, it clearly demonstrates the tension between the desire of political parties to determine their own organizational procedures and the perceived interest of the state in limiting the degrees of freedom to do so.
13. See, for example, Memmott 2010.
14. See, for example, Vance 2010. Vance is a former state chair of the Republican Party.
15. The extent of Wilbur's Tea Party activism is a matter of dispute. However, what is not disputed is that the new vice chair, Laura Sample, was indeed a very active Tea Party member. See Muir 2011.
16. Party spending is determined by a formula based on the number of registered voters in a district.
17. Although Americans for Prosperity did disclose its payments to the PDC, it did so as a "grassroots organization" and not as a Political Action Committee. However, the charges placed Attorney General McKenna in the uncomfortable position of having to decide whether to bring suit against the state chair of his own party.

References

Anderson v. Milliken, 59 P.2d 295 WA (1936).

Appleton, Andrew, and Ashley Grosse. 2004. "Washington State Parties." In *Washington State Government and Politics*, edited by Cornell W. Clayton, Lance T. LeLoup, and Nicholas P. Lovrich. Pullman: Washington State University Press.

Associated Press. August 20, 2010. "Didier Holds Off On Rossi Endorsement." *Spokesman-Review*. spokesman.com/stories/2010/aug/20/didier-may-throw-support-behind-rossi-senate.

Bennett, James T. 2009. *Not Invited to the Party: How the Demopublicans Have Rigged the System and Left the Independents Out in the Cold*. New York: Springer.

Berg-Andersson, Richard E. "The Green Papers." thegreenpapers.com/P12/WA-R.

Black, Benjamin D. 1996. "Developments in the State Regulation of Major and Minor Political Parties." *Cornell Law Review* 82(1): 109–81.

California Democratic Party v. Jones, 530 U.S. 567 (2000).

Democratic Party of Washington State v. Reed, W.D. Wash. 2002.

Faulkner, Debbie, and Ginger McCall. "Commentary: Washington State Grange v. Washington State Republican Party (06-713)" *Liibulletin*. topics.law.cornell.edu/supct/cert/06-713.

Galloway, Angela. September 25, 2002. "State's Public Disclosure Law Draws Praise." *Seattle PI*. seattlepi.com/default/article/State-s-public-disclosure-law-draws-praise-1096955.php.

Heavy v. Chapman, 611 P.2d 1256 WA (1980).

Isackson, Adam. February 7, 2011. "Analyzing the Washington State Elections and the Future of the Republican Politics." *RedState*. redstate.com/aisackson/2011/02/07/analyzing-the-washington-state-elections-and-the-future-of-republican-politics.

La Raja, Raymond. 2008. *Small Change: Money, Political Parties, and Campaign Finance Reform*. Ann Arbor: University of Michigan Press.

Memmott, Mark. August 16, 2010. "Washington State's 'Top-Two' Primary May Thwart Tea Party." *NPR.org*. npr.org/blogs/thetwo-way/2010/08/16/129234729/washington-state-s-top-two-primary-may-thwart-tea-party.

Moscow-Pullman Daily News. May 15, 2003. "Study Ranks Washington State Tops for Integrity." *Moscow-Pullman Daily News*.

Muir, Pat. January 25, 2011. "Yakima Woman Elected State GOP Vice Chairwoman." *Yakima Herald*. yakima-herald.com/blogs/checks-balances/posts/yakima-woman-elected-state-gop-vice-chairwoman.

Oldham, Kit. February 17, 2009. "Washington Holds First Top-Two Primary Election on August 19, 2008." *Historylink.org*. historylink.org/index.cfm?DisplayPage=output.cfm&file_id=8937.

PDC (Public Disclosure Commission). 2010. "Contribution Limits." www.pdc.wa.gov/filers/page2.aspx?c2=159.

Rasmussen Reports. 2010. "Washington Survey of 750 Likely Voters August 31, 2010." rasmussenreports.com/public_content/politics/elections/election_2010/election_2010_senate_elections/washington/washington_senate_rossi_r_48_murray_d_46.

Salka, William. April 17, 2011. "Minor Parties in US House Elections: An Examination of the Influence of Ballot Access Laws and Other State Level Variables." Paper presented at the Annual Meeting of the Western Political Science Association, San Antonio, Texas.

Smith, Erik. October 27, 2010. "A Mind-Bogglingly Complex Scheme Allows Labor and Allies to Funnel $2.7 Million into Legislative Races—Berkey Case is Just the Beginning."

Washington State Wire. washingtonstatewire.com/home/5859-a_mind_bogglingly_ complex_scheme_funnels_27_million_for_labor_and_its_allies_in_legislative_races_-_ berkey_case_is_just_the_beginning.htm.

———. January 31, 2011. "Wilbur and Fellow Republicans Lay Out Battle Plans at Roanoke Conference—New Chairman May Offer a Few Surprises." *Washington State Wire.* washingtonstatewire.com/home/7412-wilbur_and_fellow_republicans_lay_out_ battle_plans_at_roanoke_conference_-_new_chairman_may_offer_a_few_surprises.htm.

SOSa (Secretary of State). "History of the Blanket Primary in Washington." www.sos.wa.gov/ elections/bp_history.aspx.

SOSb (Secretary of State). "History of Washington State Primary Systems." www.sos. wa.gov/_assets/elections/History of Washington State Primary Systems.pdf.

Spokesman-Review. January 4, 1974. "Highest State Court Backs Initiative 276." *Spokesman Review.*

Toeplitz, Shira. September 13, 2010. "Didier Still Not Endorsing Rossi." *Politico.com.* politico. com/news/stories/0910/42080.html.

Vance, Chris. November 22, 2010. "Why the GOP Tide Fell Short in Washington State." *Crosscut.com.* crosscut.com/2010/11/22/elections/20385/Why-the-GOP-tide-fell-short- in-Washington-state.

Washington State Republican Party v. Washington State Grange, No. 2:05-cv-00927-JCC, W.D. Wash. (January 11, 2011). sos.wa.gov/_assets/elections/Courts%20Order%20 1-11-11.pdf.

Washington State Statutes Cited
RCW 29A.04.086
RCW 29A.42.020
RCW 29A.56
RCW 29A.80.011
RCW 29A.80.020
RCW 29A.80.51

CHAPTER FOUR

Interest Groups in Washington State: The Political Dynamics of Representation, Influence, and Regulation

Clive S. Thomas and Richard Elgar

Introduction

PICK UP A NEWSPAPER like the *Seattle Times*, turn on the radio or TV, go online to read a political blog and you will likely find stories about the activities of interest groups and lobbyists in Olympia—from school boards to business lobbies, from nonprofit organizations to public agencies. Plus, around the streets of Olympia are the offices of a host of interest groups and lobbyists. As the *Seattle Post-Intelligencer* put it, "Lobbying is big business in [the] state" (McGann 2007).

Interest groups are often a major force in what policies are considered or enacted in Washington. Historically, interest groups representing railroads, mining, lumber, and other extractive industries were a dominant force in Washington politics. This is no longer the case, but understanding interest groups can provide an important perspective on where political power resides in the state.

For many people, interest groups represent the abuse of power and the representation of narrow "special interests" at the expense of the common good. Yet Washingtonians join interest groups by the hundreds of thousands and Americans by the tens of millions. Indeed, Americans see it as their political birthright to band together to influence government, as guaranteed in the First Amendment to the U.S. Constitution. So the attitude toward interest groups is not entirely negative, but one of ambivalence. This public ambivalence has produced a political dynamic centered on the issues of representation of interests, their influence, and the regulation of groups. Our chapter explores this representation–influence–regulation dynamic, and what it tells us about the role of interest groups in Washington's public policy making process.[1]

Lobbying in Washington

Interests and interest groups operate in a democracy by lobbying—conveying their views through a process of advocacy to government and its elected and appointed officials for the purpose of influencing public policy decisions. Lobbying involves four stages that often overlap in practice:

1. gaining access to policy makers;
2. building a relationship with them;
3. providing them with information on an issue or cause; and
4. influencing their actions.

To facilitate advocacy, two types of tactics are usually employed: direct tactics (approaching policy makers personally) and indirect tactics (such as using the media to convey a message to policy makers).

There is, however, no generally accepted definition of an interest group among scholars (Thomas 2004). The term is usually defined narrowly to include only those groups required to register under state laws. Yet many groups and organizations engage in lobbying but are not required to register. The most important are those representing various levels and agencies of government. Washington State, for example, does not require public officials at any level of government to register as lobbyists. Therefore, in this chapter we utilize the following broad definition: An interest group is an association of individuals or organizations, or a public or private institution, which, on the basis of one or more shared concerns, attempts to influence public policy in its favor.

There are three categories of interest groups operating in most democracies, including Washington State:

1. The *membership groups*, made up of individuals promoting a host of economic, social, and political concerns, such as senior citizens, environmentalists, schoolteachers, nurses, or anti-tax advocates.
2. *Organizational interests* are usually composed of groups such as businesses or trade unions.
3. *Institutional interests* comprise both private and public entities such as businesses, think tanks, universities, state and federal agencies, and local governments. They are the largest category of organized interests operating in state governments (Gray and Lowery 2004).

A *lobby* is a collection of interests concerned with a similar area of public policy—traditional, organizational, or institutional interests or a combination of all three. For example, the higher education lobby in Washington is comprised of student and faculty groups, as well as institutions such as Washington State University and the University of Washington. Lobbying takes place throughout the government, including the legislature and executive branch agencies (Nownes and Freeman 1998).

In Washington, traditional interests, such as agriculture, business, "old" labor (blue collar), education (teachers and school boards), and local governments (individual cities and towns and their statewide organizations like the Association of Washington Cities), have been lobbying for generations. In addition, new groups have developed or have come to prominence in Washington since the 1950s, such as those representing minorities, women, environmentalists, and good government interests.

Interests in Washington are further divided into insider groups (those with good access to policy makers with long-standing relationships in the state and often backed by major financial and other resources) and outsider groups. The latter are usually new groups or those advocating less mainstream causes, such as gay rights and animal rights. These often have minimal resources and little direct access to policymakers, so they rely on indirect tactics, including demonstrations, to influence policy. Most outsider groups work to become insider groups to increase their success. For instance, many environmental groups began as outsider groups in the early 1960s but have since become more powerful insiders.

A *lobbyist* is a person who represents an interest group in an effort to influence government decisions in that group's favor. Lobbyists include not only those required to register by law but also those representing non-registered groups and organizations, particularly government organizations. The decisions most often targeted by interest groups and their lobbyists concern public policies, but they also include decisions about who gets elected and appointed to make policies. Some lobbying techniques have proven to be most efficient and are common to all states. These include direct contact with those making decisions, strength in numbers by involving group members or forming coalitions with other groups, garnering public support for a cause, and helping those who make public policy decisions get elected, often by setting up a political action committee (PAC) to channel campaign funds to favored candidates.

The *state interest group system* is the array of groups and organizations, both formal and informal, and their lobbyists working to affect public policy in a state. The idea of a state interest group system is an abstraction, because even though there is interaction between groups and lobbyists representing various interests, never do all groups in a state act in concert to achieve one goal. However, it is the characteristics of the interest group system—its size, development, composition, methods of operating, and so on—that shape much of the politics in a state.

Public Ambivalence toward Interest Groups

Interest groups and political parties both facilitate the essential democratic function of representation—linking the citizenry with their government. Unlike political parties, however, interest groups do not exist solely for political purposes. Parties are, in essence, umbrella organizations for a collection of interest groups, and bring together people of like-mined political perspectives to win control of government. In contrast, the majority of interest groups exist for the economic, personal, recreational, or other non-political benefit of their members. For example, the Washington State Medical Association was formed to promote the professional interests of general practitioners, such as disseminating information on new medical procedures. The Washington Trails Association was formed to share information on places to walk and to organize hikes. But many groups become involved in politics because of the government affecting their activities or their need for government aid.

When interest groups get involved in politics they have one overriding goal—to influence the political process and public policy in their favor. The right of groups to present their case to government and attempt to influence policy decisions is essential to the functioning of pluralist democracy. Democracies naturally include a myriad of interests, attitudes, and values. Interest groups perform an essential public function by making representation more efficient and potentially more effective than if each person lobbied separately, providing policymakers with needed information and alternative perspectives, aiding in the process of compromise and bargaining, providing education on issues to their members, recruiting candidates for public office, and, in many cases, helping to fund election campaigns.

Yet these public roles of interest groups are purely incidental. In their private capacity the vast majority of interest groups do not exist to either facilitate or improve the democratic process. In fact, the reverse is often true. In the rough-and-tumble of interest group politics, many groups work to undermine the access and influence of their opponents, which adds to the ambivalence many people have toward them.

The public's negative view of interest groups usually comes less from illegal activities than from powerful interest groups dominating a state or town, as with the railroad, lumber, and fishing industries in Washington during territorial and early statehood days. Although the actions of some interest groups and lobbyists have created a negative image in the minds of many Americans and Washingtonians, the vast majority of groups work within the law and very few lobbyists make large salaries. Many advocacy groups are not very influential but plod away diligently, working with public officials.

Generally, public officials, especially elected officials, have a more positive attitude toward interest groups and lobbyists than the general public. This is because they see their value in the technical information groups provide and in their ability to offer an efficient mechanism to gauge the views of particular political constituencies. Public officials, however, are not blind to the potential negative effects of interest groups and lobbyists, although they are not always enthusiastic about regulating interest group activities.

Perhaps the most important consequence of the actual and perceived abuses by interest groups has been efforts to regulate them. That said, there is only so much that regulation can achieve given the nature of political power, the attitudes of some elected officials, and the guaranteed right in the First Amendment to the U.S. Constitution to petition—in effect lobby—government (also guaranteed in the Washington State Constitution, Article 1, Section 4). Nevertheless, public support for regulation of interest groups is a political reality and an important part of the political environment that produced the representation–influence–regulation dynamic of interest group activity.

The Development of Interest Group Activity in the Evergreen State from Statehood to the 1920s

Like most western states, Washington's politics were dominated in its early years by a few powerful interests—primarily railroads and natural resource extraction industries such as the Great Northern and the Northern Pacific railroads and the Weyerhaeuser Corporation (Clark 1976; LeWarne 1986). Given the laissez faire economic doctrine of the time and the desire for economic growth in the new state, the political goals of these powerful interests and those of the state were often seen as identical.

Over time, however, the dominance of these groups was challenged. Indeed, from the very beginning, regulating the railroads and the power of major corporations was a primary target of the Populist reformers who drafted Washington's constitution. Viewed as particularly unacceptable was any creation of monopolies or the use of private money to corrupt public officials. Accordingly, Article XII of the state's constitution places curbs on corporations and forbids public officials from accepting free railroad passes. Populist reforms included ownership of public utilities, which began in Tacoma in 1893 and spread rapidly (Bone 1969), and Progressive reforms, including the adoption of voter initiatives and referenda, added to the constitution in 1912 (Long 2004).

The political power of business and its clash with labor, the establishment of the popular initiative, and attempts to curb private political power and monopolies in these early years set the political stage for the evolution of the Evergreen State's interest group system. One event that would have far-reaching effects on this system occurred in 1916, when William E. Boeing established an airplane company in Seattle.

A Developing System: The 1930s to the 1960s

Five developments from the 1930s to the 1960s were important in shaping the state's interest group system. First, traditional interests solidified their regular presence in Olympia, as was also the case in most other state capitals during this period. Lobbying by other interests was minimal and intermittent. Second, the 1930s saw political lines drawn between advocates of public ownership and control of the state's energy resources and those favoring private ownership and less regulation. The fight centered on the development of hydroelectric power in the Columbia River Basin. Public power came to be represented by the Washington Public Utility Districts Association and the Northwest Public Power Association. Opposition to public power was led by the Washington Water Power Company of Spokane and the Pacific Power and Light Company of Portland. These battles continue today. Third, the rise of air travel and the development of jetliners, plus federal contracts stemming from the Cold War, led Boeing to establish itself as a prominent political force in the state by the 1960s (Gissberg and Boswell 1996). Fourth, the initiative process became increasingly used by interest groups (Bone 1969). And fifth, public suspicion about the role of interest groups in campaign financing and providing other perks to legislators led to a groundswell for more regulation of interest group activity (Gissberg and Boswell 1996; Petersen 2010).

Yet although some major developments were taking place in the 1960s, Washington State's interest group system was still underdeveloped by today's standards. The range of groups was narrow, with insider groups dominating the Olympia scene. Lobbying techniques primarily consisted of direct tactics—mainly the use of a lobbyist—although organizations like the Washington State Medical Association and labor groups also had established political action committees. All this took place without any public transparency or substantive regulation. Before 1972 there was no lobby regulation. Lobbyists did have to obtain a registration card if they wanted to enter the floor of the house, which could be obtained by simply registering with the legislature, but the list of registered organizations was not made public. Jolene Unsoeld, an independent citizen lobbyist and activist, was a major force behind moves for lobby regulation (Bone 1969; Cuillier, Dean, and Ross 2004). In terms of influence, natural resource interests (led by Weyerhaeuser), labor (blue and white collar), some agricultural interests, and business, particularly Boeing, dominated the lobbying scene.

The System Transformed: The 1970s to the Present

The representation–influence–regulation relationship of Washington's interest group system went through a major transformation after the 1960s. A confluence of circumstances led to a major expansion in the number of groups in Olympia. These included anti-Vietnam War protests, the civil rights movement, the rise of the environmental movement and challenges to uncontrolled economic development, and the rise of the role of government, particularly as a result of the Great Society Program in the mid-1960s. These developments inspired a range of new interests and stimulated others to become more active. The women's movement, minority rights groups, environmentalists, advocates for various social causes such as pro-life and pro-choice groups, gay rights groups, and groups for the disabled, as well as groups representing public employees, universities, state agencies, and good government groups like Common Cause and the League of Women Voters, all emerged during this period. Many of these groups were single-issue groups, in contrast to the traditional interests that covered a range of issues. Plus, the traditional interests began to fragment as many groups, particularly local governments and businesses with specific concerns, began to lobby as individual organizations while remaining members of their respective statewide organizations.

Changes in Washington's economy also contributed to the increased number and types of groups represented in Olympia. Most notable was the establishment of Microsoft and the high-tech industry beginning in the late 1970s. Another development was the attraction of outside businesses to Washington State. For example, in 1999 Enron came to the state, hiring a small army of contract lobbyists in an attempt to deregulate the public power industry, which would allow consumers to buy power not only from their local utility company but also from Enron (Johnson 2010).

This expansion in group activity led to greater competition among groups and encouraged the use of a broader range of lobbying techniques, including increased use of group members (grassroots lobbying), use of the press and political advertising, boycotts and demonstrations, and enhanced efforts to elect group supporters to political office. Although labor had used PACs since World War II, they became increasingly prominent in the 1970s and 1980s and a major source of campaign funds for candidates running for elected offices.

Two other group tactics that have been increasingly used since the late 1960s are the initiative and the formation of ad hoc coalitions. It was, in fact, a combination of the initiative process and a coalition that was behind the enactment of public disclosure laws in Washington State. Initiative 276, passed by the voters in 1972, had been pushed by a broad coalition of good government groups named the Coalition for Open Government (Cuillier, Dean, and Ross 2004). From this initiative came the Public Disclosure Act of 1972 and the Public Disclosure Commission (PDC).

The Contemporary Interest Group System

Today Washington's interest group system is one of the most diversified, developed, and professional of all 50 states. Due to its balanced economy, which combines primary production (mainly agriculture, mining, and forestry), manufacturing, and services, plus a degree of ethnic and demographic diversity, including a large, well-educated middle class, there are a diverse range of interests operating in Olympia. In this regard, Washington is on a par with much larger, diversified states, though on a smaller scale.

Examples of individual membership groups include the Washington Chiropractic Association, which lobbies to protect, promote, and improve the chiropractic profession; the Washington Trails Association, whose mission is to preserve, enhance, and promote hiking opportunities in Washington State; and the Brotherhood Against Totalitarian Enactments of Washington, which promotes the rights of motorcyclists and freedom of choice to use crash-helmets.

Organizational interest groups are represented in Olympia by associations such as the Washington State Horticulture Association, which, as the nation's largest association of tree fruit growers and shippers, works with government officials to develop public policies beneficial to the industry and the schools, communities, and families it supports, and the Washington Public Utility Districts Association, which is concerned with protecting sources of public power, the costs and controversy over nuclear power development, and environmental issues affecting the electric industry.

An example of institutional interests lobbying in Olympia is Weyerhaeuser, one of the nation's largest forest product companies and a major private employer. Its political concerns range from keeping taxes low to pollution and environmental issues. Similarly, the Washington State Department of Transportation, through its senior staff and legislative liaison, work with the governor and legislature to secure funding for transportation projects and personnel.

As we will see below, while the number of groups that lobby in Olympia has grown over the years, the groups and interests that are influential have changed very little. Presence in Olympia and a high profile is one thing, but actual influence is often quite another.

External Interests Lobbying in Olympia, and Washington Interests Lobbying Other Governments

This chapter is primarily concerned with interest groups and lobbying in Olympia. But lobbying by Washington State interests occurs at all levels of government. Many interests in the state lobby at the local, state, and federal levels, such as Boeing and schoolteachers.

Figure 1 shows this interrelationship of lobbying by Washington interests. Of particular note in recent years is lobbying by groups from out of state.

Lobbying in Olympia by interests outside the state has a long history, beginning with the Populist and Progressive eras, and has been especially on the increase in the last 30 years. Out-of-state interests are of three types: social issue groups, such as the campaign by Mothers Against Drunk Driving (MADD); major economic interests, including Enron and outside beverage companies who lobby for favorable access to Washington markets; and ideological interest groups that push various causes such as restricting abortion rights or gay rights,

Figure 1. The Interrelation of Washington State Interest Groups and Interest Activity Across the United States

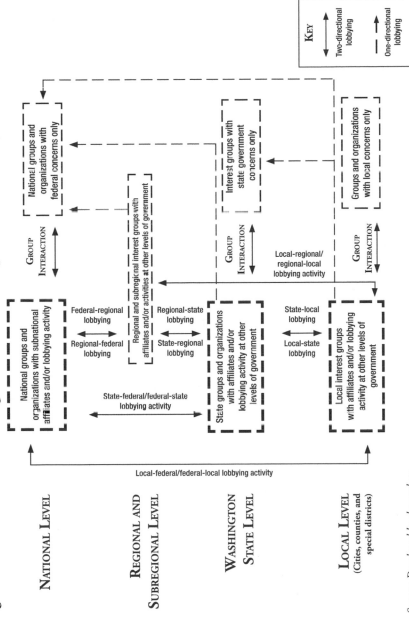

Source: Developed by the authors.

and more recently a national movement to restrict lobbying by public agencies and those receiving government funding.

The Role of the Public Disclosure Commission (PDC)

A major factor shaping the operating environment of interest groups in Washington State is the role of the PDC.[2] The PDC is the major regulatory force in the representation–influence–regulation dynamic. Agencies across the nation like the PDC cannot directly affect representation or political power within a state, but, with the right combination of laws and enforcement authority, they can use public disclosure and transparency regulations to dramatically influence the actions of interest groups and their lobbyists, preventing them from exercising undue influence. The PDC in Washington appears to be more active in this role than similar agencies in other states. In several national surveys, the PDC was ranked as the most effective of such agencies across the 50 states by the Center for Public Integrity, a campaign and lobbying watchdog (CPI 2003; Anderson 2011).

The media is certainly important in throwing light on the actions of interest groups and group relations with public officials, but it is the PDC that provides reporters with much of the information they use in their stories. Since its establishment in 1972 the PDC has administered laws and regulations relating to campaign finance, political advertising, disclosure of the finances of major public officials, and the registration and financial activities of lobbyists and their employers (Anderson 2011). In addition, although the PDC does not require those representing government to register, it does require disclosure of the funds spent for such purposes, with the exception of local elected officials (Anderson 2011). The PDC makes the actions of groups and lobbyists transparent to the public and thus enables their actions to be monitored. Nevertheless, the PDC is not free of political and other constraints, as we will discuss later.

Interest Group Strategies and Tactics

Interest groups in Washington State employ similar lobbying strategies and tactics as those in other states and in Washington, D.C. Direct contact between the lobbyist and the policy maker was the predominant and, in many cases remains, the only form of lobbying used by many organizations. But because of the increasing competition between groups, many organizations now supplement the use of a lobbyist with other indirect tactics, resulting in more complex lobbying campaigns. Indirect tactics include affiliation with or support of a political party; involvement in direct democracy campaigns such as the initiative, referendum, and recall; financial contributions or other support to help elect candidates; use of the media, public relations, and advertising campaigns to get a message across to policy makers; and protests, boycotts, demonstrations, and violence—often used by outsider groups who do not have access to policy makers but want to attract attention to their cause.

Research shows that direct contact by lobbyists with public officials is still the major tactic used by groups, with indirect tactics much less favored (Nownes, Thomas, and Hrebenar 2008). This is clearly the case in Washington State, but there are two aspects of lobbying strategy and tactics that are particularly noteworthy in Washington. These are the use of the initiative and judicial campaign activity.

Use of the initiative has become an increasingly important tactic used by a range of interest groups in Washington. It has been used by the Washington Education Association (WEA) to reduce class sizes and protect teachers' pay, by those who want to restrict the rights of public employees to spend money on political activities, those working to promote healthcare, and by both pro- and anti-tax interests. Tim Eyman is perhaps best known in the state for pushing many anti-tax initiatives in the past decade (Herold and Gombosky 2004) Among his several successes was Initiative 1053, passed in 2010, which requires a two-thirds vote by the electorate to increase state taxes and fees.

The initiative process can be used to benefit citizens as a whole, as with Initiative 276 in 1972 that established public disclosure in the state. However, often the initiative has become the captive of very specific interests pushing narrow causes. Many would argue that Eyman's efforts fall into this category. Plus, many businesses, including those from out of state, have used the initiative to promote their economic self-interest. This was the case in 2010 with Initiative 1107, which repealed food and beverage taxes enacted by the legislature and was supported by more than $16 million in funding from outside the state (PDC "Contributions").

As the result of a 1912 amendment to the Washington constitution, judicial elections are nonpartisan. The intention was to insulate judges from politics and political party control in order to protect their impartiality. However, state judicial elections have become increasingly politicized in recent years and have been the subject of targeted spending by interest groups concerned with who becomes a judge.

Until 2006, judicial candidates were not subject to the spending limits imposed on other statewide candidates, allowing interest groups to directly fund judicial campaigns. Business interests have been some of the most prominent supporters of certain judicial candidates, enabling those candidates to significantly outspend their opponents. Yet while this direct contribution loophole has now been closed, independent expenditures to support judicial candidates are still allowed. Some of these expenditures appear in advertising campaigns. For example, all the advertising that appeared on television regarding the 2006 judicial elections was paid for by independent groups (see chapter 8).

Washington State's Lobbyists

In many ways Olympia's lobbying community is similar to those in other states. In 2011, a total of 893 lobbyists representing 1,265 employers registered with the PDC in Washington.[3] The number of lobbyists has remained fairly constant since 2000 but the number of employers has increased about 50 percent (PDC "Lobbyists"; Anderson 2011). Given Washington State's socioeconomic and political diversity and the size of its population, this number of lobbyists is comparable to most states (CPI 2007). However, based on our definition of a lobbyist, the number registered with the PDC for 2011 (893) is a far lower number than those actually lobbying. The number is likely to be nearly double.

There are five different types of lobbyists (Nownes, Thomas, and Hrebenar 2008) and examples of all five can be found in Washington:

- *Contract Lobbyists*: People hired on contract for a fee specifically to lobby. They often represent more than one client. They are often former legislators, legislative aides, or have worked in the executive branch.
- *In-house Lobbyists*: Employees of an association, organization, or business who, as all or part of their job, act as a lobbyist. These represent only one client—their employer.
- *Legislative Liaisons*: Employees of state, local, and federal agencies who represent their agency to the legislative and executive branches of state government.
- *Volunteer or Cause Lobbyists*: People who represent citizen and community organizations or informal groups. They rarely represent more than one interest and are usually unpaid.
- *Private Individual Lobbyists*: People acting on their own behalf and not designated by any organization as an official representative.

Although they receive the most publicity due to their high compensation, contract lobbyists constitute only about 20 percent of the lobbying community across the states, including in Olympia. Also like other states, several contract-lobbying firms have offices near the capitol. However, as a medium-sized state in population, Washington's lobbyists and contract-lobbying firms tend to be generalists representing a range of interests and not specialized lobbyists, such as those found in large states like California and New York. In Washington, for example, a small firm might represent airlines, oil, technology, utilities, and agricultural industries, while a medium-sized firm could represent forestry, pulp and paper, telecommunications, banking, health care, mining, aviation, retail, water rights, the state lottery, land development, oil, taxes, alcohol, tobacco, and the environment. A large law and lobby firm in Seattle has close to 40 lobbying clients ranging from Citicorp and General Motors to the Pacific Northwest Ski Areas Association and the Washington State Medical Association (PDC "Lobbyists").

A recent development in the lobbying business in the larger states is the rise of multi-service lobbying firms. Such firms have long existed in Washington, D.C. They provide services at all levels of government and aid in strategies, tactics, research, and other services—a sort of one-stop lobbying firm. In Washington State the best example of such a firm is Gordon Thomas Honeywell Governmental Affairs. They lobby at the local, state, and federal level and have developed expertise in several policy areas including public safety/homeland security, technology, biotechnology, local government, utilities, and transportation.

Interest Group Power in Washington State

Scholars have found power to be one of the most elusive aspects of interest groups to study (Thomas 2004). Interest group power refers to one of three things: (1) single group power, the ability of a single group or coalition to achieve its policy goals; (2) overall individual interest power, the perceived most effective interest groups and interests overall in the state; and (3) group system power, the strength of interest groups as a whole in a state in relation to other organizations or institutions, particularly political parties. Figure 2 below shows the most effective interest groups in Washington and across the 50 states.

- *Single group power* is the ability of a group or coalition to achieve its goals as it defines them. The only important assessment of success is an internal evaluation by the group itself. Some groups can be very successful in achieving their goals but keep a very low profile in a state and not be singled out as powerful by public officials. Many groups, such as beauticians and dentists involved in the regulatory process, are very successful because they have "captured" their area of concern (control of policy making) through dependence of bureaucrats upon their expertise. Many of these do not want public attention or to be singled out as an effective group.
- *Overall individual interest power* is the aspect of group power that most fascinates the press and the public, who are less concerned with the minutiae of government and more with high-profile issues and scandals. Whereas the only important assessment of single group power is internal to a group, overall interest power is based on external assessments by informed observers. As indicated earlier, despite the major expansion in group activity, there has been little change in the type of effective groups over the past 30 years in Washington. The listings in figures 2 and 3 for Washington State alone, and when compared with the nation over the past 30 years, confirms what has been known since the first study of the power of state interest groups was conducted in the 1950s (Zeller 1954)—business and the professions remain the most effective interests. For example, Boeing has been able to sustain its influence over the years,

Figure 2. The Ten Most Effective Interests and Interest Groups Across the Fifty States Compared with Washington State from the Early 1980s to 2010

THE FIFTY STATES Ranking in 2010 Followed by Rank in Early 1980s		WASHINGTON STATE
GROUP 1: CONSISTENTLY THE TWO MOST EFFECTIVE INTERESTS		
1 – 2	General Business Organizations (State Chambers of Commerce, etc.)	1	Boeing
2 – 1	School Teachers' Organizations (NEA and AFT)	2	Association of WA Business—AWB
GROUP 2: CONSISTENTLY AMONG THE TEN MOST EFFECTIVE		
3 – 6	Utility Companies and Associations (electric, gas, water, telephone/telecommunications)	3	WA State Labor Council—WSLC (state affiliate of AFL-CIO)
4 – 4	Manufacturers (companies and associations)	4	WA Education Association—WEA (schoolteachers)
5 – 17	Hospital/Nursing Homes Associations	5	Construction industry/contractors/developers, especially Building Industry Association of Washington and Associated General Contractors of Washington
6 – 13	Insurance: General and Medical (companies and associations)	6	Public power and utilities, especially Washington Public Utility Districts Association—WPUDA
7 – 11	Physicians/State Medical Associations	7	Weyerhaeuser (forest and wood products company)
8 – 22	Contractors/Builders/Developers	8	Farmers, especially Washington Farm Bureau, Washington State Grange, wheat-growers
9 – 9	General Local Government Organizations (municipal leagues, county organizations, elected officials)	9	Private power and utilities (investor-owned), especially Puget Sound Electric (PSE), Avista, Pacific Power
10 – 8	Lawyers (predominantly trial lawyers, state bar associations)	10	Realtors, especially Washington Association of Realtors

Source: Developed by the authors using Nownes, Thomas, and Hrebenar (2008) and Morehouse (1981, 109).

although it was not always successful in pressing its case due to the strong countervailing force of labor and other interests. But contrary to some accounts (Herold and Gombosky 2004), Boeing never really declined in influence in the state. They simply chose to keep a lower profile after moving their headquarters to Chicago in 2001. Boeing still has a powerful presence, as their lobbying activities during the 2011 legislative session demonstrated (Jenkins 2011).

- *Interest Group System Power* focuses on the relationship and relative power of political institutions in a state and how this affects policy making. Several factors determine group system power. One major factor is the relationship between the group system and the strength of political parties—the stronger parties are, the more constrained are interest groups. Another factor is the political culture; states that have predominantly moralistic or communally-regarding political cultures, such as Maine, Vermont, and Washington, generally have less powerful group systems than states that have more individualistic cultures, such as Nevada and Florida. Other factors include advanced socioeconomic development, which usually increases the number of groups and reduces the likelihood that the state will be dominated by one or a few interests, a strong executive branch, and competition between groups, particularly in the more economically developed states.

When the first assessment of the power of Washington's interest group system was made (Zeller 1954) it was seen as "strong" or dominant. This was when natural resources and labor dominated the state, when the range of interests was very narrow, and before the PDC was established. The next assessment conducted in the late 1970s (Morehouse 1981) also assessed the system as strong. By this time Boeing had become the major political interest in the state (Gissberg and Boswell 1996; Bone 1969; Peterson 1987).

By the early 1980s, however, the expansion in the range and number of groups, the competition among groups, and the effects of regulation had begun to constrain the power of the group system. Since then, Washington has been in the complementary category, where groups are still significant forces in policy making but share this influence with other political institutions and certainly do not "run the state" (Nownes, Thomas, and Hrebenar 2008). So in contrast to states like Nevada and Florida, with their dominant groups systems, Washington has more of a balance between representation and influence in its group system.

Money and Washington State Interest Groups

A common belief is that lobbying is all about money; those who have a lot of it get what they want from government but those who have little or no money have minimal political influence. There is certainly some truth in this, but the reality is more complex. Nevertheless, money and the resources it commands

Figure 3. The Most Influential Interests and Interest Groups in Washington State in the Late 1970s/Early 1980s Compared with 2005–10

2005–10	LATE 1970S/EARLY 1980S
WA State Labor Council—WSLC (state affiliate of the AFL-CIO—American Federation of Labor-Congress of Industrial Organizations)	Washington State Council of Fire Fighters
WA Education Association—WEA (schoolteachers)	Washington Education Association—WEA
WA Federation of State Employees—WFSE	Washington State Labor Council—WSLC (and traditional labor in general, including the Teamsters)
WA State Building and Construction Trades Council	Association of Washington Business—AWB
Service Employees International Union—SEIU	Washington Federation of State Employees
Realtors, especially Washington Association of Realtors	Boeing Aircraft
Association of Washington Business—AWB	United for Washington (business PAC only)
Washington State Association for Justice (trial lawyers)	Utilities (public and private)
Environmentalists, especially Washington Environmental Council, Northwest Energy Coalition, Sierra Club	Forest products industry, especially Weyerhaeuser
Boeing Aircraft	
Software industry (especially Microsoft)	

Source: Developed by the authors using Nownes, Thomas, and Hrebenar (2008) and Morehouse (1981, 109).

are important factors in interest group effectiveness. The most consistently successful groups are those with money, and expenditures in Washington have been rising as the competition between interest groups increases. As the data collected by the 50 states varies widely in what is and is not included in lobby and campaign spending, comparing the Evergreen State with other states can only be approximate. Nevertheless, comparisons are useful for examining whether spending by some interest groups gives them an unfair advantage in the competition to influence public policy.

Lobby Spending in Washington State over the Years

Figure 4 shows private, public, and total spending on lobbying since 2000, when the PDC began keeping composite records. Clearly, there has been a steady rise in spending, much of which is due to increased spending on initiatives and from out-of-state interests. Three comparisons with other states are enlightening. First, in 2006 the money spent on lobbying across the 50 states passed the $1 billion mark for the first time (Laskow 2006). The total for that year in Washington State was $49 million, accounting for about 5 percent (or one twentieth) of the 50-state total. Second, according to the Center for Public Integrity (CPI), between the late 1970s and 2010, lobbying per capita expenditure, after adjusting for inflation, more than tripled across the 50 states. In 1980 Washington State expenditures were about $7 million (Peterson 1987, 125). Factoring in inflation, the state's lobbying expenditures increased about six-fold and were at the high end of the increase. Third, in 2010 Washington's per capita spending on lobbying was around $10 compared with $8 in California, $11 in Connecticut, and $25 in Alaska (Thomas, forthcoming).

Spending by Political Action Committees (PACs)

Among political scientists, the evidence of the effect of PACs on the actions of policy makers is inconclusive (Hrebenar 2004). In contrast, there is little doubt about their influence to political practitioners. They see PACs as important for access to decision-makers and a major factor in influence, hence the increasing use of PACs in recent years. By 1980 PACs were the main source of campaign funds in Washington State and have been increasing in importance ever since (Peterson 1987). Moreover, a business PAC of the 1980s and 1990s, United For Washington (UFW), was one of the most powerful interests in the state, as shown in Figure 4, although it did not engage in lobbying. The amount of money spent by PACs in Washington in the 2010 election amounted to $18,669,986.86 (PDC "Elections").

Out-of-State Money and Washington State Lobbying

It was noted earlier that Washington has been the target of spending by out-of-state money from certain interest group campaigns in recent years. As might be

Figure 4. Washington State Lobby Spending, 2001–10: Private, Public, and Total Outlays

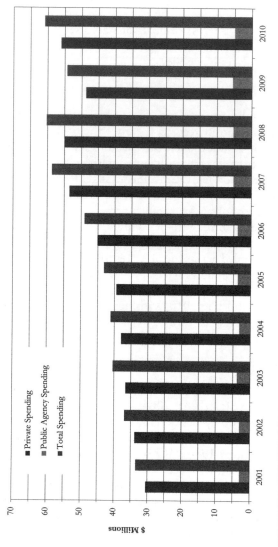

Year	2001	2002	2003	2004	2005	2006	2007	2008	2009	2010
Private Spending	30,508,436.00	33,809,294.00	36,574,357.00	37,892,328.00	39,408,494.00	45,139,598.00	53,451,475.00	54,975,732.00	48,733,671.00	56,088,574.00
Public Spending	2,984,214.23	3,055,532.15	3,819,406.53	3,227,206.38	3,736,867.87	3,860,813.65	5,212,566.93	5,305,031.42	5,556,600.71	4,854,327.71
Total Spending	33,492,650.23	36,864,826.15	40,393,763.53	41,119,534.38	43,145,361.87	49,000,411.65	58,664,041.93	60,280,763.42	54,290,271.71	60,942,901.71

Source: PDC. Yearly Comparison Chart of Total Lobbying Expenses.

expected, issues that are largely of concern only in Washington, such as those regarding education, transportation (to reduce congestion), and health issues, attract less than 20 percent of out-of-state money.

In contrast, the 2010 Stop the Food and Beverage Tax Hikes initiative gathered over $16 million in contributions, of which over 95 percent came from out of state. Most contributions came from the American Beverage Association (ABA) based in Washington, D.C., in which Pepsi Cola and Coca Cola are well represented. This extensive funding, the most ever spent on an initiative and an interest group campaign in Washington's history, was probably a major factor in the success of the initiative (PDC "Initiatives"). This case clearly demonstrates the potential of outside funding. In the future, in-state interests may have less and less control over the outcome of lobbying campaigns that have a major impact on outside interests.

Lobbyist Fees and Salaries

One source of the public's negative attitudes toward lobbyists is the size of their earnings, as reported in the press. Again, however, this perception is a distortion of the reality. These large sums apply only to contract lobbyists and then only to a small percentage of them. Most contract lobbyists earn considerably less, as do in-house lobbyists and legislative liaisons. Volunteer and individual lobbyists are usually unpaid.

Interest Groups in Washington: The Challenges and the Question of Corruption

While it was an accolade for the PDC to receive the top ranking of similar agencies across the nation, this does not mean that Washington has reached an ideal regarding the ability of regulation to maximize representation and curb the excessive power of certain interests. One challenge is a lack of consensus and understanding on what regulation should and can achieve. Perspectives on the purpose of lobby regulation range from the notion that it should even the political playing field, to the idea that it should prevent abuses by powerful interests, to the view that it should inform public officials and the public of the connections between those lobbying and those being lobbied. Whatever their perceived purposes, experience demonstrates that lobby laws cannot turn powerless groups into powerful forces, nor reduce the political clout of existing influential groups. The best that can be hoped is to restrict potential abuses and to publicize the activities of lobbyists (such as how much they spend on lobbying and whom they lobby).

Another challenge is the interaction of constitutional tensions and political realities. As mentioned earlier, the essence of the deep-rooted tension involved in regulating interest groups stems from their right to represent their cause to government, set against their potential abuses and questions of the extent to which they are biased by representing segments of society with more resources over those with fewer resources.

Yet another challenge results from the impetus for such regulation and the attitude of many elected state officials toward regulation. Rarely is there a systematic approach to enacting lobby laws and other public disclosure regulations. The main driver is political scandal or public concern with the actions of public officials, as was the motivation behind the creation of the PDC. Thus, most lobby laws are enacted on an ad hoc basis and often within a highly charged political atmosphere.

Furthermore, evidence suggests that most politicians pay only lip service to enacting lobby laws or amending existing ones; most would not deal with the issue unless pressured by constituents or public opinion, or when laws are forced on them by the initiative process (as was the case with Washington in 1972). It costs money to administer the laws, and such agencies are also often responsible for administering campaign finance and conflict of interest laws. But perhaps the major reason why such agencies and enforcement of the laws are not popular with politicians is that it is not the public that makes use of public disclosure information made available through lobby laws, but the press and candidates running against incumbents.

As a consequence of these challenges, discussions of lobby laws in Washington State revolve around the extensiveness of regulation and monitoring. Among public officials and those groups lobbying for regulation, there has been consensus on the role of regulation as partly restrictive but mainly as a monitoring device. Plus, more than most states, Washington has a systematic body of regulation that is well-enforced and generally less under attack to be changed.

Given constitutional and political limitations, increased regulation has had some effect in Washington State. As in all states, restraint in dealings with public officials, greater concern for their group's public image, and the increased professionalism of lobbyists appear to be the three major effects. Lobbyists, especially those representing powerful interests, are much less likely to use blatant strong-arm tactics, while public officials are less likely to deal with shady lobbyists and their organizations than was the case until the 1960s. This is, in part, the reason for the apparent disappearance of the old wheeler-dealer lobbyist from state politics and the increased professionalism of lobbyists in general.

How Clean or Corrupt is Washington State's Interest Group Activity?

While there is no systematic research comparing the extent of corruption involving lobbyists across the states, we can combine two sources to provide a credible answer to this question. First, research by the U.S. Justice Department and private organizations over the past decade or so indicate that the level of convictions of public officials ranks Washington as one of the cleaner states in the nation (Marsh 2008). Second, judging by lobbying scandals that hit the press, and prosecutions by the PDC, the Evergreen State is very clean. Over the past 30 years or so, there have been very few lobbying scandals. Certainly there has been suspect activity. For example, there was some controversy surrounding state senator Dino Rossi's 2008 bid for the governorship and the financial support extended to him by the Building Industry Association of Washington (BIAW), which is a very influential lobby in Olympia. Following a complaint of state disclosure violations, the PDC cleared Senator Rossi of any wrongdoing, but its final report revealed how closely the BIAW skirted the law in promoting his candidacy (PDC "Case No. 09-033"). The Rossi-BIAW case appears to be an exception, however. In fact, Washington State is probably among the top ten of the cleanest lobbying states in the nation and on par with states like Vermont, Maine, Nebraska, and Minnesota.

Washington State's relatively clean lobbying activity is likely explained by the state's largely moralistic, communally-regarding political culture and both the authority and political tone set by the PDC. Over time, this combination has made sleazy and illegal lobbying activity unacceptable and politically unwise. Yet with major benefits and often millions or billions of dollars at stake in lobbying, there will always be those willing to break the law and engage in criminal and unethical conduct in all states.

Conclusion: Interest Group Activity and Democracy in Washington State—Past, Present, and Future

In many ways, Washington State's interest group system is similar to group systems in the other 49 states. The range of groups and interests is similar, as are strategies and tactics, including the role of lobbyists, the factors that shape group power, and the regulation of group activities. The variations and differences in Washington's group activity arise from the particular representation–influence–regulation dynamic of the past and present. Overall, the state's interest group system today is a far cry from the early days of statehood or even 40 years ago. The contemporary system is broadly representative of society, imposes many constraints on the excessive use and abuse of power by interest groups, and has a broad-based and effective system of transparency and monitoring of group activity.

As states go, Washington's record in enhancing democracy in relation to the potential power of many interests and interest groups is among the most successful of any state. However, it is still far from ideal, given the constitutional constraints on regulation, the inherent nature of political power, and the central role of interest groups in exercising power in any political system. In Washington, as in other states, the role of lobbyists and interest groups is one of the mixed blessings of liberal democracy. The pressures of groups wanting to be represented, and to influence policy making, is countered by the need for regulation to ensure some leveling of the political landscape.

The pace of change has slowed down considerably in most aspects. This is largely because most interests that can be organized are now organized; most of the lobbying techniques that can be used are being employed. One minor exception is the pressure to enact more stringent lobby regulations, although this demand is likely to wax and wane depending on lobbying scandals.

Despite the slower pace of changes and that the key elements of contacts and personal relationship will continue to be paramount in lobbying success, a combination of factors is likely to continue to make interest group activity and the lobbying business in Washington, as in other states, more professional and sophisticated. This will be particularly the case regarding the ways groups and interests are organized and how they approach policy makers. Important influences here are likely to be continuing and increasing competition among groups for the ears of policy makers, public scrutiny and transparency of lobbying due to surges in the enactment of lobby regulations, and the complexity of government, which produces increased reliance on interest groups by public officials for technical and extensive political information.

The patterns of interest group power that have been more or less constant over the past 40 years are also likely to continue in Washington State. Once again, it is important not to confuse the visibility of a group or its popularity with the media with its influence. Certainly, some outsider groups and those with minimum resources will from time to time score political victories. However, it will be those groups and interests with major resources—financial, organizational, and political, mainly through contacts and their access to government—that will exercise influence on a year-to-year basis. This means that, for some time to come, Washington State's interest group system, like its counterpart in Washington, D.C., will continue to favor business (including agri-business), the professions, some sectors of labor, and various government agencies.

Endnotes

1. The authors thank Norma Wallace, senior legislative assistant, Washington House of Representatives, for her extensive research and aid on this chapter and Steve Johnson, former executive director of the Washington Public Utility Districts Association, for his help and advice on the chapter.
2. The authors thank Lori Anderson, Communications and Training Office, Washington State Public Disclosure Commission, for her aid in tracking down data and her useful suggestions.
3. The PDC's data archives are extensive. However, they are only systematically tabulated regarding aggregate numbers and comparisons since 2000. Comparisons in the chapter from before 2000 use some PDC data plus other sources as cited in the text.

References

Anderson, Lori (Communications and Training Office, Washington State Public Disclosure Commission), personal interview, February 17, 2011, and subsequent phone contact and emails, April and May 2011.

Bone, Hugh A. 1969. "Washington State: Free Style Politics." In *Politics in the American West*, edited by Frank H. Jonas, 380–415. Salt Lake City: University of Utah Press.

Clark, Norman H. 1976. *Washington: A Bicentennial History*. New York: Norton.

CPI (Center for Public Integrity). May 15, 2003. "Lobby Disclosure Ranking 2003." projects. publicintegrity.org/hiredguns/nationwide.aspx.

_____. December 21, 2007. "State Lobbying Totals, 2004–2006." projects.publicintegrity. org/hiredguns/chart.aspx?act=lobbyspending.

Cuillier, David, David Dean, and Susan Dente Ross. 2004. "The History and Intent of Initiative 276." Pullman: AccessNorthwest, Edward R. Murrow School of Communication, Washington State University. washingtoncog.org/media/images/resources/ANWInit276. pdf.

Gissberg, William A., and Sharon A. Boswell. 1996. *William A. Gissberg: An Oral History*. Olympia: Washington State Oral History Project, Office of the Secretary of State.

Gray, Virginia, and David Lowery. 2004. "The Institutionalization of State Communities of Organized Interests." *Political Research Quarterly* 54(2): 265–84.

Herold, Robert, and Jeff Gombosky. 2004. "Interest Group Politics in Washington State. Emergent Urbanization and the Continuing Struggle for the Public Domain." In *Washington State Government and Politics*, edited by Cornell W. Clayton, Lance T. LeLoup, and Nicholas P. Lovrich, 45–71. Pullman: Washington State University Press.

Hrebenar, Ronald J. 2004. "Political Action Committees (PACs)." In *Research Guide to U.S. and International Interest Groups*, edited by Clive S. Thomas, 147–48. Westport, CT: Praeger.

Jenkins, Austin. May 2, 2011. "SEIU and Boeing Are Top Lobbying Spenders in Wash." Northwest News Network, National Public Radio. npr.org/templates/story/story. php?storyId=135907897.

Johnson, Stephen F. (former executive director, Washington Public Utility Districts Association), personal interview, November 5, 2010.

Laskow, Sarah. December 20, 2006. "State Lobbying Becomes Billion Dollar Business," news release. Center for Public Integrity, Washington, D.C. projects.publicintegrity.org/ hiredguns/report.aspx?aid=835.

LeWarne, Charles P. 1986. *Washington State*. Seattle: University of Washington Press.

Long, Carolyn, N., 2004. "Direct Democracy in Washington." In *Washington State Government and Politics*, edited by Cornell W. Clayton, Lance T. LeLoup, and Nicholas P. Lovrich, 73–92. Pullman: Washington State University Press.

Marsh, Bill. December 13, 2008. "Illinois Is Trying. It Really Is. But the Most Corrupt State Is Actually…" *The New York Times.* nytimes.com/2008/12/14/weekinreview/14marsh. html?_r=3.

McGann, Chris. July 1, 2007. "Lobbying is Big Business in State, Washington is Sixth in U.S. for Spending." *Seattle Post-Intelligencer.*

Morehouse, Sarah McCally. 1981. *State Politics, Parties and Policy.* New York: Holt, Rinehart, and Winston.

Nownes, Anthony J., and Patricia K. Freeman. 1998. "Interest Group Activity in the States." *The Journal of Politics* 60(1): 86–112.

Nownes, Anthony J., Clive S. Thomas, and Ronald J. Hrebenar. 2008. "Interest Groups in the States." In *Politics in the American States: A Comparative Analysis* 9th ed., edited by Virginia Gray and Russell L. Hanson. Washington, D.C.: Congressional Quarterly Press.

PDC (Public Disclosure Commission). Case No. 09-033. www.pdc.wa.gov/archive/commissionmeetings/meetingshearings/pdfs/2010/03.25.10.Enforcement.09-033.pdf.

_____. Contributions. www.pdc.wa.gov/MvcQuerySystem/CommitteeData/contributions ?param=U1RPUEZCIDUwNw====&year=2010&type=initiative.

_____. Elections. www.pdc.wa.gov/MvcQuerySystem/ElectionTotals/totals?year=2010.

_____. Initiatives. March 18, 2010. PDC Cases #09-033, #09-034, #09-035, #09-036, #09-037, #09-038, #09-039, #09-040, #09-042, #09-043, #09-044, #09-045. www.pdc.wa.gov/archive/commissionmeetings/meetingshearings/pdfs/2010/03.25.10.Enforcement.09-033.Analysis.pdf.

_____. Lobbyists. www.pdc.wa.gov/MvcViewReports/Lobbying/lobbyists.

_____. Yearly Comparison Chart of Total Lobbying Expenses. www.pdc.wa.gov/home/page2.aspx?c1=0&c2=100.

Petersen, Anne (journal clerk, Washington State House of Representatives, 1960–65), personal interview, November 11, 2010.

Peterson, Walfred H. 1987. "Washington: The Impact of Public Disclosure Laws." In *Interest Group Politics in the American West*, edited by Ronald J. Hrebenar and Clive S. Thomas, 123–31. Salt Lake City: University of Utah Press.

Thomas, Clive S. 2004. *Research Guide to U.S. and International Interest Groups.* Westport, CT: Praeger.

_____. Forthcoming. "Interest Groups and Lobbying in Alaska: How Different Is It?" In *Alaska Politics and Public Policy*, edited by Clive S. Thomas, chapter 15. Fairbanks, AK: University of Alaska Press.

Zeller, Belle. 1954. *American State Legislatures.* New York: Thomas Y. Crowell.

CHAPTER FIVE

Changing Faces of Diversity in Washington State

Luis Ricardo Fraga and María Chávez

L IKE MANY STATES ACROSS THE NATION, the 2010 census reveals that during the last decade Washington has experienced notable growth and profound shifts in its population. In 2000, it had a total population of 5,894,121; in 2010 its population rose to 6,724,540, a growth rate of 14.1%. Even more dramatic than this overall growth has been the growth in the diversity of its population. It is estimated that 73% of all population growth in the state over the last decade was due to increases in its non-white population. Over the last ten years, Hispanics/Latinos[1] increased by 37.8%,[2] Whites increased by 27%, Asians by 18.8%, people of two or more races by 8.6%, African Americans by 5.4%, Native Hawaiians/Pacific Islanders by 1.9%, and American Indians/Alaska Natives by 0.4%. Stated differently, although Whites were 78.9% of the state population in 2000, by 2010 they had declined to now comprising under three-quarters of the population at 72.5%. How does this growing racial and ethnic diversity in the Washington population affect its politics and policy-making?

Rodney Hero argues in his analysis of the role of social diversity in the study of states that previous typologies of state political culture, such as that of Daniel Elazar (1994), have not sufficiently considered how the "ethnic/racial composi-tions and configurations of the states [can] have a major impact on state politics and policy" (Hero 1998, 3). He develops the "social diversity thesis" to place demographic context central to interpretations of who wins and who loses in state politics. He continues, "I put forth and examine the claim that mixtures or cleavages of various minority and/or racial/ethnic groups within a state—the types and levels of social *diversity* or complexity—are critical in understanding the politics and policy in the states" (6). In this chapter, we build upon Hero's insights and focus specifically on how the history of settlement and current pat-terns of ethnic/racial diversity in Washington are reflected in important aspects of the state's politics and policy-making.

We begin with a consideration of how the characterization of the state as having a "moralistic" political culture needs to be modified to take into account the growing presence of ethnic and racial minority communities in the state. A moralistic political culture is one where there is a high level of consensus regarding "basic values" (Hero 1998, 17–18), especially agreement that the government should have a direct role in promoting the common good and general social welfare. Among the questions we examine in this section are: Do ethnic and racial communities fit within the state's general understanding of the common good and the public interest? If so, how do they fit? How might this vary across distinct regions of the state given that some areas have much longer experiences with ethnic and racial communities? In the second part of the chapter we examine a variety of indicators of political incorporation of ethnic and racial minority communities in the state. We outline the pace and magnitude of growth in ethnic/racial communities. We then examine a number of dimensions of the patterns of political incorporation of these communities in the state. For example, we examine levels of political participation, political representation, and policy benefit. In the third part of the chapter we conclude with a discussion of the choices state political leaders face in determining how the state's Latino, African American, Asian/Asian American, and Native American communities and their interests will be included within the state's general understanding of the common good and the public interest. What opportunities does a state such as Washington have to engage demographic changes in ways that learn from and build on experiences in larger, more diverse states? How can the state effectively engage diversity as a fundamental part of serving the state's long-term public interest? Washington State has a unique opportunity to not only politically incorporate communities of color, but to empower local communities of all classes, races, and backgrounds by the way it decides to adapt to recent demographic changes. We posit that the choices political leaders make regarding the state's growing ethnic and racial diversity will have long-term consequences for how inclusive and responsive state government will be to all citizens and residents in the state of Washington.

Reconciling Moralistic Political Culture and Growing Ethnic and Racial Diversity

As noted in the first chapter, political culture can be defined as "the mix of shared attitudes, values, behaviors, and institutions that reflects a particular history and approach to politics," and that despite the political differences found in Washington's two largest cities—Spokane and Seattle—both cities exhibit a moralistic political culture. In other words, Washington State's political culture is dominated by a sense of the "common good" as opposed to an individualistic, laissez faire orientation, or a traditionalistic one where structures of government and patterns of policy making serve to reinforce the status quo and the distribution of privileges and disadvantages that structure opportunity in a state. Furthermore, Pierce and his colleagues contend that the emphasis on the common good in Washington State promotes healthy levels of social capital, or the sense of community connectedness and trust that leads to strong levels of political participation.

But do racial and ethnic communities fit within this moralistic political culture? Are their interests included within traditional notions of the common good? Are their voices included in the arenas of policy-making where determinations are made as to how governmental power will be used to promote the common good?

Social capital has become an increasingly common measure of political and social incorporation. Trust is a key component of social capital because it links individuals to their communities, improving both individual and collective lives (Putnam 2000). However, scholars have found that social capital more effectively measures associations among people with similar backgrounds, and it may not capture the interaction of individuals in ethnically and racially diverse societies (Hero 2003). Hero found that social capital, as traditionally measured, decreased in states with diverse populations (120). Where do the diverse communities in Washington fit on the question of political culture and political incorporation? How effectively are Washington's diverse communities being engaged within Washington's body politic?

A growing body of empirical research has developed in recent years examining the phenomenon of minority political incorporation. Rufus Browning and his colleagues define political incorporation as "the extent to which group interests are effectively represented in policy making" (1984, 25). A number of prominent scholars conclude that minority communities continue to be marginalized, given little evidence that their interests are effectively represented (McClain and Stewart 1995; Barker, Jones, and Tate 1999; Hero 1992, 1998; Fraga 2005; Fraga et al. 2010; Schmidt 2000; Schmidt et al. 2010; Chávez 2011).

Ramírez and Fraga (2008) developed a multidimensional framework for examining the political incorporation of Latinos in California, and then applied it to the 20-year period of 1990 to 2010. They define political incorporation as "the extent to which self-identified group interests are articulated, represented, and met in public policy making." They continue, "Political incorporation has three *descriptive* dimensions: electoral, representational, and policy-based" (64). Each of these is a distinct arena in which influence can be exercised: voting, descriptive representation, and policy benefit. They further specify three distinct analytical dimensions within each of these arenas to more precisely gauge how much political incorporation is present. The three *analytical* dimensions are access, opportunity, and institutionalization. Access refers to identifiable potential influence, opportunity refers to the actual exercise of influence, and institutionalization refers to the presence of that influence over an extended period of time (65–7). Although it is possible for these dimensions to "exist in a direct positive relationship" (66), it is also possible that gains on each of these dimensions can be uneven, or that changes in governmental structure or procedures can produce reversals to gains that have been attained. We draw heavily on this conceptual work and prior application to California in our analysis of conditions for people of color in the Evergreen State.

Finally, how should one assess sub-state variation in which social groups are included in discussions of the common good? In between Seattle and Spokane lies the Yakima Valley, Tri-Cities, and other areas where there is a long history of race and ethnic-based tensions arising from the split between growers and other major employers and their workers, many of them migrant farm workers whose livelihood and job prospects are often extremely limited. It is reasonable to posit that in this region of the state, a traditionalistic political culture may operate in local politics. It may be that this political culture that has historically marginalized, and likely continues to marginalize, communities of color, especially Hispanics/Latinos, can coexist with a larger statewide moralistic culture; the local political culture may well address an exclusive common good that does not incorporate the interests of Hispanics/Latinos.

Demographic Change and Political Incorporation

In 1970, communities of color were estimated to constitute only 6.5% of Washington's population. That percentage has been steadily rising, as indicated in Figure 1. In 1980 it was 9.5%, in 1990 it was 13.5%, and in 2000 it was approximately 20.7%.[3] As stated earlier, non-White communities now comprise an estimated 27.5% of the state's population. Further examination of Figure 1 indicates that the growth in the non-White population is driven largely by increasing populations of Latinos and Asians. Latinos were estimated to comprise only 2.1% of the state population in 1970. At present, the 2010 census estimates that they now are now 11.2%. This represents a dramatic growth rate of slightly more than five times over the last 40 years. It is likely that this growth will continue well into the future. If current birth, death, and immigration rates are maintained, Hispanics/Latinos are estimated to comprise 14.5% of the population in 2020 and 17.8% in 2030. Asians were approximately 1.3% of the state population in 1970, and in 2010 are now 7.1%; this represents an even more dramatic growth rate of five and a half times over the last 40 years. If the Asian population continues to grow at the same rate, Asians are likely to comprise 8.7% of the population in 2020 and 9.7% in 2030. The non-Hispanic White population in the state has declined substantially since 1970, going from 95.6% in 1970 to 72.5% in 2010. Using straight-line projections we estimate that they are likely to comprise 65.3% of the population in 2020 and 59.4%

Figure 1. Population Growth in Washington, 1970–2030

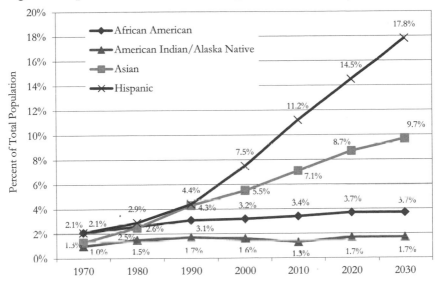

Source: Office of Financial Management, State of WA, and straight-line projections using 2010 Census data.

in 2030. The population of the state is becoming more ethnically and racially diverse, and less White, than ever before in its history since territorial days.

The distribution of this increased racial and ethnic diversity in the state varies greatly. As indicated in Table 1, there are three counties where racial and ethnic groups comprise a majority of the population. These counties are Adams County, where 61.2% of the population is non-White, Franklin County at 56.8% non-White, and Yakima County at 52.3% minority population. Grant County also has a substantial non-White population of 42.7%, and King County, the most populous county in the state, has a non-White population of 35.2%. Four of these five high-minority counties are in the politically conservative area of eastern Washington.

Table 2 lists the ethnic and racial distributions of the population in the five counties with the highest percentages of Latinos, the largest ethnic group in the state. Four of these counties also appear in Table 1 indicating that, with the exception of King County, Latinos are the largest segment of the non-White population in these high-minority counties. Interestingly, all five of these counties are located in the eastern part of the state.

This dramatic population growth among the state's minority citizenry has not led to a concomitant growth in the political incorporation and political influence of ethnic and racial communities in the state's politics, as the data to be reported next clearly indicate. Table 3 displays the rates of registration

Table 1

Five Most Non-White Counties in Washington, 2010

	Adams County	Franklin County	Yakima County	Grant County	King County
Total Population	18,728	78,163	243,231	89,120	1,931,249
White	7,262	33,804	116,024	51,066	1,251,300
Black or African American	47	1,339	1,743	710	116,326
American Indian and Alaska Native	76	357	9,072	779	12,931
Asian	99	1,384	2,359	783	280,029
Pacific Islander	3	92	142	54	14,068
Other Race	18	96	331	95	4,688
Two or More Races	124	1,087	4,090	1,470	79,529
Hispanic	11,099	40,004	109,470	34,163	172,378
Total Non-White Population	11,466	44,359	127,207	38,054	679,949
% non-White	61.22%	56.75%	52.29%	42.70%	35.21%
% Hispanic/Latino	59.26%	51.18%	45.01%	38.33%	8.93%

Source: U.S. Census, 2010.

Table 2

Five Most Hispanic/Latino Counties in Washington, 2010

	Adams County	Franklin County	Yakima County	Grant County	Douglas County
Total Population	18,728	78,163	243,231	89,120	38,431
White	7,262	33,804	116,024	51,066	26,070
Black or African American	47	1,339	1,743	710	85
American Indian and Alaska Native	76	357	9,072	779	293
Asian	99	1,384	2,359	783	269
Pacific Islander	3	92	142	54	51
Other Race	18	96	331	95	52
Two or More Races	124	1,087	4,090	1,470	598
Hispanic	11,099	40,004	109,470	34,163	11,013
Total Non-White Population	11,466	44,359	127,207	38,054	12,361
% non-White	61.22%	56.75%	52.29%	42.70%	32.16%
% Hispanic/Latino	59.26%	51.18%	45.01%	38.33%	28.66%

Source: U.S. Census, 2010.

and voting in the 2008 presidential election as determined by responses to the Current Population Survey of the Census Bureau. Among citizens, significant disparities exist in the voter registration rates of African Americans, Latinos, and

Table 3

Registration and Voting in Washington, 2008

	Total Population	Total Citizen Population	% Registered Citizens	% Voted (Total 18+)	% Voted (Citizen 18+)	% Voted Registered Citizens)
Total	4,912	4,600	71.7%	62.6%	66.8%	93.1%
White, non-Hispanic/Latino	3,801	3,729	73.3	69.2	70.6	94.4
Black	157	123	46.3	36.3	46.4	100.0
Asian	344	262	63.7	38.5	50.5	79.0
Hispanic/Latino (of any race)	404	280	57.1	36.6	52.7	92.5

Source: U.S. Census Bureau, Current Population Survey, November 2008.

Asian Americans as compared to Whites. The highest rates of voter registration among citizens who are 18 years of age or older are Whites at 73.3%. The registration rate for Asian adult citizens is 63.7%, for Latinos is 57.1%, and for African Americans is a surprisingly low 46.3%.[4] It is interesting, however, that the disparities in voter registration reduce considerably when one compares rates of voter turnout among those who are registered. Interestingly, it is African Americans who have the highest rates of voter participation in 2008 among those who are registered. It is still the case that among the major impediments to the exercise of further electoral influence by ethnic and racial minority groups is the act of voter registration.

It is also true that ethnic and racial minority groups in Washington are not particularly well represented at any level of government. It was only in 2010 that the first Latina was elected to Congress. She is the only minority member of the state's congressional delegation. There are two Asian Americans and one Latina serving in the state senate, comprising only 6% of the 49-member body. There are also three Asian Americans, one Latina, one Latino, one African American, and one Native American serving in the 98-member state house of representatives. Together they comprise only 7% of all the members of the house. It is important to recall that 27.5% of the population of the state is comprised of ethnic and racial minority communities.

Table 4 reveals the levels of representation of Latinos in local governments in 2010. In that year there were five mayors, two mayors pro-tem, eighteen city council members, one municipal court judge, and sixteen school board members—for a total of 42 local officials. Of the 25 elected officials serving at the city level, eight of them come from one city, Wapato (on the Yakama Indian Reservation). This is an anomaly in the state. Four elected city officials serve in Granger, and three serve in each of the cities of Harrah and Mabton, two serve in Warden, two in Grandview, and one each in Toppenish, Port Townsend, and

Table 4

Latina/o Local Elected Officials in Washington, 2010

Office	Number
Mayor	5
Mayor Pro-Tem	2
Councilmember	18
Municipal Court Judge	1
School Board Member	16
Total	42

Source: National Association of Latino Elected and Appointed Officials, 2010.

Sunnyside. Stated differently, these 25 local government officials serve across nine cities. Also as indicated in Table 4, only 16 Latinos were serving on school boards in 2010. The Mabton School District had three Latinos serving as board members, the largest number in any school district in the state. There were two Latino/as serving in each of the districts of Wapato, Grandview, and Sunnyside. There was only one Latino serving on the school boards of Othello, Toppenish, Wenatchee, Mount Adams, Union Gap, Yakima, and Grandview. Given that the State Department of Education estimated that Latinos were 18.2% of all the students enrolled in K-12 public schools in Washington in 2010, it is reasonable to conclude that there is considerable underrepresentation of Latinos on the state's school boards.

Another way of gauging the political incorporation of communities of color is by closely examining levels of material well-being that, in part, result from the distribution of national- and state-level policy benefits. The data set forth in Figure 2 display disparities in poverty rates for major racial/ethnic segments of the population in 2010. Overall, an estimated 15% of all people living in Washington live at or below the federally-established poverty level. Based on cross-group comparisons, Latinos have the highest poverty rates in the state; it is estimated that 30% of all Latinos live below the official poverty level. While 12% of Whites live at or below the poverty level, over a quarter (27%) of African Americans live at or below the poverty level.

The percentage of Washington residents who do not have the benefit of health insurance is displayed in Figure 3. Again, it is Washington's Latinos who have the most severe disparities relative to Whites. While it is estimated that 14% of all residents in the state of Washington are currently uninsured, more than a third (35%) of Latinos are currently uninsured. In stark contrast, it is estimated that only 11% of Whites in Washington do not have the benefit of health insurance coverage. Comparable health insurance coverage data for African Americans was not available at this writing. Data reported by Washington Kids Count, a joint effort of the Children's Alliance and the Washington State

Figure 2. Poverty by Race and Ethnicity in Washington

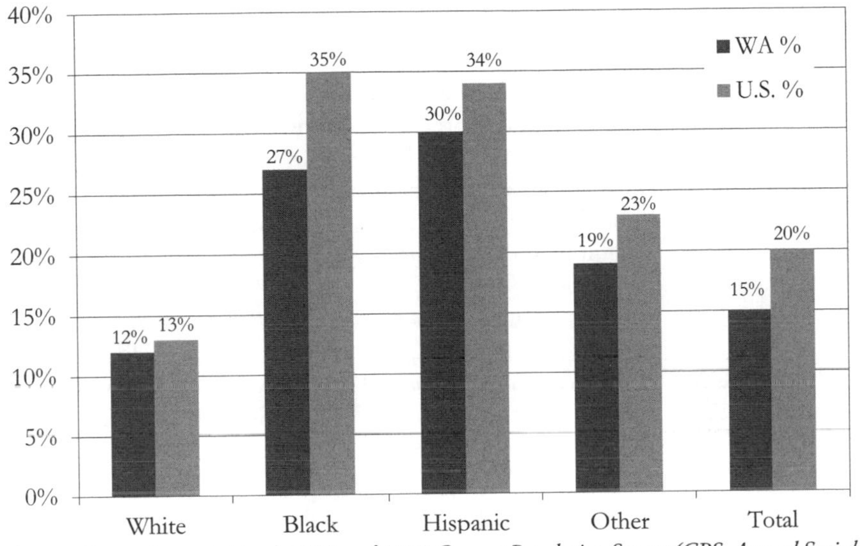

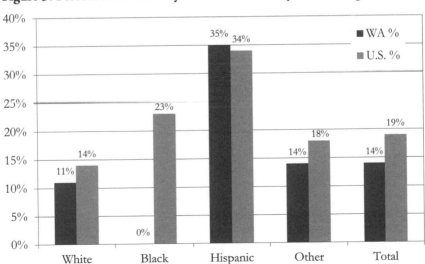

Source: *Census Bureau's March 2009 and 2010 Current Population Survey (CPS: Annual Social and Economic Supplements).*

Figure 3. Percent Uninsured by Race and Ethnicity in Washington

Source: *Urban Institute and Kaiser Commission on Medicaid and the Uninsured estimates based on the Census Bureau's March 2009 and 2010 Current Population Survey (CPS: Annual Social and Economic Supplements).*

Budget and Policy Center, reports that in 2008 22.4% of Native American and Alaska Native children had no health insurance, and neither did 17.7% of children who were Hispanic, 8.6% of those who were Asian, and only 6.2% of those children who were White (Manza 2010).

Lastly, the data displayed in Figure 4 document rates of unemployment by racial ethnic group. Statewide, both Hispanics and African Americans have unemployment rates that are noticeably higher than that of their White counterparts. It is estimated that 9.2% of Hispanics across the state are unemployed, whereas the figure for Whites out of work is 6.4%. African Americans have the highest estimated unemployment rate of any racial/ethnic group, registering 12.3% at the time of writing.

Figure 4 also displays estimated unemployment rates for selected counties across the state. We take particular note of the racial/ethnic disparities in Yakima County. It is reported that 13.3% of Hispanics/Latinos of working age are unemployed in this county, whereas only 7.6% of Whites are unemployed. The rate of unemployment for African Americans in Yakima County is below that of Hispanics, estimated to be at 8.6%.

In sum, measures of policy benefits regarding poverty rates, the uninsured, and those who are unemployed reveal that Latinos and African Americans do

Figure 4. Percent Unemployed by Race and Ethnicity in Five Most Minority Washington Counties

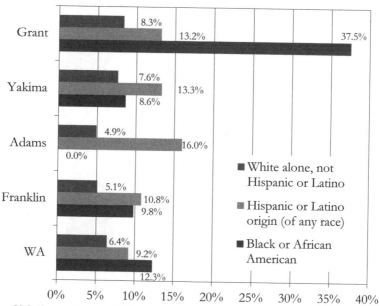

Source: *U.S. Census Bureau, 2005–2009 American Community Survey.*

considerably worse than Whites in the state of Washington. Undoubtedly, this pattern of systematic inequity in condition can be documented in virtually every state in the nation. Our point here, however, is that it is quite clear that the general characterization of the state as moralistic—leading it to utilize government to promote the common good—nonetheless leaves two of Washington's major ethnic and racial minority communities, Latinos and African Americans, with significant challenges to overcome their socioeconomic disparities relative to Whites. If comparable figures were available for Native Americans in the state, it is very likely that the same could be said of both reservation- and non-reservation residing Native Americans in Washington.

To further gauge the political incorporation of communities of color in the state, we provide narratives of perceptions of the political incorporation of racial and ethnic communities in the state generated from a series of personal interviews with persons of color.[5] We found three common themes across our numerous interviews: marginalization, tokenism, and minority community assumption of collective responsibility. A woman who first came to Yakima in 1982 to work in the fields stated that relations between Caucasians and Latinos have "gone from bad to worse." She continues, "The Americans are leaving us. They are racist and they want to leave us alone. They're retreating and they're leaving us, the city, and the town…A lot of people don't like us, but they don't mind that we do their work for them in the fields." She gives examples of perceived discrimination stating, "People don't like us, police target us." She also gave the example of people going by her house and screaming "beaner." Despite these perceptions of marginalization, she wants to stay in Yakima because it provides a better life for her and her family compared to what they would have in Mexico. She concluded:

> We have hope here because we're not leaving. And if they kick us out we'll come back…We don't have papers but they still take taxes out of our checks. They take out about half of what we earn, but we still don't get services.

Tokenism was another recurring theme among a number of respondents. When a Latina member of the Yakima city council reflected on her experiences as a public official she stated:

> It was a little bit of a negative because…[being a Latina] is how I was always defined. It overshadowed and took away from all the other things that I am, which is a business person, a lawyer, well-educated, an active member of the community, a parent. I mean, Latina or not I was qualified for the position. I'm not going to say race for sure had something to do with it, but when you start to go down the checklist—well did I make bad decisions? No. Did I take unpopular positions? No. Was it because I was a woman? No. When you go down the checklist you start to believe it [was race] because it seems so hard to see what else it could have been.

Being perceived as the "token" Latina council member took its toll and overshadowed her many accomplishments while on the council. She continues:

> What was really challenging from the beginning was that I was so defined by my ethnic background that it took away from my other qualifications to hold that position. So it really became a point of polarization...I worked hard to educate myself on the issues. I felt like I had to be really on the ball on the issues. I always felt like people were going to scrutinize me even more because I was so defined by my ethnic background. I was always referred to this way by the media. I tried really hard to get up to speed on everything and really know my stuff. I enjoyed being on the council and I felt like I had a positive impact on the city. I was only on the council for ten months, but I brought to the table adopting an ethics policy, some awareness of the gang issue, and how we would tackle it city-wide because the gang issue hampers the city's progress. I also tried to figure out where we could save money in the budget, especially with jail costs, court costs, and public safety costs.

She believes she was perceived as a threat to the status quo, so many of her supporters did not come out publicly in support of her campaign for election. She stated, "The people who needed to stand by me weren't in a position to do that. The people who would stand by me, the liberals, well, it would almost hurt my campaign. My campaign committee consisted of my daughter, myself, my husband, and my dog and maybe two other friends." She was defeated by an opponent without any political experience or previous leadership position, who didn't actively campaign, and who also had a DUI record and a charge of domestic violence, according to the local newspaper.

When asked what the greatest challenges were in her election campaign she stated, "Yakima has a long way to go and there is an obvious perception, you know, people who are used to being in power are not like me [racially/ethnically] and maybe I was perceived as a threat to the status quo." She also noted with sadness: "People used to tell me to take my husband's name [Caucasian surname] and then I wouldn't have [a Latino surname] when I ran for re-election."

A further example of perceptions of marginalization and tokenism was provided by a former commissioner of one of the ethnic/racial commissions in the governor's office. In this last legislative session the governor proposed consolidating all of these commissions into one multicultural group. The former commissioner stated:

> The commissions grew out of a progressive tradition in our populist state. The core idea was a good one. But, institutional racism still exists, so the [minority] commissions aren't taken as seriously as they should be in the policy-making arena. They are not being engaged in policy discussions in substantive ways. The central problem with the commissions is that they are gubernatorial artifacts, so they can't have an entirely independent point of view. They cannot act independently without risk, either.

The commissions represent a great, progressive idea that grew out of our populist past, but in practice it has never reached its potential. So when you look at it this way, if the commissions were gone tomorrow, it would be a loss, but not as great a loss as some might fear. Symbolically, the loss would be great. In terms of real public policy impact for communities of color, I doubt the loss would be profound.

In the end, the legislature did not embrace the governor's proposal to consolidate the minority commissions as a cost-cutting measure.

A final theme that appeared in our interviews was community responsibility. A number of our respondents observed that effective political incorporation also depended on racial and ethnic minority communities taking more direct responsibility for their own futures. As the Latina former councilwoman stated, "I think we do have to be in a position to organize ourselves to really promote good leadership and develop good leadership. Not because we expect someone to represent the entire Latino community, but we need to have a voice and be part of the government. So that we're not left out." The current director of the Commission on Hispanic Affairs took this line of argument a step further. He stated that what is needed most of all is to get "the Latino community, particularly the professionals, to be proactive when it comes to improving educational levels among Latinos." He continued:

I think that in order for you to be civically engaged you have to be informed... Many of us Latinos who are professionals, we have forgotten about *el barrio*. Giving back can take many forms. You can teach people to defend themselves. There are too few of us who have taken the burden on. The education is all the way through. Get the parents involved. Get the children involved. As my father always used to tell us that all of us can work together...We have to make our situation better. I remember my Dad telling me, what happens to water when it doesn't move? *Se azeda* (it gets rancid). You have to keep moving, because [if you do not] then you become useless.

The former commissioner on African American Affairs shared similar sentiments:

We have done a lot of good work around education policy through the African American Commission. The governor appoints all members of the commission board and selects the chair. When a recent board had no educators, we went to the community and recruited people who care about schools and would work with the commission to change education policy. These people were not commissioners. They were just community volunteers who cared and who supported the commission. So, we leveraged the commission to develop a volunteer group that became the Black Education Strategy Roundtable. Their goal was to be a voice for improving schools through public policy change at the state level. That volunteer group ran on fried chicken and potato salad, eventually coming to the attention of the Bill & Melinda Gates Foundation. The result was a small grant that kept a body of work on education reform alive, even as state funds to the commission were diminished by the deep recession.

Our form of government is about stability. When you go up to try and make change in Olympia, the whole process is set up to kill your bill. Limiting change is what the process does best. In the black community we have many single moms, men locked up, people with low incomes, families struggling to make ends meet, small community organizations struggling to make payroll. We don't have the same level of social and political capital as other groups. It's harder for us to press for change. The advocacy community around educational change also is not diverse or well equipped to engage the black community in making schools better for our kids. That's why a group like the Black Education Strategy Roundtable is important. That's also why it's good to have a commission that can nurture community involvement in this way. The slow grind of government becomes a benefit to communities when it helps people be heard.

At the end of the day, the ethnic commissions still are government agencies that must conform to that reality. The next step for communities of color is to better organize ourselves around public policy change. Our communities need influence beyond that controlled by any one elected or appointed official. We will be better served by pleading our own cause from outside of government. That's the key pathway for advocates who want to foster major public policy change in our state.

This interviewee further noted that the traditional political process did not provide adequate representation for the interests of any of the ethnic and racial communities in Washington. In response to a question about the adequacy of current political representation, she said:

If it is through the legislative environment—No, because we only have one representative. If it is the economic sector—No, because there is still a lot of nepotism…In every sphere the answer would be NO because there is still a lot of institutional and systemic racism. We're going backwards now. We had three black legislators in the 1980s, and we've got one now. There is underrepresentation in the legislature for all of the ethnic groups in Washington. The Latino community isn't represented adequately either in the legislative arena. At all levels of state and local government there are only twenty elected black officials in Washington. I know them all. So there isn't any sphere as far as I'm concerned where black people and other people of color have adequate representation.

Our last way of examining the political incorporation of ethnic and racial communities is by reviewing major legislative initiatives in the 2011 session that dealt specifically with immigrant, and especially Latino immigrant, communities. Washington's most recent legislative session was particularly harsh on immigrants and the poor because of the approach taken by lawmakers to focus on budget cuts instead of focusing on identifying new sources of revenue. It is estimated that one in ten residents of Washington is an immigrant. Six major programs serving immigrants were affected by the budget cuts enacted in the 2011 session. These minority-serving programs included:

- Washington New Americans Program: Reduced by 30% to $396,000 for the 2011–2013 biennium.
- DSHS Naturalization Program: Reduced by 40% to $3.4 million for the 2011–2013 biennium.
- Medical Interpreter Services: Reduced by 20% to approximately $37 million for the 2011–2013 biennium.
- Apple Health for Kids for 27,000 immigrant children: Now requires premium covering the full cost of coverage for undocumented children between 200% and 300% of the federal poverty level.
- State Food Assistance: Benefit level reduced by 50% to $31 million for the 2011–2013 biennium.
- LEP Pathways/Refugee Services: Reduced by 50% to $5 million for the 2011–2013 biennium. (Guevin 2011)

The implications of these budget cuts are enormous for immigrants and communities of color, many of whom are already disproportionately living in poverty. According to the Washington State Commission on Hispanic Affairs 2009 Assessment,[6] the median annual earnings in 2007 for Hispanics was $20,238 a year, for African Americans it was $25,298 a year, and for Whites it was $32,482. The Commission on Hispanic Affairs 2009 Assessment further indicated that 31% of Hispanic children younger than 17 years of age are living in poverty, 33% of black children are living in poverty, and 10% of white children are living in poverty.

Nonetheless, there were several protective (moralistic) legislative actions taken that directly served the interests of immigrant and minority communities, reflecting that deep tradition in the state's politics. Among these were a bill that would benefit or at least protect immigrants from unfair sentencing practices, a bill that would help prevent immigrants from being victimized by fraudulent practices by unqualified *notarios* (notary publics) who mislead immigrants into thinking they have training in immigration law, and the successful effort to defeat a bill seeking to make it illegal for undocumented immigrants to continue to obtain driver's licenses. Clearly, Washington State is not as xenophobic as many other states across the country. For example, in Alabama the state legislature recently enacted an immigration bill that will require children to provide documentation before being enrolled in public school, bar landlords from renting to people who are undocumented, permit police officers to ask about one's immigration status based on "reasonable suspicion" of being undocumented (similar to Arizona's SB 1070), denies businesses tax deductions on wages paid to unauthorized immigrants, criminalizes the failure of an immigrant to carry documentation proving their legal status on their person, and criminalizes the knowing transport of illegal immigrants (Chávez-Pringle 2011).

There are, however, strongly non-moralistic governmental actions being taken in Washington State as well. Currently eight counties in Washington have agreed to become part of the Immigration and Customs Enforcement (ICE)

"Secure Communities" program.[7] This program will allow state and local police authorities to fingerprint anyone booked into a jail and have the fingerprints checked against a Department of Homeland Security (DHS) immigration database. The agreement also allows people who are booked to be held for 48 hours until the DHS completes its review. Another local setback for immigrants is the recent adoption of E-Verify by the Yakima City Council for all city contractors and their workers. These local policies will have disproportionate effects on immigrant communities in counties with high concentrations of Latinos.

Strategic Choices and the Future of Washington's Diverse Communities

We began our analysis of the demographic changes in Washington with a simple, but clearly important question: Do ethnic and racial communities fit within the state's general understanding of the common good and the public interest? After reviewing the pace and magnitude of growth in ethnic/racial communities and examining a number of dimensions of the patterns of political incorporation of these communities in the state, we conclude that there are still major challenges faced by these communities to be consistently and significantly included in understandings of the long-term public interest of the state consistent with its characterization as operating as a moralistic political culture.

It is clear that despite considerable demographic shift to being a much more ethnically and racially diverse state, the political incorporation of communities of color as measured by political participation, political representation, and policy benefits still has much more progress to make. There are some signs of hope, such as the defeat of some legislation that was likely to further marginalize immigrant communities. However, the pattern of program cuts that will disproportionately affect lower income communities, in combination with some local government actions that clearly target immigrant communities, demonstrates that not all political leaders see the interests of ethnic and racial communities as part of a larger understanding of the common good and the public interest.

We offer findings drawn from the Washington portion of the Latino National Survey[8] to suggest a way for the state's political leaders to better understand how Latinos, the largest ethnic/racial group in the state, have attitudes and preferences that are clearly consistent with building a better future in the state, with traditional notions of the common good and the public interest. It is often claimed that Latinos do not want to learn English. The data set forth in Figure 5 reveal that this is simply not true. The vast majority of Latinos residing in the state, upwards of 80%, and across generations,[9] believe that it is "very important" that everyone in the United States learns English. This is especially the case among the first generation where 92.3% feel that this is very important. This valuing of learning English, however, coincides with a similarly strong desire to maintain Spanish and sustain one's cultural identity. The data displayed in

Figure 6 reveal that substantial majorities of Latinos also prefer that their family members maintain the ability to speak Spanish. This sentiment is highest among the first generation at 89.7%, drops to 71.1% among the second generation, drops further to 63.4% for Latinos in the third generation, and then increases

Figure 5. Importance of Learning English among Latinos by Generation
Question: How important do you think it is that everyone in the United States learns English?

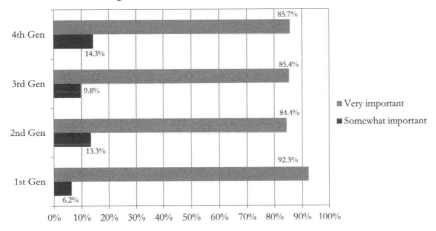

Source: Fraga et al. 2006.

Figure 6. Importance of Retaining Spanish Among Latinos by Generation
Question: How important do you think it is for you or your family to maintain the ability to speak Spanish?

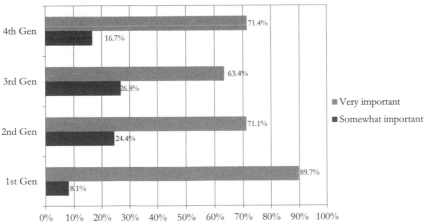

Source: Fraga et al. 2006.

to 71.4% in the fourth generation. Latinos in the state of Washington feel that it is very important to *both* learn English and maintain Spanish.

In a similar fashion, findings from the Latino National Survey reveal that Latinos in Washington State indicate that it is important to blend into the larger society while also maintaining a distinct culture as a group. As revealed in the survey findings displayed in Figure 7, it is in the first generation where the largest percentage, well over half (60.9%), think that it is very important to blend into the larger society. This figure drops to 36.4% of the second generation, 37.5% of the third generation, and 22.5% of the fourth generation. However, substantial portions across all generations think that it is somewhat important to blend into the larger society. It is noteworthy that the findings set forth in Figure 8 reveal that simultaneous with the support for "blending in" is very strong support for maintaining a distinct culture. This combination of desires to fit in and remain proud of one's Latino heritage exists across all generations. A full 79.5% of the first generation feel that it is very important to maintain a distinct culture, 80% of the second generation, 70.7% of the third, and 71.4% of the fourth. Again, the desire to blend into the larger society and maintain a distinct culture coexists among the state's Latinos.

Lastly, despite the claim often made that many Latino parents do not have high aspirations or expectations as to how their children will do in school, the Latino National Survey provides systematic evidence that this is not the case (see Figure 9). When asked the question, "How far would you like to see this child go in school?" a clear majority (58.7%) of all Latino respondents in Wash-

Figure 7. Importance of Blending Into Larger Society Among Latinos by Generation

Question: How important is it for (Hispanos or Latinos) to change so that they blend into the larger American society?

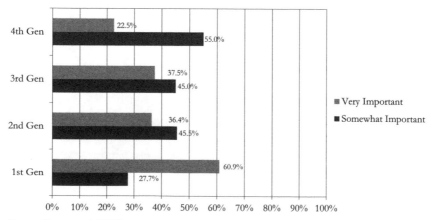

Source: Fraga et al. 2006.

Figure 8. Importance of Maintaining Distinct Culture Among Latinos by Generation

Question: How important is it for Hispanics/Latinos to maintain their distinct cultures?

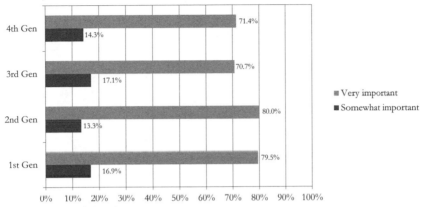

Source: Fraga et al. 2006.

ington with a child currently in school stated that they aspired for their child to receive a graduate or advanced degree, and 33.6% said that they aspired for their child to graduate from college. When asked the follow-up question, "How far do you think your child will actually go in school?" over a third (37.4%) of respondents indicated that they expected that the child would earn a graduate or advanced degree, and 36.1% expected that their child would graduate from college. These overwhelmingly high aspirations and expectations among Latino parents indicate that there is a very strong foundation in Latino communities to have their youth excel in higher education. If this commitment can be properly harnessed by public officials and educational leaders to overcome the very significant educational challenges faced by Latinos in the state, there is little doubt that the entire state would benefit greatly from a better educated work force, contributing even more to the state's economic growth and building a stronger civil society.

It may be that the state is at a critical juncture to determine whether its politics and policy-making processes have the capacity to effectively engage its growing ethnic and racial diversity within a traditional understanding of the common good and the public interest. The choices made by the state's political leaders will directly affect whether the state can still be characterized as a moralistic political culture or whether it will lean toward a traditionalistic political culture to maintain longstanding differentials in class and cross-group social standing. Washington State has a unique opportunity to not only actively politically incorporate communities of color, but also to empower local communities of all

Figure 9. Parental Aspirations of Child's Education Among Latinos
Question: How far would you like to see this child go in school?

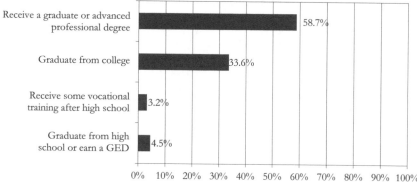

Source: Fraga et al. 2006.

Figure 10. Parental Expectations of Child's Education Among Latinos
Question: How far do you think your child will actually go in school?

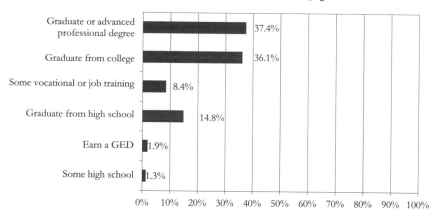

Source: Fraga et al. 2006.

classes, races, and backgrounds by the way it decides to adapt to demographic changes. Our analysis demonstrates that Washington is perhaps at a tipping point regarding which direction it will go. Washington State political leaders can broaden their conception of the moralistic political culture, or it can turn toward a more stratified and segregated style of political life. Whatever path the state's political leaders choose, the results of their decisions over the course of the next decade will be with Washington's ethnically, racially, and linguistically diverse citizens and residents for generations.

Endnotes

1. The terms Hispanic and Latino will be used interchangeably in this article. The Latino National Survey (Fraga et al. 2006) found that 35% of all Hispanics/Latinos living in the United States preferred the term Hispanic, 13.4% chose Latino, 32.5% found either term acceptable, 18.1% don't care, and 1.1% do not know.
2. All Hispanics/Latinos are counted in this group. Data for all other groups excludes Hispanics, i.e., non-Hispanic Whites, non-Hispanic Asians, non-Hispanic African Americans, etc.
3. In 2000 it was estimated that 2.9% of the population was of two or more races. In 2010, Native Hawaiians and other Pacific Islanders were 0.6% of the state population; those who indicated some other race were 0.2%, and those who indicated two or more races were 4.5%.
4. These rates are unusually low given that African Americans citizens are estimated to be registered at a rate of 69.7% nationwide.
5. The interview participants include: a Latina former councilwoman, a former executive director of the Commission on African American Affairs, and the current executive director of the Commission on Hispanic Affairs. These interviews were conducted in 2011. We also use narratives from numerous interviews conducted in eastern Washington with recent immigrants. These individuals were found in public spaces such as laundromats, Mexican businesses, shopping centers, and open air markets known as "swap meets." Sixteen interviews were conducted in this fashion in 2004.
6. This report can be downloaded at cha.wa.gov/?q=statistics_reports.
7. The counties are Yakima, Lewis, Benton, Franklin, Gray's Harbor, Island, Pacific, and Walla Walla.
8. The Latino National Survey (Fraga et al. 2006) is the first-ever state stratified national survey of representative samples of Latinos in 15 states and the Washington, D.C., metropolitan area. Washington was one of the states included in the survey. Representative samples for each state and the D.C. area were developed. When aggregated, the survey covered approximately 87.5% of all Latinos living in the United States. The sample size for Washington was 400.
9. The term first generation refers to Latinos who were born outside of the United States. Second generation Latinos were born in the United States, but their parents were born outside of the United States. Third generation Latinos were born in the United States and have at least one parent who was also born in the United States. Fourth generation Latinos were born in the United States and have at least one grandparent who was also born in the United States.

References

Barker, Lucius, Mack H. Jones, and Katherine Tate. 1999. *African Americans and the American Political System.* Upper Saddle River, NJ: Prentice Hall.

Browning, Rufus P., Dale Rogers Marshall, and David H. Tabb. 1984. *Protest Is Not Enough: The Struggle of Blacks and Hispanics for Equality in Urban Politics.* Berkeley: University of California Press.

Chávez, Maria. 2011. *Everyday Injustice: Latino Professionals and Racism.* Lanham, MD: Rowman & Littlefield.

Chávez-Pringle, María. June 11, 2011. "Democracy or Authoritarianism: What are We Becoming?" *Racism Review.* racismreview.com/blog/2011/06/11/democracy-or-authoritarianism-what-are-we-becoming.

Elazar, Daniel. 1994. *The American Mosaic: The Impact of Space, Time, and Culture on American Politics*. Boulder, CO: Westview Press.

Fraga, Luis Ricardo. 2005. "Racial and Ethnic Politics in a Multicultural Society." In *Diversity in Democracy: Minority Representation in the United States*, edited by Gary M. Segura and Shaun Bowler, 278–301. Charlottesville: University of Virginia Press.

Fraga, Luis R., John A. Garcia, Rodney Hero, Michael Jones-Correa, Valerie Martinez-Ebers, Gary M. Segura. 2006. Latino National Survey. dx.doi.org/10.3886/ICPSR20862.v4.

_____. 2010. *Latino Lives in America: Making it Home*. Philadelphia, PA: Temple University Press.

Guevin, Toby. June 14, 2011. *OneAmerica's State Immigration Policy Update*. OneAmerica. statevoices.salsalabs.com/o/66/t/0/blastContent.jsp?email_blast_KEY=368.

Hero, Rodney E. 1992. *Latinos and the U.S. Political System: Two-Tiered Pluralism*. Philadelphia, PA: Temple University Press.

_____. 1998. *Faces of Inequality: Social Diversity in American Politics*. New York: Oxford University Press.

_____. 2003. "Social Capital and Racial Inequality in America." *Perspectives on Politics* 1(1): 113–122.

Manza, Maria. May 26, 2010. "Native American Children Lead Ranks of Uninsured in WA." *Children's Alliance*. childrensalliance.org/no-kidding-blog/native-american-children-lead-ranks-uninsured-wa.

McClain, Paula D. and Joseph Stewart Jr. 1995. *"Can We All Get Along?": Racial and Ethnic Minorities in American Politics*. Boulder, CO: Westview Press.

Putnam, Robert. 2000. *Bowling Alone: The Collapse and Revival of American Community*. New York: Simon and Schuster.

Ramírez, Ricardo, and Luis Ricardo Fraga. 2008. "Continuity and Change: Latino Political Incorporation in California Since 1990." In *Racial and Ethnic Politics in California: Continuity and Change* Vol. 3, edited by Bruce E. Cain and Sandra Bass, 61–93. Berkeley, CA: Institute of Governmental Studies Press, University of California Berkeley.

Schmidt, Ronald. 2000. *Language Policy and Identity Politics in the United States*. Philadelphia, PA: Temple University Press.

Schmidt Sr., Ronald, Yvette M. Alex-Assensoh, Andrew L. Aoki, and Rodney E. Hero. 2010. *Newcomers, Outsiders, and Insiders: Immigrants and American Racial Politics in the Early Twenty-first Century*. Ann Arbor: University of Michigan Press.

CHAPTER SIX

Media and Politics in Washington in the Post-*Post-Intelligencer* Age

Kathleen Searles and Austin Jenkins

I N 2009 THE *Seattle Post-Intelligencer* (*PI*) became the first major American newspaper to go online-only (SeattlePI.com 2011). This shift meant a dramatic decrease in staffing and the relegation of veteran observers like Joel Connelly, a long-time *PI* politics reporter, to the web where competition for readers is fierce. To maintain viability in a competitive market, the *PI* outsourced some local and entertainment news to other media outlets and increasingly relied on reader content and blogs to supplement coverage.

Abandoning print news was a dubious distinction for the *PI*, but the challenges facing this institution of Washington State media are not unique. In fact, the decision to move to web-only content exemplifies an era of great uncertainty for print news and for American media at large. The reality is that market demands drive the American media system, and Washington State is not immune to these pressures. Unfortunately for citizens of Washington, these pressures have made it difficult for the statehouse press corps to fulfill their civic obligation and difficult for political reporters to keep their jobs.

Trends in the coverage of news in Washington State are similar to those across the nation. Public affairs coverage can be costly and the demand for it minimal, while there is no shortage of attention-grabbing soft news. Although the press in America has long labored to maintain high standards in the coverage of political affairs and the production of civic information, that tradition is undeniably being shaped by weak regulation and increasing market pressures. When combined with the proliferation of cable television and internet sources of news (Bennett and Iyengar 2008), the dramatic shift of the *PI* to online-only content illustrates the extent to which the future of news media in Washington is one marked by great insecurity.

The news media in Washington is inextricably linked to state politics. News coverage shapes the behavior of state and local politicians, and the behaviors of politicians shape the content and tenor of news coverage (Zaller 1999). Though media consumers increasingly opt not to watch political news, their demands indirectly affect the content of news and can indicate public approval or disapproval of the political actors who are covered. Additionally, as American political parties have become weaker institutions the media has stepped in to fill the vacuum left behind, ushering in an era of media-based campaigning. For these reasons, no discussion of politics in Washington State is complete without an understanding of the vital and dynamic role played by the media. We begin our discussion with a general overview of media in Washington and the United States before delving into the changing landscape of Washington media with a focus on the diminishing role of the Capitol Press Corps.

Media in Washington

Mass media encompasses a range of communication including the internet, magazines, newspapers, television, and radio. In the state of Washington, citizens receive their news from three main media outlets. The first, print media, is perhaps the most trusted form of news and includes newspapers and magazines. Examples of Washington print media include the *Seattle Times, Yakima Herald-Republic, Snohomish Times, Northwest Business Monthly*, and *Capitol Hill Times* (USNPL 2011a).

The newspapers with the highest print circulation are as follows (Mondotimes 2011b):

Seattle Times	251,697
Seattle Weekly	109,000
Seattle Stranger	90,309
Tacoma News Tribune	82,855
Spokane Spokesman-Review	74,386

By comparison, the *Wall Street Journal* has the highest print circulation nationally with more than two million readers (Mondotimes 2011a). Print newspapers in Washington reach approximately 1.4 million readers; in 2009 there were 46 million newspaper readers nationwide (Mondotimes 2011b; NAA 2011). This represents a dramatic decline from the peak in 1990 when daily newspaper circulation was 62 million (NAA 2011). All of the top 25 newspapers in the nation, with the exception of the *Wall Street Journal*, have experienced a decline in print circulation in recent years (Arango 2009). Although newspapers remain an important source of news for many and continue to set the agenda for other media outlets, their viability in the current media market is tenuous.

The second most important media outlet for the state of Washington is broadcast media, which covers all television news. Watching television news is an important factor in political knowledge, and watching local television news is more likely to motivate political participation regardless of whether or not viewers think highly of their local television broadcast (Moy et al. 2004).

There are 20 local television stations in Washington, six of which are in Seattle (USNPL 2011b). Of the four major network affiliates in Seattle only KING TV (NBC) airs a weekly public affairs show, *Up Front with Robert Mak*, though KIRO (CBS) and KOMO (ABC) both have veteran reporters on staff with long experience covering Washington politics and the statehouse. These three stations also field aggressive investigative teams that often target state government waste, fraud, and abuse. KCTS 9 (PBS) diligently covers public affairs on programs like *KCTS Connects with Enrique Cerna* and airs a popular quarterly program called *Ask the Governor*. Another trustworthy broadcast news source is Washington State's Public Affairs Network, TVW, which strives to counteract the effects of diminishing legislative coverage by traditional news outlets. TVW is a cable-only network, accessible to 99 percent of Washington households, offering original programming and an expansive searchable online archive.

Washingtonians get their news from local television more than any other source. There are some characteristics of television that shape the content of news; the regulatory framework of broadcast media is also important (Iyengar et al 2009). The Federal Communications Commission (FCC) is the regulatory authority over electromagnetic emissions, upon which television and radio rely. As the public airwaves are a limited resource, the FCC has some control over concentration of media ownership and content. Over the years the FCC has taken an increasingly hands-off style to regulation, only asking that broadcast-ers air some programming that meets the public's need for civic information. Broadcasters are required to offer time to political candidates on equal terms, but they are not required to give equal time if the candidates cannot afford the cost. Ownership of media outlets is important because publicly-funded media are required to provide a minimum amount of public affairs information whereas private media is not. For this reason, market-oriented media is more likely to under-produce serious news.

The third major source of political news in Washington is the internet. Each day millions of Americans use the internet to get their news. More than 71 percent of Washingtonians use the internet at home, and more than 81 percent use the internet at home or elsewhere (NTIA 2007). Only the states of New Hampshire and Alaska have higher rates of internet use. Internet consumers can access print news electronically via sites like nytimes.com. In fact, the online presence of print newspapers has boosted readership, although modestly (Pew Research Center 2010). Individuals can also track breaking news in real time, using social networking sites such as Twitter. As yet another option, interested readers can keep up with specific issues via blogs that match their interests.

The greatest advantage of internet news is that it accommodates greater depth and allows for constant updating. Additionally, internet media is highly responsive because it can utilize reader feedback and track consumption rates to adapt to reader interests. Labeled "narrowcasting" by scholars, this is the ability (also shared by broadcast television and to a lesser extent newspapers) to focus on a specific segment of the population when delivering news content. In this way internet media offers news that matches consumer interest rather than offering news that delivers a certain standard of public information. This ability to micro-target has contributed to the increased popularity of internet news niche-outlets that target partisan readers (Della Vigna and Kaplan 2007). However, the internet facilitates individual selective exposure to news that confirms existing attitudes. Many argue that inasmuch as the internet enables niche-reporting and selective exposure to information, it contributes to misinformation and the polarization of political attitudes. However, others counter that for every consumer that uses the internet to confirm their world view, hundreds of other consumers use it for educational purposes (Wayne 2000).

In the state of Washington and across the country, young people are more likely to access their news via the internet, as are individuals with a college education and those living in households with an income of $75,000 or more (Focus 2010). In 2010, 6 in 10 American adults were reported to be wireless internet users (Smith 2010). The United States is fifth in the world for internet accessibility, trumped only by Norway, Sweden, Finland, and the Netherlands (Focus 2010). The burgeoning growth of the internet has not passed by Washington's traditional media. In fact, many of the changes in the press in Washington are due to changes brought on by the proliferation of choice on the internet; some argue the internet has hastened the decline of Olympia's Capitol Press Corps. We discuss these changes from the perspective of those charged with arming the public with information—the reporters—in the section that follows.

Another One Bites the Dust—A View from the Trenches: Dramatic Changes in Olympia's Capitol Press Corps

Washington's Olympia press corps is located in two converted houses on the capitol campus. The "Blue House" and the "White House"—named after their original paint colors, and the second later officially named to honor Associated Press reporter John White—were once single-family residences occupied by denizens of the capital city. For decades, legions of reporters have cycled through the press houses. Some logged short stints on their way to jobs with national media in Washington, D.C.; others stayed several years before getting lured to what journalists jokingly refer to as "the dark side"—a better paying job in public relations, usually with a state agency. And then there are the creatures of Olympia—reporters who settle in for decades and possess an institutional memory that is hard to come by in a city that turns over on two- and four-year election cycles.

While the cast of characters has changed, the two press houses have consistently operated at full occupancy. Year-to-year, the press corps averaged 15 full-time reporters. This staffing level held fairly constant until the past decade when things began changing and the internet age finally caught up to the newspaper business. As consumers began turning to Craigslist instead of the back of the newspaper to find a job or a used Volkswagen, the centuries-old financial model of newspapers was broken.

By 2008, reporters in bureaus and newsrooms throughout Washington could see the writing on the wall. That's the year the *Seattle Times*, the state's largest newspaper, announced a significant downsizing. The paper reported its own bad news on April 8, 2008: "The Seattle Times Co., reeling from continued declines in advertising revenue, announced Monday it will slice its flagship newspaper's staff by nearly 200 and make other cuts aimed at saving $15 million" (Pryne 2008). The *Times* also announced it was closing its suburban Seattle bureaus. Some staff took early retirement packages. Others were simply shown the door. This was just the first round of layoffs that year. In November, the newspaper announced it was cutting another 130 to 150 employees (Perry 2008).

In Olympia, 2008 marked the beginning of an exodus from the White and Blue Houses. First to go, that April, was longtime Associated Press reporter David Ammons, the "dean" of the Capitol Press Corps. After 37 years covering state government, he was crossing the street to take a job as communications director for Secretary of State Sam Reed. "I'm stunned because it is hard to imagine this place without Dave," wrote David Postman, the *Seattle Times* chief political reporter, on his blog minutes after Ammons announced his departure. "It'll be tough for those who can't rely on his institutional memory and constant good humor and positive attitude" (Postman 2008a).

Next to go was Ralph Thomas of the *Seattle Times*, an eight-year veteran of the Olympia beat. That September, he took a job with a communications consulting firm run by a former *Times* reporter whose largest client was Microsoft. Once again, Postman had the news: "Politicians and readers should mourn Ralph's departure. He worked as hard as anyone I know to always be fair. He got a lot of enjoyment out of finding just the right well-turned phrase or even from the studied choice of a single word in a story" (Postman 2008b). Eight days later, the headline on Postman's blog flashed: "Another One Bites the Dust." This time it was Postman himself who was departing after 14 years at the *Times*. "I'm also leaving journalism, at least for the next phase of my career," wrote Postman. "I am going to work for Vulcan, Inc." (Postman 2008c). In an ironic twist, Postman had found his new job on Craigslist.

For the Capitol Press Corps this was a one, two, three punch. David Ammons, Ralph Thomas, and David Postman were three highly respected reporters. All different in their demeanor and approach, they nonetheless commanded the respect of elected leaders and top-level staff. They wrote about Olympia and Washington politics with conviction and confidence. And they were not afraid to call it how they saw it. Ammons, at nearly four decades, was undoubtedly the longest serving member in the history of the press corps. In all those years, he says he never tired of his "front row" seat and his reporting reflected that. He strived to give his readers an up-close look at how their state government functioned—or did not, in some cases.

That optimism was Ammons's trademark. But he was not naïve. He understood intrinsically the role of money in politics and how it can influence decision making. That was one prism through which he viewed Olympia. Another prism was the budgets—operating, capital, and transportation. Ammons (2011) noted that a keen read of the budget reveals "the pressure points and the political drama and tradeoffs" going on behind the scenes. When he was not covering the legislature, Ammons focused his reporting on broader trend lines and emerging newsmakers. For instance, he charted the rise and fall, and rise again, of anti-tax initiative king Tim Eyman. For nearly 20 years he also wrote a weekly column, Ammons on Politics, carried in newspapers across the state.

The Seattle Times' Ralph Thomas paid close attention to the role of special interests in Olympia. Some of his most important work charted the rise of state employee unions, especially the growing clout of the Service Employees International Union (SEIU) in Washington.

Postman's reporting legacy dated back to the O.K. Boys Ranch scandal of the mid-1990s. Dubbed a "house of horrors" by the *Times*, the O.K. Ranch was a home for troubled youth in Olympia where the boys were physically and sexually abused. Postman and his colleagues chronicled how the Department of Social and Health Services repeatedly turned a blind eye to the "horrors" and failed to protect the young residents of the home.

In May 2005, Postman revolutionized political coverage in Washington while covering the gubernatorial election contest trial between Democrat Christine Gregoire and Republican Dino Rossi. Postman blogged live from the courtroom in Wenatchee for the entire five day trial. In the end, the court's decision gave Gregoire a 133-vote victory over Rossi, and Postman had reinvented himself. In 2006, inspired by his experience during the election contest, Postman became a full-time political blogger for the *Seattle Times*. In short order, he established himself as the state's political blogger of record. Thus his departure in 2008 was all the more surprising. Postman says when he decided to leave the *Times* in 2008 he was not leaping for a life raft. "I didn't think cuts would go so deep to close our [Olympia] bureau. But the business was changing and I felt our collective ambition was suffering."

It was a different story for *Tri-City Herald* reporter Chris Mulick. His decision to leave, a few weeks after Postman's, was motivated by financial security. Mulick, a new father, revealed his internal agony in a candid blog post titled "My Sorrowful and Unthinkable Goodbye" (Mulick 2008).

> To be sure, this move isn't about selling out, cashing in, personal politics or personal gain. This is about putting family before all else. I can't point to one

single reason that fueled this decision…But certainly, the financial troubles plaguing this industry have created considerable uncertainty.

A more dramatic turn of events occurred in January 2009 when Hearst Corporation put the venerable *Seattle Post-Intelligencer* up for sale. The company said if no buyer came forward within 60 days, the newspaper would be shut down. The *PI*'s reporter in Olympia, Chris McGann, did not wait to find out how this story would end. Six days after the announcement, he took a job with the newly elected state treasurer, Jim McIntire. McGann had been on the Olympia beat just a couple of years, but had made his mark writing "follow the money" stories.

PI managing editor David McCumber announced McGann's departure on his blog. McCumber then went on to write a self-flagellating analysis of how things in the newspaper business—and in particular at the *PI*—had reached a crisis point:

> I can't help feeling as though we've done something badly wrong to get to this position…It's easy to blame our potential demise on forces beyond our control, and newsroom conversations would confirm there are no shortage of targets—the overall decline of print, the economy, the dysfunction of the JOA [Joint Operating Agreement with the *Seattle Times*], the corporation. But the truth is, we have to shoulder our share of it…I think as an industry we started our slide from a place of arrogance and self-importance. I think that nationally and locally, we've been slow to respond to changes in the market, in readers' needs and in technology. I think larger papers, like the P-I, gradually ossified by demanding years of experience for any opening, and paid too little attention to diversifying, in terms of age, ethnicity and gender, to better reflect the communities they serve. I think we haven't done a good job of marketing ourselves, of making sure people understand that what we do actually is valuable. I think we got trapped between serving the readers we wanted to attract and the readers we actually had. (McCumber 2009)

By the time the 60-day March deadline rolled around, no savior for the *PI* was found. Hearst announced the 146-year-old newspaper would immediately stop publishing, but would continue to exist online with a skeleton staff.

The Blue and White Houses on the capitol campus were now feeling empty. Unlike in previous years, the reporters who left were not replaced. The steady drumbeat of departures continued in the summer of 2009. Adam Wilson of the *Olympian*, another reporter with a young family, accepted a job as Governor Chris Gregoire's speechwriter. "Olympia Press-Corps Loses another Voice" was the headline on The Politics Blog, maintained by Wilson's colleague Brad Shannon. In bidding Wilson adieu, Shannon went on to lament the dwindling press corps and the state of the newspaper business: "Now a word on the downside. My back-of-the-envelope tally is this leaves the state with about eight full-time Olympia-based journalists to cover the Capitol, less than half what we had a year ago. Wilson leaves after the worst 12-month stretch I've known in my years in the business. Just since June 2008, we've had three downsizings at the paper" (Shannon 2009). Like a plague sweeping through a village, the question on everyone's mind was: who would be next? The answer came ten days later. "Capitol Press Corps Loses Another" read the headline at Rich Roesler's Eye on Olympia blog. After nearly nine years with the *Spokesman Review*, Roesler had accepted a job with the state's elected insurance commissioner. He too cited the uneasy times in the newspaper business as his reason for leaving: "I love what I do, and am deeply grateful to the *Spokesman-Review* and to everyone who's clicked on this blog or read my stories. But given the worrisome state of newspapers—round after round of layoffs, a pay cut, a furlough—it would have felt irresponsible to not jump at a job that feels like a good fit and a new opportunity" (Roesler 2009).

Now, not only had the statehouse press corps lost much of its venerable, experienced old guard, but also the next line of defense in Mulick, Wilson, and Roesler. This trio may have worked for smaller papers, but they were experienced reporters who pushed the envelope by producing multimedia stories, investigating malfeasance by hometown legislators, and shinning a light on state agencies. Unlike many younger reporters, they also were not using Olympia as a way station but had a passion for state government and politics.

By late 2008 if there was such a thing as an "old newspaperman" remaining in the Capitol Press Corps, it was Joe Turner of the *Tacoma News Tribune*. More snappish than gruff, Turner could often be heard throughout the White House yelling at someone on the other end of the phone line—so loud, in fact, that the public radio reporters upstairs sometimes had to wait for him to hang up to record their stories. But for all his cantankerousness, Turner was arguably the best sourced reporter in Olympia. During legislative sessions, he would often set up his laptop in the old Pritchard Library, the domain of lobbyists, and spend the day blogging the tips, tidbits, and morsels fed to him by members of the so-called Third House (lobbyists or other special interests). He was also known for his mastery of the state budgets—operating, capital, and transportation. He was a budget reading machine, pouring through the thousands of pages that comprised the competing proposals from the governor, house, and senate. "Sometimes I was looking for daily stories," says Turner. "Other times I was saving up ideas for stories to do during the interim" (Turner 2011). Like Ammons at the AP, Turner understood intrinsically that a budget at its core is a political document. Embedded in that big boring bill were a thousand stories of hopes realized, dreams dashed, and a whole lot of political horse trading. Turner had a nose for unearthing those stories and shining a light on them. But in October of 2009, Turner announced his retirement:

Don't get me wrong. The remaining members of the Olympia press corps are top notch…But there are too few of them. And newspapers are not going to replace all of the reporters who have left, even after the economy improves…A former newspaper colleague, after he had worked in state government for several years, once told me, "You don't know even 10 percent of what goes on behind the scenes." I believe him. And that's what distresses me. Government is sneaky… That's why the press is supposed to be a watchdog. We're supposed to find out what they're doing and alert everyone. I hope the 10 percent that we reporters do find out about is the most important 10 percent of what government is doing to and for us. But I'm also sure we miss a lot. I fear that those state workers in whom I have so much faith won't be able to find a reporter when they need to alert someone to what is going on. And if they need find a reporter, he or she won't have the time to closely examine what needs scrutiny. (Turner 2009)

Whereas in the past, statehouse reporters who left were usually replaced, the economic reality was the vacancies remained unfilled. There were a couple of exceptions. Jim Camden, a veteran political reporter from Spokane, took over from Rich Roesler, and Jordan Schrader, a young reporter out of North Carolina, was recruited to fill Turner's big shoes.

If 2008 was the tipping point, the ebb of the statehouse press corps had actually begun years earlier. Former AP reporter David Ammons says he noticed signs of change as far back as the 1980s. "It was 'oh, *The Oregonian* isn't sending anybody to cover session this year.' And we'd say 'oh that's too bad,'" recalls Ammons. Back in those days, the Seattle TV stations—KING, KIRO, and KOMO—had cubbyhole bureaus in the statehouse and sent reporters to Olympia for the duration of the session. Commercial radio stations also had a full-time presence. "So it was blanket coverage," says Ammons. "I think there was a steady erosion of coverage and commitment to Olympia throughout the years. First commercial radio and TV stations—but later also newspapers—conducted audience research surveys and found statehouse coverage wasn't a top priority. To news managers, Olympia started seeming like a frill" (Ammons 2011).

There are contrarian voices to this view. "I think the narrative is just too convenient…you're swatting at myths to some degree," argues Peter Callaghan, who has been a political reporter and columnist at the *Tacoma News Tribune* since 1985. To make his point, Callaghan points to a copy of the July/August 1998 issue of *American Journalism Review* with a cover that says "Overmatched: The Shrinking Statehouse Press Corps." The cover art shows an outgunned reporter squished amid a sea of lobbyists in suits (Callaghan 2011).

Callaghan believes statehouse and political coverage has, in fact, "suffered less" from newspaper layoffs than other areas of coverage like sports. His theory is publishers and editors feel that one of the core functions of American newspapers is to serve as a watchdog over government. The biggest change Callaghan has noticed over the years is the coverage of political campaigns. Gone are the days when reporters would essentially embed with a campaign and spend days at a time on the campaign trail.

Today, a newspaper reporter might embed with a campaign for a two-day bus tour. But it is often more irregular, even on statewide marquee races. Jim Brunner has been a roving political reporter at the *Seattle Times* since 1998. In 2010, he covered the U.S. Senate contest between incumbent Democrat Patty Murray and former two-time Republican gubernatorial candidate Dino Rossi. Brunner laments the loss of several veteran political reporters at the *Times* through layoffs and attrition. Nonetheless, Brunner and his colleagues produced groundbreaking reporting during the 2010 senate campaign—including an investigation headlined "Patty Murray's Former Aides Cash in on Connection." The story chronicled the revolving door of Murray staffers who had left her office, become lobbyists, and then used their connections to Murray to help their clients (Brunner and Martin 2010).

Perhaps the biggest change for a reporter like Brunner is that the competitive landscape has been dramatically altered. In the Seattle newspaper world, the folding of the print version of the *PI* was akin to the collapse of the Soviet Union. The Cold War between the two papers was finally over. "I always thought maybe my job would get easier if the *PI* folded," says Brunner. "But I'm not sure that it has." Continuing the national security analogy, Brunner and the *Times* now face a balkanized media landscape. The competition is a bunch of smaller, scrappy—often ideological—start-ups that don't necessarily play by the old rules. "In a way there's more competition and in a way there's less," notes Brunner. "But you don't have the classic competition with, for instance, the *Seattle PI*" (Brunner 2011).

Brunner recounts the story of covering a Rossi for Senate event at a shipyard on Whidbey Island. Rossi had been railing relentlessly against the Democrats' federal stimulus spending. As it turned out, the shipyard he was touring had received stimulus dollars. Brunner says he debated filing a quick blog post about this "irony," but decided against it. But by the time he made it back to Seattle, *PubliCola*—a start-up political news website—already had the story. "Rossi Tours Company that Got $800,000 in Stimulus Money" blared the headline (Feit 2010).

PubliCola founder and writer Josh Feit, a former editor at Seattle's liberal weekly the *Stranger*, had not been on the tour, but says he researched Rossi's schedule and the shipyard. On the one hand Brunner views *PubliCola*'s scoop as a result of a cozy relationship with Democratic Party operatives. The fact *PubliCola* had broken the shipyard stimulus story forced Brunner's hand—he blogged about it the next day. But then he later also incorporated the scene into his profile of Rossi.

Feit rejects the idea that *PubliCola* is an organ for the Democratic Party. "We're trying to expand to more general political readers…we make a concerted effort to reach the Republicans," says Feit. It is no coincidence that *PubliCola* launched in 2008 when the newspaper business was in tremendous flux. Feit recounts sitting in a pitch meeting with potential investors on the day the *PI* announced it would cease printing. "I'm in this meeting saying, look, Postman is leaving, Ammons is leaving. It's a threat to democracy. It's a scary situation. And then we get a call that the *PI* is closing," recalls Feit. "Talk about an alignment. Newspaper bureaus were shutting down and papers were shutting down. The print world was just shaky, shaky, shaky. Meanwhile the online and digital worlds were coming into their own. It seemed like a perfect time to go for it" (Feit 2010).

PubliCola got early backing from a couple of angel investors—green developer Greg Smith and tech-company founder Rajeev Singh. An article in the *Stranger* about *PubliCola* noted that it was the first online publication to gain a coveted press credential from the statehouse press association.

But right out of the gates there were questions about *PubliCola*'s ability to provide impartial news. One of the co-founders was former *Stranger* staffer Sandeep Kaushik, who had become a Democratic political consultant. Feit admits *PubliCola*'s origins are unorthodox, but he argues that this is the new media reality. Unlike a traditional newspaper where there are firewalls between the reporting staff and the editorial staff, at *PubliCola* they are one in the same. Feit gives the example of how *PubliCola* provided standard coverage of the Murray-Rossi senate race but then "we simultaneously wrote an endorsement of Patty Murray—surprise, surprise. So clearly while I'm the guy who's doing the reporting, I'm also weighing in heavily on the editorial side…it's a trick. I can compartmentalize in my head, it's not a problem for me. But it can be confusing to readers." Feit admits "it's an uphill battle in terms of image" but he notes that several Republican officeholders participated in *PubliCola*'s end-of-year coverage in 2010 (Feit 2010).

In a burgeoning world of nonprofit or so-called "public" media, it's perhaps surprising that *PubliCola* aims to turn a profit. If and when it does make a profit, Feit's goal is to grow the staff and start publishing more long-form stories:

> Traditional journalists were worried that on-line journalism would lower the standard of reporting. What we're doing is bringing traditional journalism standards to bear to raise the chops of on-line journalism. We think there's a sweet spot between the fake objectivity (of traditional media) and partisan advocacy as practiced by publications like *The Stranger*. (Feit 2010).

PubliCola is just one of several Washington-based news websites that have cropped up in recent years. Some—like the *Olympia Newswire*—came and went in a matter of months (Grygiel 2010). Others have demonstrated staying power. *Crosscut.com* is the most visible and largest. The brainchild of *Seattle Weekly* founder David Brewster, *Crosscut* is part news-aggregator and part original content. Launched in early 2007 as a for-profit and now run as a nonprofit, it aims to cover the "News of the Great Nearby"—a geographic reference to the three Northwest states plus Montana and British Columbia. In many respects, *Crosscut* is a prime example of the democratization of journalism.

Unlike a traditional newspaper with a staff, *Crosscut* is powered by an array of regular and occasional contributors. Some have old-school journalism credentials. Others, like former Republican Party Chair Chris Vance, represent a new breed of writer-journalist who are experts in a particular field. Vance, for instance, writes lengthy political analysis and handicapping pieces. The goal at *Crosscut* is simple: lead the public policy conversation. The rule is also simple: writers disclose who they are and their potential conflicts in a short bio at the end of their piece. To stay financially afloat, Brewster has adopted a public radio model of funding: grants, underwriting, and member support.

If *PubliCola* is popular with the left and *Crosscut* aims to be pan-partisan, then the *Washington State Wire*—another relative newcomer on the political coverage scene—falls into the right-of-center, pro-business camp. Financially backed by a couple of business lobbyists, the *Wire* is essentially a one-man operation. Erik Smith, a former reporter for the *Tri-City Herald*, cranks out blog posts and lengthy coverage of issues that are of particular interest to the business community: workers compensation, unemployment insurance, the regulatory climate, political spending by unions. "Basically I'm writing about the issues that are of concern to the business community," says Smith. "But I'm trying to do what I would consider a balanced job. I try to get in both views." Coming from a newspaper background, Smith says he's found writing for the web very liberating. He ignores the rule that on the web you have to write short and, instead, does just the opposite. "On the Internet ink is free. Frankly, there's a thirst for longer stories that explain things—like the complexities of workers' compensation—in great detail than you can get anywhere else" (Smith 2010).

But Smith is candid that *Washington State Wire* is still an experiment and he has zero job security. He notes a big story might get 2,000 hits. "I guess I'm still disappointed by the readership. It could be a thousand times bigger," he laments. Like *PubliCola*, the *Wire* aims to be a for-profit operation.

If you visit the Associated Press office on the first floor of the White House on the Washington State capitol campus, you'll see a pictorial guide to the press corps. Many of the faces are covered over with a sticker that shows a frowning face. These are the reporters who have left. To be sure, they outnumber those who remain.

With the parade of departures, "coverage has gotten worse" says Joe Turner, formerly of the *News Tribune*. "Not because of the caliber of the reporters," he adds quickly, but because there are not enough of them. Turner makes a prediction: "Years from now, something important will come to light, something that we missed during our hectic coverage and reporters probably will be accused of being asleep at the switch. It won't be true, of course, but there simply will have been too many other things to cover" (Turner 2011).

Outgunned is another way to think about it. Reporters have always been outnumbered by lawmakers, lobbyists, and bureaucrats. But that ratio has grown. "I don't think there is any doubt that the coverage is much thinner that it was 10 years ago," says Chris McGann, formerly of the *Seattle PI*. "My hunch is it gives interest groups and think tanks a louder voice in public discourse…and then you've got the establishment itself providing information with relatively no filter, check or balance. It seems like a lose-lose for the public" (McGann 2011).

Despite the reshuffling and downsizing there are optimists to be found. David Ammons (2011) believes the quality of reporting and writing about Washington politics and government has improved over the decades: more nimble, less turn-of-the-screw. For Joe Turner the advent of political blogging stands out as a positive development. A reluctant blogger at first, he embraced that new medium in the final years of his career. "Blogs allow a reporter to speculate about what's really going on, what newsmakers are actually doing and suggest that all important 'why'" (Turner 2011).

A truism in journalism is that bad news sells. In that sense, the Great Recession proved good for statehouse coverage as the second decade of the 21st century commenced. Three years of deep state budget cuts triggered a mini-resurgence in attention to what was happening in Olympia. Suddenly, it seemed, the broadcast media rediscovered the state capital. Television crews, once scarce, returned. But instead of working out of cubbyhole bureaus like the old days, they would retreat to vans to produce their stories and then report live with a shot of the dome as their backdrop. Seattle's PBS station also stepped up its coverage of the statehouse. Meanwhile TVW, the state's C-SPAN network, saw an opportunity to step into the breach. In January 2009, TVW launched a weekly public affairs program called *The Impact*. The channel, known for its gavel-to-gavel coverage of the legislature, also began producing documentaries on hot button issues like education and health care.

As the 2011 regular session was ending, there were other hopeful signs. The Associated Press announced it was hiring back to Olympia a young reporter named Mike Baker. A Washington native, he had covered Olympia for one session before being dispatched to AP's bureau in Raleigh, North Carolina. Also, former *Seattle PI* reporter Paul Shukovsky announced he would be covering Washington State government—with a focus on regulatory affairs—for the Bureau of National Affairs, a specialized subscription-based news service for professionals in business and government.

The mass exodus of 2008 was over. But it is too early to know how things will evolve. Which start-ups will survive? Which will fail? "I think efforts like *Washington State Wire* or *PubliCola* are a bit more likely to be the future," predicted a hopeful Erik Smith of the *Wire*. "You have a couple of people with their own portfolio, who find sponsors and who begin churning out copy. Maybe they can turn it into a business. Who knows? It's just beginning. But from where I sit, I can see that the revolution doesn't come from top down. It comes from the bottom up, from guys like me and the folks at *PubliCola*" (Smith 2010).

Though the future of *PubliCola* and other similar start-up outlets can be debated, it is without question that the landscape of Washington State media has changed significantly.

Conclusion: Implications for Changes in Washington State Media

The decline of the Olympia Capitol Press Corps underscores the degree to which market demands govern American media, and that Washington State is not immune to these pressures. As major news outlets such as the *Seattle Post-Intelligencer* quit the sinking print industry, they join other internet-only niche outlets such as the *Washington State Wire* and *PubliCola*. Additionally, reporters find that more and more content is moving to the blogosphere. These changes, compounded with the exodus of experienced reporters who leave the news industry for the security of private sector and government employment, have caused concern. Critics lament the proliferation of for-profit niche-reporting outlets and the increasing popularity of news blogs, which they claim do not subscribe to the same dictates of civic obligation as more traditional news outlets (Bennett and Iyengar 2008). Though such criticisms are debatable, these outlets are viable news providers in an otherwise shaky news environment. One thing is clear, in light of the diminishing Capitol Press Corps, internet-only news sources and bloggers will continue to provide a civic function in reporting breaking news.

References

Ammons, David. March/April 2011. Interview by Austin Jenkins.

Arango, Tim. April 27, 2009. "Fall in Newspaper Sales Accelerates to Pass 7%." *New York Times*. nytimes.com/2009/04/28/business/media/28paper.html.

Bennett, Lance W., and Shanto Iyengar. 2008. "A New Era of Minimal Effects? The Changing Foundations of Political Communication." *Journal of Communication* 58(4): 707–31.

Brunner, Jim. March/April 2011. Interview by Austin Jenkins.

Brunner, Jim, and Jonathan Martin. September 29, 2010. "Patty Murray's Former Aides Cash in on Connection." *Seattle Times*. seattletimes.com/html/localnews/2013032208_murraylobbyists30m.html.

Callaghan, Peter. March/April 2011. Interview by Austin Jenkins.

Della Vigna, Stephano, and Ethan Kaplan. 2007. "The Fox News Effect: Media Bias and Voting." *The Quarterly Journal of Economics* 122(3): 1187–234.

Feit, Josh. September 16, 2010. "Rossi Tours Company that Got $800,000 in Stimulus Money." *PubliCola*. publicola.com/2010/09/16/rossi-tours-company-that-got-800000-in-stimulus-money.

Focus. February 2, 2010. "State of the Internet." *Focus*. focus.com/fyi/state-internet.

Grygiel, Chris. March 31, 2010. "Olympia Newswire to Go On Hiatus." *Seattle PI*. blog. seattlepi.com/seattlepolitics/2010/03/31/olympia-newswire-to-go-on-hiatus.

Iyengar, Shanto, Kyu Hahn, Hanz Bonfadelli, and Mirko Marr. 2009. "'Dark Areas of Ignorance' Revisited: Comparing International Affairs Knowledge in Switzerland and the United States." *Communication Research*. doi:10.1177/0093650209333024.

Layton, Charles, and Mary Walton. July/August 1998. "State of the American Newspaper: Missing the Story at the Statehouse." *American Journalism Review*. ajr.org/Article. asp?id=3279.

McCumber, David. January 15, 2009. "Sixty Days: Taking another Punch." *Seattle PI*. blog. seattlepi.com/thebigblog/2009/01/15/sixty-days-taking-another-punch.

McGann, Chris. March/April 2011. Interview by Austin Jenkins.

Mondotimes. 2011a. "The Highest Circulation Newspapers in the United States." mondotimes.com/newspapers/usa/usatop100.html.

_____. 2011b. "Highest Circulation Washington Newspapers." mondonewspapers.com/usa/circulation/washington.html.

Moy, Patricia, Michael R. McCluskey, Kelley McCoy, and Margaret A. Spratt. 2004. "Political Correlates of Local News Media Use." *Journal of Communication* 54(3): 532–46.

Mulick, Chris. September 29, 2008. "My Sorrowful and Unthinkable Goodbye." *Tri-City Herald*. tri-cityherald.com/2008/09/28/331448/my-sorrowful-and-unthinkable-goodbye. html#ixzz1FrfVHBkf.

NAA (Newspaper Association of America). 2011. "Total Paid Circulation." naa.org/-/media/NAACorp/Public%20Files/TrendsAndNumbers/Circulation/Total-Paid-Circulation.ashx.

NTIA (National Telecommunications and Information Administration). 2007. "Households Using the Internet In and Outside the Home, by Selected Characteristics: Total, Urban, Rural, Principal City, 2007." ntia.doc.gov/reports/2008/Table_HouseholdInternet2007.pdf.

Perry, Nick. November 3, 2008. "Seattle Times Co. to Cut Work Force by About 10%." *Seattle Times*. seattletimes.com/html/businesstechnology/2008345566_webtimes03m.html.

Pew Research Center. September 12, 2010. "Americans Spending More Time Following the News." pewresearch.org/pubs/1725/where-people-get-news-print-online-readership-cable-news-viewers.

Postman, David. April 11, 2008a. "Dave Ammons to Leave AP." *Seattle Times*. blog. seattletimes.nwsource.com/davidpostman/2008/04/dave_ammons_to_leave_ap.html.

_____. August 27, 2008b. "Another One Bites the Dust." *Seattle Times*. blog.seattletimes. nwsource.com/davidpostman/2008/08/27/another_one_bites_the_dust_1.html.

_____. September 4, 2008c. "Another One Bites the Dust." *Seattle Times*. blog.seattletimes. nwsource.com/davidpostman/2008/09/04/another_one_bites_the_dust_2.html.

Pryne, Eric. April 8, 2008. "Seattle Times Announces Layoffs." *Seattle Times*. seattletimes. nwsource.com/html/businesstechnology/2004333926_times08.html.

Roesler, Richard. July 9, 2009. "Capitol Press Corps Loses Another…" *Spokesman-Review*. spokesman.com/blogs/olympia/2009/jul/09/capitol-press-corps-loses-another.

SeattlePI.com. 2011. "About SeattlePI.com." seattlepi.com/facts.

Shannon, Brad. June 30, 2009. "Olympia Press Corps Loses Another Voice: Adam Wilson." *Olympian*. theolympian.com/2009/06/30/897436/olympia-press-corps-loses-another. html#ixzz1GWhLsnZQ.

Smith, Aaron. July 7, 2010. "Mobile Access 2010 Part 1: The Current State of Wireless Internet Use." pewinternet.org/Reports/2010/Mobile-Access-2010/Part-1/The-current-state-of-wireless-internet-use.aspx.

Turner, Joe. October 1, 2009. "Joe Turner's Come and Gone." *Tacoma News Tribune*. blog. thenewstribune.com/politics/2009/10/01/joe-turners-come-and-gone.

_____. March/April 2011. Interview by Austin Jenkins.

USNPL (US Newspaper Links). 2011a. "Newspapers by State." usnpl.com/wanews.php.

_____. 2011b. "TV Stations by State." usnpl.com/tv/watv.php.

Wayne, Leslie. May 21, 2000. "On Web, Voters Reinvent Grass-Roots Activism." *New York Times*. nytimes.com/2000/05/21/us/on-web-voters-reinvent-grass-roots-activism. html?scp=1&sq=On%20Web,%20Voters%20Reinvent%20Grass-Roots%20 Activism&st=cse.

Zaller, John R. 1999. "A Theory of Media Politics: How the Interests of Politicians, Journalists, and Citizens Shape the News." Unpublished manuscript. sscnet.ucla.edu/polisci/faculty/ zaller/media%20politics%20book%20.pdf.

Section II

CHAPTER SEVEN

Washington's Constitution: The Politics of State Constitutional Interpretation

Cornell W. Clayton and Lucas McMillan

Introduction

THE UNITED STATES has always been a system of dual constitutionalism. State constitutions pre-existed the federal document and were the primary instruments for distributing and limiting government power during most of the 19th century. Despite this long history of constitutional dualism, Americans know relatively little about state constitutions or state constitutional law. Indeed, leading constitutional commentaries focus almost exclusively on the federal document and many Americans do not realize that their states have constitutions. The lack of knowledge about state constitutionalism undoubtedly is the result of the nationalization of American politics that took place in the first half of the twentieth century, a period that culminated in the 1960s and 1970s when the Warren and Burger Courts expanded federal constitutional law into seemingly every aspect of American life. Since that time, however, there has been a revival of federalism in the United States and a revitalization of the political role played by state courts and state constitutions.

Today it would be a mistake to think that state constitutions are unimportant or that they simply mirror their federal counterpart. State constitutions differ from the federal document in important ways. They have their own histories, their own structures and concerns, and they restrict government power in wholly different ways. Moreover, with the revitalization of state governments, state constitutions have taken on new importance. A new "judicial federalism" has emerged in which state courts have begun to independently interpret their own constitutions to offer greater protection of individual rights than that afforded under federal law (Tarr 1997). Recent decisions by high courts in Massachusetts, California, Connecticut, Iowa, and elsewhere to protect the right of same-sex couples to marry under state constitutional law is only one controversial area in which this new judicial federalism has manifest itself.[1] Importantly, the "rediscovery" of the right-protecting role of state constitutions has occurred against a political backdrop of an increasingly conservative U.S. Supreme Court and the retrenchment of federal protection of certain rights under the Rehnquist and Roberts Courts. Not surprisingly, this new judicial federalism has become the subject of growing political controversy and a fierce debate has emerged over how to interpret state constitutions (Gardner 1992; Kahn 1996).

Washington's Supreme Court was an early leader in developing an independent state constitutional jurisprudence, and its efforts have not been without political controversy (Clayton 2002; Spitzer 1998; Utter 1992). Studying recent developments in the state's constitutional law should therefore tell us not only much about Washington's political system but also about the promise and problems of a system of dual constitutionalism in the 21st century.

Washington's Constitutional History and the Concerns of its Framers

Efforts to create a state in the territory that eventually became Washington began immediately following the Civil War. Measures calling for a state constitutional convention appeared on territorial ballots as early as 1869 and one was finally passed in 1876. The first convention was held in Walla Walla in June 1878. After 40 days of deliberation the 15 delegates to that convention produced a lengthy draft constitutional document (Beckett 1968). Statehood, however, would be stalled for another decade as a delicately balanced Congress was unwilling to admit new states into the Union. Democrats controlled the U.S. House of Representatives and were reluctant to admit new states that were perceived to be Republican-leaning (including Washington), while Republicans maintained control of the U.S. Senate and refused to acquiesce to states that might possibly elect Democrats to their chamber. The impasse broke in 1888, when Republicans gained control of both houses of Congress and the presidency. On February 22, 1889, Congress passed statehood-enabling legislation for Washington, Montana, and North and South Dakota.

A second constitutional convention convened in Olympia on July 4, 1889. The 75 delegates in Olympia were selected by a special election; two-thirds were Republican and one-third Democrat. The constitution they drafted was overwhelmingly approved by a special election of voters in the state on October 1, 1889, by a margin of 40,152 to 11,879 (Beckett 1968). On November 11, 1889, President Benjamin Harrison proclaimed Washington admitted to the Union as the 42nd state of the union.

Although a transcriber took detailed notes of the convention debates, the person was never paid and the notes were lost. Contemporaneous news accounts and other historical documents, however, shed light on the attitudes of those at the convention. Many of the debates in Olympia echoed those in other state conventions during the same period.[2] Indeed, late 19th-century state constitution makers operated self-consciously in a context of constitutional pluralism and constitutional borrowing. Delegates in Olympia were of course familiar with the federal constitution, and its influence on the structure and language of the state constitution was ubiquitous. Not only did the framers of Washington's constitution copy certain structural features of the federal document, such as a separation of powers into three branches and a bicameral legislature, but several provisions of the state constitution were drawn nearly verbatim from the federal text (e.g., article I, section 3 "No person shall be deprived of life, liberty, or property, without due process of law").

Delegates at these constitutional conventions also engaged in systematic analysis of other state constitutions and borrowed freely from the provisions that had been successful elsewhere (Fritz 1994; Utter and Spitzer 2002). This spirit of comparative constitutional construction clearly infected the delegates in Olympia. Scarcely any of the provisions in Washington's constitution can claim originality. From the various individual rights found in article I, to the restrictions placed on corporations under article XII, to the design of the executive branch and the titles assigned to various state officers in article III—nearly all of its provisions had appeared in other states' constitutions before. In fact, prior to the convention, former territorial judge W. Lair Hill drafted a model constitution which was distributed to the delegates; that draft drew heavily on California's constitution from 1879 (Knapp 1913). Hill's draft eventually provided the exact wording for 51 sections and substantively similar wording for 41 sections of Washington's constitution. In all, the constitution of California provided wording for at least 45 provisions, Oregon's constitution accounted for 23 provisions, Wisconsin's for 27, and Indiana's for 7 (Clayton 2002).

The basic structural features of Washington's constitution also were borrowed from elsewhere. These provided for a bicameral legislature. the house consisting of between 63 and 99 members, each serving two-year terms (art. 1, sec. 2); the senate, one-third to one-half this size, would consist of senators serving four-year terms, and half the seats would be elected every two years (art. I, sec. 6). Regular legislative sessions would be biennial and limited to 60 days (art. I, sec. 12). The convention also decided to disperse the executive authority among the office of governor, who was elected to a four-year term (art. III, sec. 2), and seven other independently elected officers. These included the lieutenant governor, secretary of state, treasurer, auditor, attorney general, superintendent of public instruction, and the commissioner of public lands (art. III, sec. 1).

There was lively debate about the veto power. In the end, the convention granted the governor a broad power to veto any bill or single item of any bill, and required a two-thirds vote of those present in both legislative houses to override a veto (art. II, sec. 12). The court systems, drawing on the California model, consisted of a supreme court of five members (later expanded to nine) and lower superior courts (art. IV). Supreme court justices were to be elected to six-year terms and superior court judges to four-year terms (art. IV, secs. 3, 5).

The general social and political attitudes of late 19th-century America are also evident in the work of the Olympia convention. Two particularly contentious issues of the period—women's suffrage and the prohibition of alcohol—were the subject of heated debates in the convention. Two separate articles dealing with these issues were offered to voters but both were defeated at the polls (Beckett 1968).

Other social and political attitudes of the period, however, did find their way into the constitution. America was going through an era of wrenching social and economic change. The nation was shifting from an agrarian economy to industrial capitalism and the period was marked by increasing concentrations of wealth, rising corporate power, and corruption in government. In response to these problems, Progressive-era third parties had sprung up throughout the United States, and Washington was no exception. State chapters of the Grange, the Farmers Alliance, and the Knights of Labor were all established in territorial Washington and their ideas animated much of the debate at the convention (Schwantes 1982).

Influenced by Progressive-era attitudes, the delegates in Olympia thus had different concerns about the relationship between democratic institutions and private power than did the federalist framers of the American constitution a century earlier (Avery 1962; Dolliver 1992). While the federalists had been influenced by the ideas of civic republicanism and a fear of Populist majorities, the delegates in Olympia were advocates of popular sovereignty and direct forms of democracy. They feared too much power in government, especially the legislature, but they feared concentrations of corporate power and the corruption of special economic interests even more. Liberty, they believed, was best secured through open, democratic government that was capable of strong regulation of corporations and private concentrations of power (Dolliver 1992; Snure 1992). Similar to other Western state constitutional conventions of the period, delegates in Olympia thus sought to balance the desire for economic development with their desire to protect citizens against concentrations of private power and wealth (Bakken 1987; Tarr and Williams 1998).

Understanding this historical milieu and the Progressive political culture of the era can help make sense out of several otherwise disparate provisions of Washington's constitution. In drafting the constitution the delegates focused on four priorities:

Individual Rights

The delegates made rights their first concern. Article I of the constitution is a broadly phrased declaration listing 27 individual liberties, ranging from traditional legislative prohibitions on bills of attainder and ex post facto laws (sec. 23), to specific proclamations of individual liberties, including a right to assemble (sec. 4), a right to speak freely (sec. 5), a right to religious freedom (sec. 11), a right to trial by jury and other due process restrictions (sec. 3, 21, 22, 26), a right to bear arms (sec. 24), and a right to privacy (sec. 7). Unlike the federal bill of rights, which is phrased mostly as restrictions on Congress (e.g., "Congress shall make no law…abridging the freedom of speech"), the rights provisions in Washington's constitution are phrased as broad affirmations of liberty (e.g., "Every person may freely speak…") and can therefore be interpreted as protections against both government or private exercises of power.

Democracy

In contrast to the republican institutions created by the federal constitution, the framers of Washington's constitution provided for direct democratic control of all three branches of the government. This included the direct election of both houses of the legislature (art. II, sec. 4, 6), the popular election of judges (art. IV, sec. 3, 5) and the separate election of all major offices in the executive branch (art. III, sec. 1). Democratic control of government was further enhanced by amendments 7 and 8 in 1912, which allowed citizens to directly legislate through the initiative and referendum processes (art. II, sec. 1) and made all state-wide elected officials, except judges, subject to popular recall (art. I, sec. 23).

The Legislature and Special Interests

The framers attempted to keep the legislative branch from becoming a tool of corporate interests. For example, the legislature was constitutionally prohibited from lending public money or credit to private companies (art. XII, sec. 9; art. VIII, sec. 5), from contracting convict labor to companies (art. II, sec. 29), from authorizing lotteries and granting divorces (art. II, sec. 24), and from passing "private or special legislation" involving taxes, highways, mortgages, corporate privileges, deeds and wills, interest rates, fines and penalties, adoptions, or civil and criminal actions (art. II, sec. 28). Moreover, the constitution imposed structural restrictions on the legislative process, such as a provision requiring open meetings (art. II, sec. 2), an anti-"log-rolling" provision that prohibited bills from embracing more than one subject (art. II, sec. 19), and specific prescriptions against bribery and corruption of government officials (art. II, sec. 30, 39).

Restricting Corporate Power

Finally, the framers adopted an entire article (art. XII) and several other separate provisions that aimed directly at restricting the power of private corporations. These included barring the formation of monopolies and trusts (sec. 22), prohibiting companies from discriminating in the rates that they charge customers (sec. 15), prohibiting railroads from consolidating lines (sec. 16), requiring stockholders to assume liability for corporate debts (sec. 4, 11), prohibiting companies from receiving public subsidies or credit (sec. 9), and prohibiting the use of the government's eminent domain powers on behalf of private companies (art. I, sec. 16). In one of the more unique provisions in a state constitution the delegates also prohibited private companies from "organizing, maintaining or employing an armed body of men" (art. I, sec. 24). This last restriction was aimed at preventing the reoccurrence of an event in 1888, when mining companies in Cle Elum and Roslyn employed armed strikebreakers to resolve a labor dispute (Dolliver 1992).

Structural Differences between the State and the Federal Constitution

In addition to reflecting a distinct history and the different political attitudes of the era, Washington's constitution differs from the federal document in several structural respects as well. Understanding these differences is crucial to understanding constitutional politics at the state level.

Restricting or Empowering Government

Constitutions can either authorize or restrict government power. The federal constitution established a government of limited or "enumerated powers," so that when Congress chooses to regulate in an area it must have a specific grant of constitutional authority to do so.[3] The opposite is true of state constitutions. It is assumed that state governments possess plenary legislative authority, or general "police powers" (powers that the federal government does not possess) to legislate in any area, unless they are specifically restricted from doing so by the constitution (Grad 1968). The delegates in Olympia understood this basic difference between the two constitutions, which is one reason why the state document is so much more detailed in its restrictions on legislative authority (Utter 1985). Members of Washington's Supreme Court have recognized this difference too, as former Justice Andersen noted:

> [As] this court has often observed, the United States Constitution is a grant of limited power authorizing the federal government to exercise only those constitutionally enumerated powers expressly delegated to it by the states, whereas our state constitution imposes limitations on the otherwise plenary power of the state to do anything not expressly forbidden by the state constitution or federal law. (*State v. Gunwall* 1986, 815)

Because of this structural difference in the state constitution, when legislative enactments in Washington are challenged in court the focus of inquiry is not whether the state has authority to enact the law but whether it is specifically prohibited from doing so by the constitution. Thus, in contrast to federal jurisprudence, the burden falls squarely on those challenging a state statute to find specific restrictions on state authority (Grad 1968). Secondly, unlike the federal level where judges tend to interpret grants of government authority expansively (e.g., the Supreme Court's modern commerce clause jurisprudence), constitutional specifications of authority at the state level often act as limitations on what the government may do. In a constitution of plenary authority, an authorization to pursue one course of action may by negative implication preclude others (Tarr 1998, 6–9; Utter 1985).

This structural difference also forces interpreters of the two constitutions to think differently about provisions for individual rights. In federal jurisprudence the absence of a specific grant of legislative authority under the constitution acts as an implicit protection of individual liberty. At the state level, however, protection from legislative power is found solely in express constitutional affirmations of liberties, which is one reason why the state constitution goes much further in specifying individual rights.

Positive Rights

At the federal level rights are nearly always thought of as restrictions on governmental action. This is because the rights found in the federal Bill of Rights are generally "negative"—prohibitions against government taking certain action (e.g., "Congress shall make no law respecting..."). State constitutions, by contrast, often contain positive affirmations of certain freedoms as well as provisions that require government action or provision of public resources. Indeed, of the 35 sections in Washington's Declaration of Rights, only three were expressed as negations of government authority (art. I, sec. 8, 12, 23). All others are phrased as general affirmations that the state is required to actively enforce and not simply refrain from breaching. Moreover, in contrast to the federal document, the Washington constitution contains several provisions that expressly require the state to take action to provide resource or protections. For example, article II, section 35 provides that "The legislature shall pass necessary laws for the protection of persons working in mines, factories and other employments dangerous to life or deleterious to health." Similarly, article XIII, section I provides that educational, reformatory, and penal institutions, as well as state mental hospitals, "shall be fostered and supported by the state"; while article IX, section 1 declares it to be "the paramount duty of the state to make ample provision for the education of all children residing within its borders."

What do positive rights provisions mean for the courts in Washington? In one landmark case, *Seattle School District No. 1 v. State* (1978), Washington's Supreme Court held that the state had breached its constitutional duty to ensure a "basic education" to students under article IX, and it required the legislature to appropriate more money for public schools. In general, however, Washington courts have been reluctant to enforce the positive rights provisions of the state's constitution, fearing that their active enforcement would violate doctrines of separation of powers and judicial restraint (Talmadge 1999). Whether such concerns are appropriate within the Washington context is debatable. Unlike their federal counterparts, Washington judges can point to clear textual commands in the constitution when they enforce such rights, and, moreover, they would be doing so as democratically elected officials rather than political appointees (Clayton 2002).

Length and Fluidity

Washington's constitution is much longer, more detailed, and more diverse in the concerns it addresses than the federal constitution. The state document contains 32 separate articles and over 100 amendments, compared to only 7 articles and 27 amendments in the federal document. The state constitution runs to nearly 40,000 words, compared to approximately 6,000 in the federal constitution. The provisions of the state document range from relatively clear and specific commands (e.g., article III specifies the governor's salary) to open-ended clauses that require pure political judgments to interpret (e.g., article I's statement that a "frequent recurrence to fundamental principles is essential to the security of individual rights and the perpetuity of free government").

Even more troubling for those charged with interpreting Washington's constitution is its fluidity. The document has been amended more than 100 times since its adoption in 1889, and its amendments also vary in detail and subject matter. The area with the most amendments is public expenditure and finance, with more than 25 separate amendments. Other areas in which there have been multiple amendments include courts and judges (11), local governments (9), compensation of public officials (5), voter qualifications (5), and filling vacancies in elective offices (4). In all, more than 78 of the constitution's 247 original sections—nearly one-third of the entire document—have been altered by amendment, and at least 26 of these amendments themselves have been subsequently amended or repealed (Clayton 2002).

Moreover, unlike federal constitutional history, there are no historical periods of tectonic constitutional change or reconstruction in Washington history that would bring coherence to the document. Scholars of the federal constitution have identified important political eras or constitutional junctures in American history—such as the Civil War or the New Deal—in which the constitution was fundamentally realigned as the result of sweeping amendments and judicial decisions (Ackerman 1991). However, no such critical junctures have brought coherence to changes made in Washington's constitution. Indeed, several efforts to fundamentally reshape the state constitution have failed. In 1918, the legislature recommended holding another constitutional convention but that proposal was rejected in a state-wide referendum. In the 1930s a Constitutional

Revision Commission appointed by Governor Clarence Martin recommended to the legislature nine sweeping reforms to the constitution (including a move to a unicameral legislature), but none were adopted. In 1965, a second Constitutional Advisory Council made a series of reform proposals, but these too failed to elicit action. Governor Daniel Evans, a strong advocate of constitutional reform, created three separate constitutional revision committees in 1967, 1968, and 1975. These too recommended changes, but none of their efforts bore fruit (Beckett and Peterson 1985).

The amendments to Washington's constitution thus stand as individual, unrelated alterations to the document. Some parts of the constitution have remained unchanged since 1889, while others have been altered on a regular basis (for example, article II has been amended at least 25 separate times). Some portions of the existing document may embody a relatively coherent constitutional perspective, while others will reflect a hodge-podge of inconsistent constitutional perspectives and values accreted over time. Judges seeking to interpret the constitution may thus confront the task of constructing rather than discovering its coherence. Moreover, to the extent the state constitutional provisions do not embody a coherent set of political perspectives, an interpreter cannot look to the whole to illuminate the meaning of its parts. State judges are thus often forced to adopt a "clause-bound" interpretive approach in which each provision must be interpreted in isolation rather than relying on a uniform interpretive process (Tarr 1998, 189–94).

The Politics of Developing an Independent State Constitutional Jurisprudence

Recent interest in state constitutions dates back to a speech by former U.S. Supreme Court Justice William Brennan in 1977. In that speech Brennan urged state judges to look past the federal constitution to the protected rights in their own state charters; he especially urged them not to interpret state constitutional provisions in lock-step fashion with how federal courts had interpreted analogous provisions of the federal Bill of Rights (Brennan 1977). His call ushered in a renaissance in state constitutional law as one state high court after another began plumbing the language and history of their constitutions to find new ways to protect rights (Tarr 1997; Williams 1996).

Washington's high court was an early leader in this movement. In 1983, former Justice Robert Utter addressed a state judicial conference and urged Washington's judges to begin developing an independent state constitutional rights jurisprudence (Utter 1984). Even before this, Washington's Supreme Court had begun interpreting provisions of the state constitution so as to confer greater individual rights on Washington's citizens. In one early case, *Alderwood v. Washington Environmental Council* (1981), the court held that the free speech clause of Washington's constitution required owners of a private shopping center to accommodate the free expression rights of political activists, even though the First Amendment of the federal constitution offers protection only against government suppression of free expression. Writing for the court, Justice Utter rejected the use of the so-called "state action" requirement of the federal constitution when interpreting the state's free speech provision. The federal constitution, he wrote, "only establishes the minimum degree of protection that a state may not abridge" but state courts "are obliged to [independently] determine the scope of [rights] in their state constitutions" (113).

In establishing an independent constitutional jurisprudence in these early cases the court also began to assert the primacy of state protections. In *State v. Coe* (1984), for example, the court used the state's free speech provisions to bar a trial judge's gag order in a highly publicized murder trial. Writing for the court, Justice Utter articulated several reasons why the court should look first to Washington's constitution before considering the federal First Amendment:

> First, state courts have a duty to independently interpret and apply their state constitutions that stems from the very nature of our federal system…Second, the histories of the United States and Washington Constitutions clearly demonstrate that the protection of the fundamental rights of Washington citizens was intended to be and remains a separate and important function of our state constitution…Third, by turning first to our own constitution we can develop a body of independent jurisprudence…Fourth, we will be able to assist other states that have similar constitutional provisions develop principled, responsible body of law…Finally, to apply the federal constitution before the Washington Constitution would be as improper and premature as deciding a case on state constitutional grounds when statutory grounds would have sufficed, and for essentially the same reasons. (359)

From the outset, however, the revived interest in state constitutions carried with it political undercurrents. Justice Brennan's call was viewed by conservative critics as part of a political agenda to use state constitutional law to counter the increasingly conservative drift of federal constitutional jurisprudence since the 1980s. Critics of the new judicial federalism complained that it was unprincipled, result-oriented jurisprudence. Washington's Supreme Court was not exempt from such criticism (Kahn 1996; Spitzer 1998). For example, in a highly publicized search and seizure case, *State v. Ringer* (1983), Justice Carolyn Dimmick chided her colleagues for their "sudden leap to the sanctuary of our own state constitution" rather than rely on familiar federal Fourth Amendment analysis. By adopting a different interpretation of analogous state provisions, she wrote, "we confound the constabulary and, by picking and choosing between state and federal constitutions, change the rules after the game has been played in good faith."

In the state legislature, critics of the court's new jurisprudence introduced legislation to curb the court's power of judicial review (Talmadge 1999). Although those efforts were unsuccessful, a more serious challenge came when four new justices were elected to the court in 1984 and 1985. Three of these were former prosecutors and all of them considered themselves conservatives opposed to the court's liberal interpretations of the state constitution (Sheldon 1988; Spitzer 2006). The personnel changes created a deep cleavage in the court over constitutional interpretation, and by 1986 the court began retreating from some of its earlier decisions.[4] In one highly publicized case, *Southcenter Joint Venture v. National Democratic Policy Committee* (1989), the court's majority reversed its *Alderwood* decision that had recognized free speech protections against private property owners. Appealing to "general principles of constitutionalism," the court held that the state constitution's free speech protections only applied to "state action" after all.

In order to convince critics that its new jurisprudence was principled rather than political, the court in 1986 developed a set of criteria to guide its decisions in the future. In *State vs. Gunwall* (1986), Justice James Andersen said the court would look to "six neutral and nonexclusive criteria" when it interpreted state constitutional provisions that had analogous provisions in the federal document: (1) the text of the state constitutional provision at issue; (2) differences in the text of the parallel provision in the federal constitution; (3) differences in constitutional and common law history of the two constitutions; (4) differences in preexisting state law; (5) differences in the structure between the two constitutions; and (6) differences that may emerge from matters of particular state interest or local concern.

Although the *Gunwall* criteria were intended to assure critics that state constitutional decisions were principled rather than political, almost immediately a debate broke out over how the criteria should be applied. Justice Utter, who had argued for state constitutional primacy in *Coe*, and Justice Barbra Madsen, elected to the court in 1992, became the leading proponents of the view that the *Gunwall* criteria were merely interpretive tools that the court should use to foster and advance the development of an independent jurisprudence. On the other side, Justice Barbra Durham, who joined the court the same year as *Gunwall*, and Justice Richard Guy, who joined the court three years later, became leading proponents for the view that the criteria posed a procedural hurdle that litigants must pass before the court would move beyond the federal constitution to consider independent state grounds (Spitzer 2006). The criteria thus would serve as a brake to slow the development of an independent state rights jurisprudence.

Initially, those who saw *Gunwall* as a hurdle prevailed in this debate. Just two years after *Gunwall*, in *State v. Wethered* (1988), the court refused to even consider a state constitutional claim raised by a criminal defendant because the attorney had failed to brief all the criteria—signifying that briefing all the criteria was necessary before the court would consider independent state constitutional grounds. Indeed, between 1986 and 1997, more than 65 percent of the court's 109 decisions that cited *Gunwall* refused to interpret the state constitution. Even in the 39 cases during this period where the *Gunwall* criteria had been fully briefed and the court analyzed the state constitution, it reached a different result from federal constitutional analysis in only 8 cases (Spitzer 1998).

The debate over *Gunwall* eventually erupted in a 1995 case involving double jeopardy. Writing for the court's majority in *State v. Gocken* (1995), Justice Guy began by analyzing the case under the double jeopardy provisions of the federal constitution. Then, after a perfunctory examination of the six *Gunwall* criteria, he announced that the factors did not support a broader protection for criminal defendants under the state's double jeopardy clause. In dissent, Justice Madsen criticized the court for using "*Gunwall* as a talisman" preventing any serious analysis of the rights protected by the state constitution. The court, she argued, should begin with an independent analysis of the state's charter first, and only after that should it proceed to a review of analogous federal provisions if necessary to decide the case. The court, she said, should "preference independent resolution of state constitutional questions under a longstanding body of state law" rather than leave it "lost somewhere in the ever-shifting shadow of the federal courts which are no less political and perhaps more so than our own state courts."

Gocken, however, became the high-water mark for those who viewed *Gunwall* as a procedural barrier, and Justice Madsen's dissent would eventually become the view of the majority. Justice Guy retired in 2001, and the entire *Gocken* majority had left the court by the end of 2002. New justices joining the court relaxed their insistence on the *Gunwall* criteria. In *State v. Jackson* (2003), for example, the court's majority said that once broader rights in a state constitutional provision had been recognized in a case, a *Gunwall* analysis was no longer necessary in subsequent cases under that provision. Then, in *Eggleston v. Pierce County* (2003), the court excused a party's failure to brief the *Gunwall* factors when the analysis was provided by an amicus curiae intervener.

Eventually the court reversed *Gocken*, essentially adopting Justice Madsen's dissent. In *City of Woodinville v. Northshore United Church of Christ* (2009), the court reversed a lower court decision that declined to interpret Washington's religious freedom provision because the parties had failed to brief the *Gunwall* criteria. Writing for the court, Justice James Johnson said that a "strict rule" requiring a complete *Gunwall* analysis in every case would turn "briefing into an antiquated writ system where parties may lose their constitutional rights by failing to incant correctly." The court should turn first to the state's constitution's protections, he said, and *Gunwall* "was better understood to prescribe appropriate arguments…(in) how Washington's constitution provides greater rights." But, he added, "failing to subhead a brief with each factor does not foreclose constitutional argument."

Toward a Coherent Approach to State Constitutional Interpretation

With *Gunwall* removed as a procedural barrier, the court is in a position now to proceed with developing a more thoughtful state constitutional rights jurisprudence. Figure 1 illustrates the court's shifting use of *Gunwall* from being a barrier to becoming an instrument for advancing an independent constitutional interpretation. Between 1986 and 2010, the court cited *Gunwall* in over 206 cases. The line in Figure 1 represents the percentage of cases in which the court cited *Gunwall* but refused to interpret the state's constitution, relying instead on analogous federal provisions to decide the case. Although there is variation from term to term there has been a steady decline in the court's use of *Gunwall* as a barrier since the mid-1990s; from a high of 86 percent of cases in 1993 to a low of zero cases during the 2008 and 2009 terms.

If *Gunwall* no longer poses a barrier as it once did to state constitutional interpretation, it remains to be seen whether it will lead to the development of a principled and coherent constitutional jurisprudence. Ultimately, constitutional interpretation must proceed out of a general theory of a particular constitution's goals and purposes. One of the problems with the court's reliance on *Gunwall* as the lodestar for state constitutional interpretation is that it forced the court to constantly examine a panoply of competing approaches or modalities of constitutional argument rather than helping it focus on development of a general theory of Washington's constitution that could guide the interpretive enterprise.[5] University of Washington law professor Hugh Spitzer points out that each of the six *Gunwall* criteria embodies a different interpretive approach. The first and second criteria of *Gunwall*, for example, force the court to adopt a textualist approach to interpreting the constitution, which finds constitutional meaning in the document's words. The third criterion requires a historical approach that looks to the intentions of the framers of the constitution, or an ethical approach that would derive rules from basic moral principles. The fourth *Gunwall* criterion requires a doctrinal approach that would apply rules generated

Figure 1. Cases Citing *Gunwall* that Refused to Interpret the State Constitution

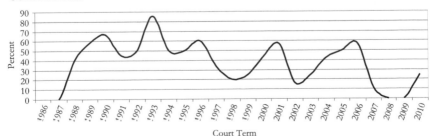

Court Term

from previous court decisions. The fifth criterion requires a structural approach that would infer rules from the relationships that the document creates between the institutions of government and citizens. Finally, the sixth criterion requires prudentialist analysis, or a balancing of the costs and benefits of particular court actions (Spitzer 2006).

Using one interpretive approach over another will produce very different outcomes. For example, a textual approach to the state constitution's free speech clause would apply its protections against both the government and private corporations that sought to restrict free expression, much as the court did in its decision in *Alderwood*. However, if the court adopts a structural approach, as it did in *Southcenter*, it would conclude that the free speech provisions apply only to state action and not to private actors such as shopping centers.

The difficulty is that *Gunwall* does not provide guidance to the court about which modality or interpretive approach to use. The court's past insistence that all six criteria are briefed was especially problematic as it diverted attention away from discussing which theory or interpretive approach was most appropriate under the circumstances. The impact of the court's use of the *Gunwall* criteria is seen in the degree of fragmentation created in the court's jurisprudence. On collegial courts like Washington's Supreme Court, fewer opinions in a case indicate a higher degree of consensus about the law. A unanimous decision with a single opinion for the court is authoritative and it signifies agreement among the justices over how the law should be interpreted. A fragmented decision with multiple dissents or concurrences indicates disagreement among the justices and uncertainty about how to interpret the law. Figure 2 illustrates the degree of fragmentation or cohesion in the court's decisions between 1986 and 2010. The data indicate the number of separate concurring and dissenting opinions in each case. If we exclude cases in which the court cited *Gunwall*, it decided a total of 2,931 cases over the 25 year period. In those cases, members of the court wrote 519 concurring opinions and 1,283 dissenting opinions—a total of 1,802 separate opinions or an average of .62 separate opinions per case in addition to the opinion for the court. During the same period the court decided 209 cases in which it cited *Gunwall*. In these cases members of the court wrote 149 dissenting and 91 concurring opinions—a total of 240 separate opinions or an average of 1.18 separate opinions per case. In other words, decisions that relied upon *Gunwall* were nearly twice as fragmented and were likely to produce nearly double the number of separate concurring and dissenting opinions as other decisions by the court.

Moreover, the data indicate that fragmentation in the court's decision-making under *Gunwall* has been increasing in recent years as the court has moved from using the criteria as a barrier to using them as an interpretive guide. Thus, rather than producing a consensual constitutional jurisprudence, *Gunwall's* legacy appears to be a more fragmented court with little agreement over constitutional interpretation.

Figure 2. Separate Opinions: *Gunwall* Cases versus All Cases, 1986–2010

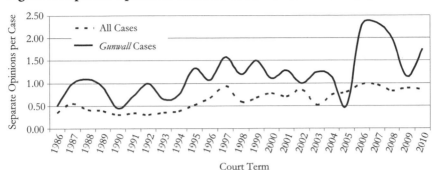

Disagreement on the court is not necessarily an indicator that the court is engaged in an unprincipled or politically-oriented jurisprudence. Individual justices may each hold strong views about how best to interpret the state's constitution but no single approach has yet to be embraced by the court as a whole. One reason for adopting the criteria approach of *Gunwall* was to allay concerns that judicial resort to the state's constitution was principled and not simply an effort to advance liberal policy outcomes. To examine this, Table 1 provides data on the outcomes of cases in which the court cited *Gunwall* between 1997 and 2010 and the opinion joining behavior of the nine justices serving on the court in 2010 in those cases. Opinions that cited *Gunwall* during this period were coded for whether they interpreted the state constitution or not, whether the court adopted a primacy approach when it interpreted the state constitution or whether it also interpreted an analogous provision of the federal constitution, whether the outcome would have been different under the federal constitution alone, and whether the independent interpretation of the state constitution advanced a liberal outcome in the case (defined as an outcome favoring the individual rights claim against the state).

Of the 101 published cases that cited *Gunwall* during this period, the court declined to interpret the state constitution in 41 cases (40.6%) but did interpret the state constitution in 60 cases (59.4%) (see Table 1, column A). Of these 60 cases, it adopted a primacy approach and decided the case on state constitutional grounds alone without interpreting the analogous federal provision in 19 cases (31.7%) (column C2). In 5 cases (8.3%) the court interpreted both state and the analogous federal provisions and found the state provision to offer more protection (column C3), while in 36 cases (60%) it interpreted the two provisions to provide the same protection (column B). Thus, when interpreting the state constitution during this period, the court came to a different outcome than it would have under the federal constitution alone in 24 out of 60 cases, or 40 percent of the time (column C1). In these 24 cases the court reached a liberal outcome in 17 cases, or 70.8 percent of the time (column D1).

Table 1

Case Outcomes and Justice Joining Behavior in Cases Citing *Gunwall*, 1997–2010

Opinions for the Court

[A] 60 Cases Interpreted the State Constitution (59.4%)

[C1] 24 Cases Resulted in Different Protection under the State Constitution (40%)
[C2] 19 decided on strict primacy (31.7%)
[C3] 5 state constitution offers more protection (8.3%)

[B] 36 Cases Resulted in Similar Protection under State and Federal Constitutions (60%)

[D1] 17 Cases Resulted in a Liberal Outcome (70.8%)
[D2] 7 Cases Resulted in a Conservative Outcome (29.2%)

	[A] Cases that Interpreted State Constitution[1]	[B] Result Similar to Federal Constitution	[C1] Result Different than Federal Constitution	[C2] Strict Primacy	[C3] State Offers More Protection	[D1] Liberal Outcome	[D2] Conservative Outcome
Opinions for the Court 101 cases	60 (59.4%)	36 (60%)	24 (40%)	19 (31.7%)	5 (8.3%)	17 (70.8%)	7 (29.2%)
Individual Justice Joining Behavior[2]							
Gerry Alexander elected 1995; 100 cases	39 (39%)	21 (53.8%)	18 (46.2%)	14 (35.9%)	4 (10.3%)	14 (77.8%)	4 (22.2%)
Tom Chambers elected 2001; 56 cases	17 (30.4%)	6 (35.3%)	11 (64.7%)	10 (58.8%)	1 (5.9%)	8 (72.7%)	3 (27.3%)
Mary Fairhurst elected 2003; 45 cases	25 (55.6%)	16 (64%)	9 (36%)	9 (36%)	0	6 (66.7%)	3 (33.3%)
Charles Johnson elected 1991; 101 cases	44 (43.6%)	23 (52.3%)	21 (47.7%)	17 (38.6%)	3 (6.8%)	15 (71.4%)	6 (28.6%)
James Johnson elected 2005; 34 cases	13 (38.2%)	7 (53.8%)	6 (46.2%)	6 (46.2%)	0	5 (83.3%)	1 (16.7%)
Barbra Madsen elected 1993; 101 cases	44 (43.6%)	27 (61.4%)	17 (38.6%)	16 (36.4%)	2 (4.5%)	13 (76.5%)	4 (23.5%)
Susan Owens elected 2001; 56 cases	32 (57.1%)	16 (50%)	16 (50%)	14 (43.8%)	1 (3.1%)	10 (62.5%)	6 (37.5%)
Richard Sanders elected 1996; 101 cases	23 (22.8%)	6 (26.1%)	17 (73.9%)	13 (56.5%)	3 (13%)	14 (82.4%)	3 (17.6%)
Debra Stephens elected 2008; 13 cases	7 (53.8%)	2 (28.6%)	5 (71.4%)	5 (71.4%)	0	5 (100%)	0

[1] Out of 101 total cases citing *Gunwall* between 1997 and March 2010. Cases where *Gunwall* was not cited in the opinion for the court were excluded from this part of the analysis.

[2] Under each justice's name is the year they were elected and the number of cases citing *Gunwall* in the opinion of the court during the justice's term. Column [A] shows the total number of cases in which the justice joined the opinion of the court and the percentage of the cases since they took office.

There is a wide variation in the willingness of individual justices to join an opinion that reaches an interpretation of the state constitution. For example, Justices Mary Fairhurst and Susan Owens appeared to be most willing to engage in state constitutional analysis, authoring or signing onto such opinions more than 50 percent of the time each. Former Justice Richard Sanders and Justice Tom Chambers, on the other hand, appeared to be least willing, joining such opinions only 22.8 percent and 30.4 percent of the time respectively. There is also wide variation in the willingness to adopt a primacy approach and to decide a case on state constitutional grounds alone. Justice Debra Stephens was most willing to write or join opinions relying upon the state constitution alone, doing so in 5 of the 7 cases (71.4%) she participated in. Justice Gerry Alexander was least willing to sign an opinion foregoing an analysis of similar federal provisions, doing so in 14 of the 39 cases (35.9%) in which he participated. Interestingly, two of the justices who were least likely to sign an opinion that interpreted the state constitution, Tom Chambers and Richard Sanders, were most likely to join opinions that adopted a primacy approach when they did (58.8% and 56.5% respectively). One of the most frequent interpreters of the state constitution, Justice Mary Fairhurst, was also one of the least likely to sign an opinion that adopted a primacy approach (36%).

Despite the variance between individual justices, it is clear that all of them, as was the case with the court as a whole, tended to reach liberal outcomes when they joined opinions interpreting the state constitution independently from the federal document. Indeed, for the justices on the court in 2010, Justice Stephens wrote or joined opinions that advanced the liberal outcome 100 percent of the time, while Justice Owens, who was least likely to join an opinion with a liberal outcome, still did so 62.5 percent of the time.

There are many reasons why the court's independent interpretations of the state constitution would tend to advance liberal outcomes. Not the least of these may be a case selection bias inherent in a court with discretion over its docket. The government tends to overwhelmingly prevail in lower courts, and the Supreme Court disproportionately accepts appeals of cases where they intend to correct a perceived error in the lower court. So the fact that the court's independent constitutional jurisprudence tends to advance liberal policy outcomes is not itself evidence of politically strategic or result-oriented decision-making. Measuring the sincerity and consistency with which individual justices hold their jurisprudential views is difficult given the many contextual factors that shape each case. Such an analysis is beyond the scope of this chapter. Nevertheless, if the court had hoped the *Gunwall* criteria approach would shield it from the critics' charge of result-oriented decision-making or would produce a coherent and consensual approach to state constitutional interpretation, those hopes seem to have gone unfulfilled.

Conclusion

The American constitutional historian Edward Corwin once observed that "one of the greatest lures to the westward movement of population was the possibility which federalism held out to the advancing settlers of establishing their own undictated political institutions" (Corwin 1950, 22). Washington's constitution has a distinct history. Its structure and purposes differ in important respects from the federal constitution.

The promise of dual constitutionalism is that states can learn from each other and from the federal experience. Former Justice Utter recognized this promise in his opinion in *Southcenter*. Federalism, he argued, "allows the states to operate as laboratories for more workable solutions to legal and constitutional problems. As part of our obligation to interpret our State's constitution, we have the opportunity to develop a jurisprudence more appropriate to our own constitutional language" (1303–6).

Washington's effort to develop an independent constitutional rights jurisprudence, however, also indicates the problems attendant with dual constitutionalism. At the national level, commitments to federalism principles are notoriously political and strategic. Political conservatives, for example, favor federalism when it comes to abortion rights or welfare policy, but favor strong national government when it comes to the war on drugs or preventing physician-assisted suicide. Liberals generally hold the opposite views about the role of the federal government in these disputes. There is no reason to suppose that such strategic commitments to constitutional principles at the federal level do not also apply to constitutional politics at the state level, leading both liberals and conservatives to favor state constitutionalism only when it advances their respective agenda. Whether or not such fears are warranted with respect to the Washington Supreme Court, the *Gunwall* criteria approach has not allayed them.

Interest in state constitutions and the new judicial federalism is nevertheless here to stay. As with other constitutional developments, the interest is linked to broader political and economic changes in America that have forced Americans to rethink the locus and forms of governmental power. As in the past, this challenge will require new generations of Washington citizens to define themselves and give voice to their political goals and aspirations. That voice, as in the past, will continue to be reflected in the state's constitution and discourse about its meaning.

Endnotes

1. See *Goodridge v. Dept. of Public Health* (2003); *In re Marriage Cases* (2008); *Kerrigan v. Commissioner of Public Health* (2008); *Varnum v. Brien* (2009).
2. The best general discussions of the convention and prevailing attitudes of the day are found in two unpublished sources, Fitts (1951) and Airey (1945). See also Dolliver (1992). For an account of the convention's day-to-day actions see Rosenow (1962).
3. The literature on this aspect of the federal constitution is vast, but some of the more interesting discussions include Abrams (1984), Howard (1982), and Lessig (1995).
4. For example, *State v. Stroud* (1986); *State v. Kennedy* (1986); *Southcenter Joint Venture v. National Democratic Policy Committee* (1989).
5. The idea of modalities of "constitutional argument" is derived from Bobbit (1982).

References

Abrams, Kathryn. 1984. "On Reading and Using the Tenth Amendment," *Yale Law Journal* 93(4): 723–43.

Ackerman, Bruce. 1991. *We The People. Vol. 1: Foundations.* Cambridge, MA: Harvard University Press.

Airey, Wilfred J. 1945. "A History of the Constitution and Government of Washington Territory." Ph.D. Thesis, University of Washington.

Avery, Mary W. 1962. *History and Government of the State of Washington.* Seattle: University of Washington Press.

Bakken, Gordon Morris. 1987. *Rocky Mountain Constitution Making: 1850–1912.* New York: Greenwood Press.

Beckett, Paul Louis. 1968. *From Wilderness to Enabling Act: The Evolution of a State of Washington.* Pullman: Washington State University Press.

Beckett, Paul L., and Walfred H. Peterson. 1985. "The Constitutional Framework." In *Political Life in Washington: Governing the Evergreen State*, edited by Thor Swanson, William F. Mullen, John C. Pierce, and Charles H. Sheldon, 19–34. Pullman: Washington State University Press.

Bobbit, Philip. 1982. *Constitutional Fate: Theory of the Constitution.* New York: Oxford University Press.

Brennan, William J. 1977. "State Constitutions and the Protection of Individual Rights." *Harvard Law Review* 90(3): 489–504.

Clayton, Cornell W. 2002. "Toward a Theory of the Washington Constitution." *Gonzaga Law Review* 37(1): 41–88.

Corwin, Edward S. 1950. "The Passing of Dual Federalism." *Virginia Law Review* 36(1): 1–24.

Dolliver, James M. 1992. "The Mind of the Founders: An Assessment of the Washington Constitution of 1889." In *Washington Comes of Age: The State in the National Experience*, edited by David Stratton, 135–51. Pullman: Washington State University Press.

Fitts, James Leonard. 1951. "The Washington Constitutional Convention of 1889." Master's thesis, University of Washington.

Fritz, Christian G. 1994. "The American Constitutional Tradition Revisited: Preliminary Observations on State Constitution-Making in the Nineteenth-Century West." *Rutgers Law Journal* 25(4): 945.

Gardner, James A. 1992. "The Failed Discourse of State Constitutionalism." *Michigan Law Review* 90(4): 761–837.

Grad, Frank P. 1968. "The State Constitution: Its Function and Form for Our Time." *Virginia Law Review* 54(5): 928–73.

Howard, A.E. Dick. 1982. "The States and the Supreme Court," *Catholic University Law Review* 31(3): 380.

Kahn, Paul. 1996. "State Constitutionalism and the Problems of Fairness." *Valparaiso University Law Review* 30(2): 459–75.

Knapp, Lebbeus J. 1913. "The Origin of the Constitution of the State of Washington." *Washington Historical Quarterly* 4(4): 227–75.

Lessig, Lawrence. 1995. "Translating Federalism: United States v. Lopez," *Supreme Court Review* 1995: 125–215.

Rosenow, Beverly. 1962. *Journal of the Washington State Constitutional Convention, 1889.* Seattle: Book Pub. Co.

Schwantes, Carlos A. 1982. "Protest in a Promised Land: Unemployment, Disinheritance, and the Origin of Labor Militancy in the Pacific Northwest, 1885–1886." *Western Historical Quarterly* 13(4): 373–90.

Sheldon, Charles H. 1988. *A Century of Judging: A Political History of the Washington Supreme Court.* Seattle: University of Washington Press.

Snure, Brian. 1992. "Comment: A Frequent Recurrence to Fundamental Principles: Individual Rights, Free Government and the Washington State Constitution." *Washington Law Review* 67(3): 669–90.

Spitzer, Hugh D. 1998. "Which Constitution? Eleven Years of Gunwall in Washington State." *Seattle University Law Review* 21(4): 1187–1215.

_____. 2006. "New Life for the 'Criteria Tests' in State Constitutional Jurisprudence: 'Gunwall is Dead-Long Live Gunwall!'" Rutgers Law Journal 37(4): 1169–1202.

Talmadge, Philip A. 1999. "Understanding the Limits of Power: Judicial Restraint in General Jurisdiction Court Systems." *Seattle University Law Review* 22(3): 695–739.

Tarr, G. Alan. 1997. "The New Judicial Federalism in Perspective." *Notre Dame Law Review* 72(4): 1097–1118.

_____. 1998. *Understanding State Constitutions.* Princeton, NJ: Princeton University Press.

Tarr, G. Alan, and Robert F. Williams. 1998. "Forward: Western State Constitutions in the American Constitutional Tradition." *New Mexico Law Review* 28(1): 191.

Utter, Robert F. 1984. "Freedom and Diversity in a Federal System: Perspectives on State Constitutions and the Washington Declaration of Rights." *University of Puget Sound Law Review* 7(3): 491–525.

_____. 1985. "Swimming in the Jaws of the Crocodile: State Court Comment on Federal Constitutional Issues When Disposing of Cases on State Constitutional Grounds." *Texas Law Review* 63(5): 1025.

_____. 1992. "The Practice of Principled Decision-Making in State Constitutionalism: Washington's Experience." *Temple Law Review* 65(1): 169.

Utter, Robert F., and Hugh D. Spitzer. 2002, *The Washington State Constitution: A Reference Guide.* Westport, CT: Greenwood Press.

Williams, Robert F. 1996. "Looking Back at the New Judicial Federalism's First Generation." *Valparaiso Law Review* 30(2): xiii.

Cases Cited

Alderwood Associates v. Washington Environmental Council, 635 P.2d 108 (1981).

City of Woodinville v. Northshore United Church of Christ, 166 Wn.2d 633 (2009).

Eggleston v. Pierce County, 148 Wn.2d 760 (2003).

Goodridge v. Department of Public Health, 798 N.E.2d 941 (Mass. 2003).

In re Marriage Cases, 183 P.3d 384 (Ca. 2008).

Kerrigan v. Commissioner of Public Health, 957 A.2d 407 (Conn. 2008).

Seattle School Dist. No. 1 v. State, 90 P.2d 71 (1978).

Southcenter Joint Venture v. National Democratic Policy Committee, 780 P.2d 1282 (Wash. 1989).

State v. Coe, 679 P.2d 353 (Wash. 1984).

State v. Gocken, 896 P.2d 1269 (Wash. 1995).

State v. Gunwall, 720 P.2d 808, 815 (Wash. 1986).

State v. Jackson, 150 Wn.2d 251 (2003).

State v. Kennedy, 726 P.2d 445 (Wash. 1986).

State v. Ringer, 674 P2d 1240 (Wash. 1983).

State v. Stroud, 720 P.2d 436 (Wash. 1986).

State v. Wethered, 755 P.2d 797 (Wash. 1988).

Varnum v. Brien, 763 N.W.2d 862 (Iowa 2009).

CHAPTER EIGHT

The Washington State Judiciary: Decentralization, Responsiveness, and Independence

Simon Zschirnt, J. Mitchell Pickerill, and Carl J. McCurley

Introduction

W HILE THE WASHINGTON JUDICIAL SYSTEM has been characterized by considerable continuity in terms of its institutional structure, caseload, and output, the changing dynamics of judicial elections have raised questions regarding whether this institutional structure continues to serve its intended purpose or is in need of reform. This chapter examines the state's judicial hierarchy and structure, the development and decentralization of the judiciary, and the potential challenges posed to the system's integrity by increased campaign spending and special interest influence in judicial elections. Despite the decentralization of the state judicial system, it has responded to a range of challenges and adopted a number of important reforms with deftness. Like the judiciaries of other states across the country, the Washington judicial system faces a number of challenges as it moves further into the 21st century. We conclude that the state has a unique blend of decentralization, responsiveness, and judicial independence.

The Structure of the Judiciary

The Washington judicial system is structured as a four-tiered system consisting of two levels of trial courts at the lower end of the hierarchy and two levels of appellate courts at the upper end. The first and lowest tier of the judicial system consists of district and municipal courts; superior courts make up the second tier; the third tier is comprised of the Washington Court of Appeals; and at the top of the judicial hierarchy sits the Supreme Court of Washington. In this section, we describe the structure of the Washington judicial system in depth and explain the essential features and functions of each tier of the system.

The Structure of Washington State Courts

Supreme Court of Washington
9 justices sit en banc
- Discretionary appellate jurisdiction over all Washington Court of Appeals decisions
- Discretionary appellate jurisdiction over all decisions involving state officers, decisions declaring a statute or ordinance unconstitutional, and decisions in cases presenting conflicts of law
- Exclusive jurisdiction over bar discipline
- Jurisdiction over certified questions
- Mandatory appellate jurisdiction over all decisions imposing the death penalty

Washington Court of Appeals (3 divisions)
22 judges sit in panels
- Mandatory appellate jurisdiction over all superior court decisions

Superior Courts (30 districts)
172 judges
- Original jurisdiction over all felony criminal cases, juvenile cases, and civil cases involving claims of greater than $50,000
- Appellate jurisdiction over all municipal court and district court decisions

Municipal Courts (127)
110 judges and commissioners
- Original jurisdiction over all cases involving violations of municipal ordinances

District Courts (49)
107 judges and commissioners
- Original jurisdiction over all misdemeanor criminal cases, civil cases involving claims of less than $50,000, small claims, petitions for protection and no contact orders, change of name petitions, and lien foreclosures

Trial Courts

District and municipal courts are known as "courts of limited jurisdiction" and serve as trial courts for misdemeanor criminal cases, cases involving traffic and parking infractions, civil cases involving claims of less than $50,000, and small claims. District courts, which have jurisdiction over both criminal and civil cases, are county courts that serve specific territories within counties. Municipal courts, which have jurisdiction over violations of municipal ordinances, serve specific municipalities. While all of the state's 107 district court judges are elected through nonpartisan elections to four-year terms, the state's 110 municipal court judges may either be elected or appointed to four-year terms. Judges serving on courts of limited jurisdiction include both professional and lay judges (also known as commissioners). Courts of limited jurisdiction presided over by lay judges differ from other courts of limited jurisdiction in that they do not produce written records of their proceedings. Thus, any appellate review of their decisions is de novo and may involve review of issues of both fact and law. On the other hand, appellate review of the decisions of courts of limited jurisdiction presided over by professional judges is limited to issues of law. In 2009, the number of district and municipal court filings totaled 2,485,602 and the disposition of these cases generated approximately $264,000,000 through filing and other fees and through fines, forfeitures, and penalties; thus, these filings are a major source of revenue for state and local governments.

More serious cases are tried in the state's superior courts, which serve as trial courts for felony criminal cases, juvenile cases, and civil cases involving claims of greater than $50,000. Superior courts also hear appeals from courts of limited jurisdiction. The state of Washington has 30 superior court districts. While most counties comprise a single superior court district, some districts in sparsely populated areas of the state encompass two or more counties. The state's 172 superior court judges are professional judges elected to four-year terms and are required to be attorneys admitted to the state bar association and thus licensed to practice law in the state of Washington. In 2009, the number of superior court filings totaled 303,655. Almost half (about 47%) of these filings were civil matters involving tort claims, commercial cases, distribution of property from a meretricious relationship, property rights, petitions for protection from civil harassment or domestic violence, and petitions to review rulings by state administrative agencies. Thirteen percent were criminal cases. The remaining cases consisted of adoption, domestic, guardianship, juvenile, mental illness, and probate cases.

Washington's district, municipal, and superior courts thus serve primarily as trial courts, whose function in the court system is distinct from that of appellate courts. In particular, trial courts are charged with making determinations regarding issues of fact and applying the law to their findings of fact. In a bench trial, a judge acts alone and is responsible for conducting the trial, making findings of fact, determining guilt or innocence, and imposing penalties in traffic and other types of minor cases. In more serious cases judges may preside over a jury trial in which the judge acts in concert with a jury of laypersons. In jury trials, the jurors serve as finders of fact while the judge oversees the trial by applying the law to make decisions regarding the admission of evidence and other procedural issues. Judges also provide jurors with instructions to help guide them in applying the law to their factual findings. The losing party at trial generally has the right to request appellate review of the trial court proceedings.

Although trial courts are where formally adjudicated cases originate, it is important to note that most legal disputes do not result in a trial. Most disputes are resolved due to plea-bargains, settlements, dropped charges, dismissed cases, and other reasons. In most cases, the court of limited jurisdiction or superior court acts to approve or certify case results that do not involve actual trial. In 2009, about 3 percent of cases filed in Washington superior courts (including about 5 percent of felony criminal cases) and less than 1 percent of cases filed in limited jurisdiction courts culminated in either a jury or bench trial.

Courts of Appeal

Appellate courts—also referred to as "courts of appeal"—hear appeals from lower courts, usually brought by the losing party. Appellate review is ordinarily limited to issues of law. This is the case in Washington as well as most other jurisdictions in the United States. Appeals courts are primarily concerned with the proper application of legal provisions and precedents to the facts of the case—as determined by the trier of fact (i.e. the trial court). Appellate courts must usually accept the findings of fact made in the superior court and review only whether the judge or jury applied the law to those facts correctly. Thus, appellate proceedings vary significantly from trials. Appellate courts generally do not hear witness testimony, accept new evidence, or make findings of fact. Instead, the parties to the appeal file legal briefs with the court that identify issues of law that may have been decided incorrectly by the trial court and make legal arguments regarding why the lower court ruling should be affirmed or reversed.

After the briefs have been filed and the judges have had the opportunity to read them, oral arguments are scheduled. During oral arguments, attorneys for both parties appear before a panel of appellate court judges to make arguments and answer questions regarding the proper interpretation and application of the law. Following oral arguments, the panel of judges discusses the merits of both parties' arguments and votes on an outcome. A simple majority is required to reach a decision. Ordinarily, one of the judges in the majority writes an opinion that explains the legal reasoning used to reach the court's decision. Other judges voting with the majority may write separate concurring opinions to explain their particular rationale or reasons for their decision. If the outcome is not unanimous, judges in the minority may write dissenting opinions explaining why they disagreed with the majority. The majority opinion is important not only because it dictates the outcome of the case, but also because the reasoning is supposed to guide future applications of the law by lower courts and other government actors. These opinions are regularly published in court reporters. The decisions of the Supreme Court of Washington are published in *Washington Reports* and *West's Pacific Reporter*, while the decisions of the Washington Court of Appeals are published in *Washington Appellate Reports* and *West's Pacific Reporter*.

Most cases appealed from superior courts are heard at the first level of appellate review, the Washington Court of Appeals. This court is divided into three divisions that each serve multiple counties, and hence multiple superior courts. Division 1, located in Seattle, and Division 2, located in Tacoma, serve the counties west of the Cascades, while Division 3, located in Spokane, serves the counties east of the Cascades. These geographical divisions are important because a losing party in a superior court must file an appeal with the appropriate division of the Court of Appeals, that is, the division that includes in its geographical boundaries the county in which the trial occurred.

The caseloads of the three divisions vary significantly. Division 1 has consistently been the busiest of the three and reviewed 1,858 cases in 2009. In contrast, Division 3 has consistently had the lightest caseload, reviewing 998 cases in 2009, while Division 2, which reviewed 1,447 cases in 2009, has had an intermediate caseload. Notably, Division 1's caseload has decreased slightly over the last decade (declining from an average of 1,946 cases for the years 1997–2001) while the caseloads for Divisions 2 and 3 have increased during this period (rising from an average of 1,348 for Division 2 and an average of 884 for Division 3 for the years 1997–2001) (May 2004).

In general, civil and criminal cases represent approximately equal shares of the Washington Court of Appeals' caseload, although it is common for criminal cases to make up a slight majority of the docket. This is notable because, among other things, criminal cases make up a much smaller percentage of filings than civil case filings in the trial courts. In other words, a much higher proportion of criminal trials result in appeals than do civil trials.

The Washington Court of Appeals docket is "non-discretionary," meaning that it must accept all properly filed appeals. This practice exists because the losing parties in trial courts are guaranteed one appeal to make sure that the lower court did not make a legal error that may have prejudiced the outcome of the trial. If an appellate court determines that a "reversible error" occurred during the trial, it may reverse the verdict or ruling in the lower court. Reversal may result in a new trial. On the other hand, if an appellate court finds no error or a "harmless error" (i.e., a minor mistake that even if remedied would not change the outcome), it will affirm the lower court's ruling or verdict.

There are 22 judges on the Washington Court of Appeals, each elected to six-year terms. The terms are staggered so only a subset of the court's membership is up for reelection in any single election year. Judges serving on the Washington Court of Appeals are required to have practiced law in the state of Washington for at least five years and must be residents of a county within their respective division for at least one year before taking office.

The State Supreme Court

The Supreme Court of Washington is at the top of the judicial hierarchy and hears appeals at its discretion. These include appeals of decisions of the Washington Court of Appeals and appeals of decisions at any level of the state court system that involve petitions against state officers, that declare a statute or ordinance unconstitutional, or that present a conflict of law. The court's "discretionary jurisdiction" is similar to that of the U.S. Supreme Court. A party who wishes to appeal to the Supreme Court of Washington is thus not guaranteed to have his or her case reviewed by the state's highest court; rather, the party must file a petition for review that makes an argument for why the court should review the case. Petitions for review are considered by panels comprised of five members of the court. If the panel fails to reach a unanimous decision either to grant or to reject the petition, the petition is considered by the entire court. In general, petitions are most likely to be granted when there is a conflict between different divisions of the Washington Court of Appeals about the proper interpretation of a law or when the justices on the court are otherwise convinced that the legal issue presented in the case is an important or ambiguous one that needs to be authoritatively resolved. The court also has mandatory jurisdiction in cases in which the death penalty has been imposed. This means the review is automatically granted and the justices do not have the discretion to reject it.

In addition, the court is specifically charged with the responsibility of making procedural rules for state courts, with general administration of the state court system, and with the disciplining of attorneys, as we discuss in more detail in the next section. The court's exclusive power to make rules of procedure has been closely guarded and has occasionally led to conflicts with the legislature. These conflicts have produced a substantial body of separation of powers case law, with the most recent addition being the court's 2010 decision in *Waples v. Yi.* In this case the court declared that restrictions on the filing of medical malpractice claims that had been enacted by the legislature were unconstitutional insofar as they conflicted with existing rules of procedure by barring cases that could otherwise be filed under the more permissive rules, established by the court, for commencing a civil action.

As the state's highest court, the Supreme Court of Washington is the final arbiter of the meaning of Washington State law. Its decisions interpreting the Washington State constitution, state statutes, and state administrative regulations therefore establish precedent that must be followed by lower courts in subsequent cases. The court's interpretations of state law are not subject to review by any higher court.[1]

There are nine justices on the Supreme Court of Washington, all of whom must be attorneys admitted to practice in the state of Washington. The justices are elected to serve six-year terms. The court is led by its chief justice, who is selected by the members of the court to serve a four-year term. The chief justice acts as the main spokesperson for the court, presides over the court's hearings and conferences, and co-chairs the state's Board for Judicial Administration. Justice Gerry Alexander, who served as chief justice from 2001 to 2010, holds the distinction of being the longest serving chief justice in the state's history. Alexander stepped down from his position in January 2011 (although he remained on the court as an associate justice), when he was succeeded by Justice Barbara Madsen as chief justice. Chief Justice Madsen was a unanimous selection by the members of the court. She was originally elected to the court in 1992 and was the third woman to be elected to the Supreme Court.

In fact, the Supreme Court of Washington has long been among the most diverse state supreme court in the nation in terms of gender. While women comprise 26 percent of state judiciaries and 31 percent of state supreme court justices nationwide (Curriden 2010), four of the court's nine current members are women. Moreover, Washington was among the first states to have a female majority on its state supreme court when five women sat on the court together between 2003 and 2005.

The number of filings received by the court has remained relatively consistent over the last five years. Between 2005 and 2009, the court received an average of 1,603 petitions annually, with a high of 1,790 in 2005 and a low of 1,468 in 2007. However, the number of cases the court decides annually has fluctuated considerably during this period, ranging from a high of 153 in 2007 to a low of 112 in 2008.

Selecting Judges in Washington: Nonpartisan Elections

As we briefly mentioned in the previous section, judges in Washington are elected in nonpartisan elections. Thus, for any given judicial vacancy, voters select judges from a list of names of candidates similarly to how they select candidates for other offices. However, unlike executive and legislative elections, no political party affiliation for judicial candidates is listed on the ballot. If a vacancy occurs for a judgeship before the term ends, the governor may appoint a judge to fill the vacancy until the next election, at which time the governor's appointee must run for the office if he or she wishes to retain the position.

This nonpartisan election model replaced a system of partisan judicial elections through an amendment to the Washington State constitution that was ratified in 1912. Like its Pacific Northwest neighbors and other states in the West, the state's move to nonpartisan elections was influenced by the values of the Progressive era. The move represented an effort to de-politicize the courts and to increase judicial independence by decreasing the influence of partisan politics without losing democratic accountability. The values underlying this system differ from those underlying executive-appointment systems that are used primarily in Eastern states as well as in the federal system. In particular, the commitment to electing judges reflects the Populist and direct democracy sentiments that pervaded Washington's political culture when the state was created and are expressed in Article I of the Washington State constitution: "All political power is inherent in the people and governments derive their power from the consent of the governed."

Although Washington's judicial elections are officially nonpartisan, the conduct of recent elections has raised concern that the process no longer functions in its intended manner, has become excessively politicized, and is subject to special interest influence. For example, the state's political parties have not only continued to blur the distinction between partisan and nonpartisan judicial elections by endorsing judicial candidates, they have also increasingly engaged in active mobilization of party supporters on behalf of selected candidates (Modie 2002). This has extended to party organizations at all levels, with most county-level Democratic and Republican organizations including statements of endorsement in judicial races on their websites. Moreover, unease regarding special interest influence has been underscored by the fact that until 2006, contribution limits for candidates for statewide office did not apply to judicial candidates, permitting interest groups to play an especially significant role in funding judicial campaigns. The 2006 amendments to the state's campaign finance laws, which closed this loophole by applying existing contribution limits to judicial candidates, were passed after Justice James Johnson's 2002 and 2004 campaigns demonstrated just how significant interest groups could be. In both races, concerted mobilization on Johnson's behalf by business interests allowed Johnson to decisively outspend his opponents, with a $95,000 contribution from the Building Industry Association of Washington, for whom Johnson had previously performed legal work, raising particular scrutiny (Skolnik 2004). Although the ability of special interests to contribute directly to a candidate for judicial office has subsequently been limited, independent expenditures on behalf of candidates by special interest groups are unlimited and have continued to generate controversy.

The growing role of special interests in judicial campaigns has been blamed for undermining public confidence in an independent judiciary, and it has also been cited as a source of voter confusion and misinformation (a particular problem in low salience and low information elections such as judicial elections). Such concerns have been raised most recently in response to extensive independent expenditures to produce political ads opposing former Chief Justice Gerry Alexander during his 2006 reelection campaign that were criticized as falsely portraying the chief justice as a "dotty old man in sympathy with child killers and drunks" (Shannon 2006). Nonetheless, such expenditures continue to be the electorate's primary source of information regarding judicial elections. Indeed, every piece of television advertising relating to judicial elections that was aired in 2006 was paid for by independent groups not formally affiliated with any candidate's campaign (Justice at Stake Campaign 2010a).

These trends are reflective of broader national trends toward increased spending and interest group influence in judicial elections. In the 21 states that continue to use elections to select judges, these trends have made judicial elections subject to growing criticism (Justice at Stake Campaign 2010b). In particular, critics have pointed to research suggesting that voter behavior in judicial elections is driven largely by partisan cues (with voters casting ballots in states employing partisan judicial elections significantly less likely to abstain from making a choice in judicial races than voters casting ballots in states employing nonpartisan judicial elections) and campaign spending, rather than by more substantive considerations such as candidates' qualifications and judicial philosophies (Champagne 2003; Geyh 2003; Klein and Baum 2001). Moreover, judicial elections have also been found to alter the behavior of judges once they take the bench in potentially problematic ways, increasing dissensus on courts by making judges more likely to author separate opinions publicizing their individual views and leading judges to compromise their principles in order to curry public favor, particularly in cases involving highly salient issues such as the death penalty (Brace and Hall 1990; Hall 1995).

Such findings have contributed to numerous organized efforts by stakeholders in the legal profession to focus public attention on the issue of judicial elections. For example, in 2000 these concerns led to the convening of an unprecedented summit of the chief justices from 15 state supreme courts to discuss judicial elections and the problems they present. In addition, in 1998, the American Bar Association commissioned a formal study of the issue and subsequently issued recommendations for judicial campaign finance reform (Bonneau 2007). A number of nonprofit organizations, such as the Justice at Stake Campaign, have also formed and been increasingly active in response to the perceived politiciza-tion of judicial elections, joining calls for more public financing of judicial elec-tions. Groups such as Justice at Stake have also observed that at the same time judicial elections have become more politicized by the influx of money from corporations and interest groups, judicial independence has also been threatened by politicians publicly attacking courts and judges more frequently and often viscerally. As a result, a chorus of high profile voices, including former United States Supreme Court Justice Sandra Day O'Connor and the president of the American Bar Association, have called for a multitude of reforms to bolster judi-cial independence at the federal and state levels (O'Connor 2010; Archer 2004).

The rising tide of cynicism regarding judicial elections has also been reflected in recent trends in institutional arrangements. In particular, the number of states employing elections to select judges has been in constant decline since reaching its peak in the middle decades of the 20th century; indeed, since 1960, 16 states have eliminated judicial elections as their method for selecting state supreme court judges and replaced elections with some form of appointive system (Bon-neau 2007). Among the 29 states currently employing appointive systems, the most popular approach has been what is commonly referred to as the "Missouri plan"—a merit system for selecting judges that was first developed and adopted in Missouri. Under the Missouri plan, judges are initially appointed to their seats by the governor, who has selected from a slate of qualified candidates presented by a nominating commission, and subsequently face periodic non-competitive retention elections. This selection system has received broad-based support among judicial selection reform advocates, including the official endorsement of the American Judicature Society (American Judicature Society 1991).

While its supporters have argued that such a system avoids many of the dangers associated with costly and politicized elections, other research has suggested that increased spending in judicial elections may not necessarily be a cause for alarm and may in fact enhance democratic accountability. Specifically, analyses of campaign spending patterns and electoral outcomes in judicial elections have indicated that campaign spending in judicial elections serves primarily to enhance the name recognition of challengers while offering little electoral benefit to incumbents (Bonneau 2007). Thus, many have argued, restrictions on campaign spending would undermine the central purpose of judicial elections by constraining the ability of challengers to mount effective campaigns, entrenching incumbents, and further dampening already low levels of interest among the electorate (Hall and Bonneau 2008). Moreover, research comparing the dynamics of non-competitive retention elections conducted under the Missouri plan with those of other types of judicial elections has suggested that their differences have been overstated. These studies indicate that while retention elections may appear to be less partisan on face value, the reality is that they simply obscure—rather than remove—the overriding influence of partisanship; this is because the results of retention elections are closely linked to fluctuations in the statewide electoral fortunes of political parties (Hall 2001).

Conflicting empirical studies such as these add complexity to the emerging debate over judicial elections and illustrate the fact that any system of judicial selection ultimately reflects political judgments regarding the proper balance between accountability and impartiality. Thus, in assessing whether the Washington court system continues to provide an adequate level of judicial independence, it is important to consider the tradeoffs associated with alternative systems. These are debates being waged across the country by a range of practitioners, scholars, and activists. No doubt national reform movements are likely to influence debates over judicial selection in Washington, but, equally without doubt, they will be counterbalanced by Washington's distinct political culture.

In his seminal work on the topic, Daniel Elazar (1984) characterizes the dominant political culture in Washington as "moralistic" in nature, meaning that Washingtonians tend to be committed to using the transformative power of the state to promote the public good. This has specific implications for judicial selection given that moralistic political cultures are also distinguished by their intolerance for political corruption and their innovation of policies designed to promote more transparent and ethical government. Both of these impulses militate in favor of the adoption of reforms such as the Missouri plan. However, moralistic political cultures are also characterized by more active civic engagement and embrace of institutional arrangements facilitating direct forms of democracy (such as the ballot initiative and referendum). These impulses militate in favor of retaining judicial elections. Washington's political culture thus pulls in both directions when considering the desirability of judicial reform. As noted in the first chapter, Washington's moralistic political culture permeates how political life is structured and carried out in the state.

Moreover, the current judicial selection system is enshrined in Article IV of the Washington State constitution and could only be altered through a constitutional amendment receiving the support of two thirds of both houses of the legislature and a majority of the electorate. Given this fact, together with the inherent tension within the state's dominant political culture discussed above, it seems likely that any successful efforts to reform the current system will be limited to more modest measures, such as campaign finance reform legislation, unless there is some focusing event (such as a major decision unambiguously influenced by campaign contributions) galvanizing public opinion against judicial elections.

Administration and Decentralization of the "Judicial Branch"

The decentralized nature of the Washington State judicial system makes it difficult to call it the "judicial branch" relative to the state's more centralized executive and legislative branches and even relative to the federal judiciary. In this section, we begin by describing the rather limited central statewide administrative apparatus of the judiciary. There are several centralized features of the judicial system that manage to keep it unified, albeit loosely so. Next, we explain how Washington's judicial system is more decentralized than other government institutions, making it difficult to characterize the Washington system as a single "branch" of state government in the conventional sense of that term.

The Supreme Court of Washington is one unifying force for the state judiciary. For example, the high court serves to unify the judicial system through its ability to promulgate uniform rules of court procedure, including, for example, rules describing how civil, criminal, and appellate matters are to be handled by the courts and rules defining when a criminal trial is "timely." Additionally, the court has the power to appoint leadership for the Administrative Office of the Courts, the Office of Public Defense (which operates the Parents Representation Program for child dependency cases, appellate indigent defense services, and criminal trial indigent defense services), and the Office of Civil Legal Aid (providing legal help to low-income residents with civil matters related to such basic needs as housing and family safety). The court also leads the budget process for the judicial branch at the state level by submitting biennial budget proposals to the legislature.

The second major unifying institution within the judicial branch is the Administrative Office of the Courts. Located in Olympia, the Administrative Office of the Courts responds to the general needs of the judicial system for budgeting and accounting of state-funded expenses, automation of case records, and reporting on the caseload of the courts. It provides consultation on court business practices, analysis of staffing and resources, forecasts of the need for judges and court commissioners, and professional training and education of court staff and judges. It also helps create a court community by bringing together judges, administrators, and staff from the cities and counties for state-level conferences.

In addition to administration support, the Washington State court system is supported by the Task Force on Canons of Judicial Ethics and the Commission on Judicial Conduct, which are responsible for preserving judicial independence by ensuring that high standards of judicial conduct are observed. The Commission on Judicial Conduct has been the more active of the two bodies. It was established by constitutional amendment in 1980 to provide a less cumbersome alternative to impeachment for violations of judicial ethics by sitting judges. In cases of misconduct, the commission may issue a formal reprimand or recommend to the Supreme Court of Washington that a judge be suspended or removed from office. The commission's most noteworthy recent imposition of discipline involved former Justice Richard Sanders of the Supreme Court of Washington, who was found guilty of violating several canons of the Code of Judicial Conduct after he toured McNeil Island Corrections Center and met personally with a number of inmates, including some who, unbeknownst to him, had cases pending before the court. As a consequence, following the court's 2006 decision affirming the Commission on Judicial Conduct's sanction in *In Re: Disciplinary Proceeding Against Sanders*, Sanders was formally reprimanded.

A variety of court associations draw their membership from across the courts and are charged with developing policy. Two associations represent judges—the District and Municipal Court Judges Association and the Superior Court Judges Association—while similar organizations exist for court administrators, such as the Washington Association of Juvenile Court Administrators, and for court clerks. These professional organizations help steer policy from a broader perspective, as has been the case with the Juvenile Court Administrators' support for rigorous quality assurance standards to apply to all juvenile probation departments. Other administrative groups created by order of the Supreme Court of Washington, in particular the Gender and Justice Commission, Minorities and Justice Commission, and Commission on Children in Foster Care, demonstrate that although the courts are decentralized, they can work together to achieve common purposes and policies.

The more day-to-day operations of the courts and other important matters, such as funding municipal, district, and superior court operations, are administered locally. Relative to other states, the level of state expenditure supporting this system is quite modest. While the full operating costs of the Supreme Court of Washington and the Washington Court of Appeals are paid out of the state budget, the state only funds half of the salaries and benefits paid to superior court judges, and a smaller percentage of the salaries and benefits paid to district and municipal court judges. According to figures for fiscal year 2007, the average percentage of funding for judicial and legal services received from state general funds is 49 percent (Kyckelhahn 2010). Indeed, four states (Alaska, Delaware, Massachusetts, and Rhode Island) rely upon their general funds to provide 90 percent or more of the funding for their judicial systems. In contrast, the Washington judicial system received just 17 percent of its funding—mainly to operate the state's appellate courts and the Administrative Office of the Courts and to pay judicial salaries—from the state general fund, while the other 83 percent was provided by county and municipal revenues (Kyckelhahn 2010). In fact, with only three-tenths of 1 percent of the most recent state budget devoted to the state's judicial system, Washington currently ranks 50th in the nation in state funding of judicial and legal services.

In combination with local court administration that operates at the pleasure of locally elected judges, reliance on local funding means that courts exercise considerable freedom in deciding how to operate. For example, local court administrators and judges have control over case calendaring, pre-trial hearings, services provided to self-represented litigants, use of problem-solving courts such as drug courts, and assignment of judges to specialized dockets. The administration of these and many other activities thus varies significantly from court to court and county to county. The decentralization of Washington's courts poses daunting obstacles to coordinating policy and the development of standards for court operations among the various courts throughout the state. Perhaps the most telling example arises with updating the automated systems used to keep track of filings, hearings, and case outcomes. The Supreme Court of Washington created the Judicial Information Services Committee, composed of multiple representatives from each court level. The committee has found it difficult to arrive at agreement on which level of court should first receive a major software update, and disagreements arise within court levels on software capabilities and vendors. Of course, decentralization is also construed as a benefit by local courts since the arrangement supports the adaptability of courts to the local context.

New Responsiveness

Despite the decentralization that characterizes the state judicial system, it has proven adept at responding to at least some problems facing the system. Tobin

(1999) identifies two major aspects of court reform: one directed at unification of the state judicial branch, and the second directed at an increasing social role for courts beyond the traditional "calling balls and strikes." As detailed above, Washington's courts are more decentralized than the courts of many other states so the first type of reform has not proceeded as far as it might. In contrast, and perhaps partially as a result of their decentralization, Washington's courts have more fully participated in the second type of reform and have modified court operations in response to the needs of individuals and communities. Although courts conserve the past by adhering to precedent, fundamental innovation does occur at times. Three current examples of reform and innovation involve pre-trial practices, the treatment of moderate and high-risk juvenile offenders, and the use of specialized problem solving courts.

First, there have been some meaningful reforms in recent years to pre-trial practices in Washington's trial courts. For example, in late 2009, Maurice Clemmons was charged with felony assault and was released from the Pierce County jail on bail while awaiting trial. While out of jail, Clemmons murdered four police officers at a coffee shop in Lakewood, Washington.[2] The incident prompted an extensive examination of pre-trial practices by a state taskforce that, in December 2009, recommended that courts provide better information to judges about the risk to community safety before making bail decisions. An existing pilot program of actuarial risk assessment—using an alleged offender's juvenile and adult conviction history to calculate risk of further offending—in the Thurston County Superior Court was then endorsed by the Superior Court Judges' Association. In 2011, funding for deployment of a risk assessment system was approved by the legislature and the program was adopted statewide. In this case, there was a convergence of public opinion, strong support among the task force members, and a well-developed and tested approach to risk assessment that enabled the courts to revise long-standing practice.

Another area of innovation in the Washington courts has involved issues relating to juvenile offenders. As part of a national trend toward blended juvenile justice approaches that combine accountability with rehabilitation, the 1997 legislature enacted the Community Juvenile Accountability Act to promote use of research-based interventions to reduce juvenile offender recidivism. The act required creation and deployment of a risk assessment process to assign youth to programs that had been scientifically evaluated; these are commonly referred to as "Evidence Based Programs" (EBP). Beginning in 2009, the state's juvenile courts worked with the Washington State Center for Court Research to create performance reporting that shows youth attributes, participation in treatment, intermediate outcomes in terms of changes to attitudes, cognition, and other crime-related attributes, and long-term outcomes such as school performance and contact with the justice system.

By 2010, after an extensive period of development, the state's juvenile courts created a system that first assesses the risk for reconviction of youth who have been adjudicated delinquent and assigned to probation supervision (Wallace et al. 2011). Moderate and high-risk offenders then receive an evaluation of needs to assess whether an available EBP can be matched to the person; if so, an assessed youth may be assigned to an EBP, such as Functional Family Therapy or Aggression Replacement Training. The transformation of juvenile courts in Washington from institutions focused on accountability and monitoring young offenders to institutions focused on preventing future offending through treatment and tracking outcomes was supported by state funds but implemented gradually by local courts as each became ready for the necessary steps. Encouragement came from repeated evaluations showing differences in outcomes between treatment and control groups.

Lastly, a third area of innovation and reform involves so-called "problem-solving courts." In contrast to the legislatively led adult pretrial risk assessment and juvenile court treatment programs described above, the spread of problem-solving courts across superior, district, and municipal courts in Washington has been through the courts. Although some courts may qualify for state funding of treatment services, it has been local leadership that has led to an expansion of problem-solving courts in Washington; each treatment court began through local initiative and an implicit affirmation that courts have a role in addressing the needs of the community. The use of problem-solving courts began with the establishment of adult drug courts in 1994. By 2010, the use of problem-solving courts had expanded around the state to include juvenile drug courts, family treatment courts, mental health courts, DUI courts, domestic violence courts, and veteran treatment courts in 25 of the state's 39 counties.[3]

Problem solving courts reflect a shifting orientation toward reducing harm rather than strict punishment. Among the defining features of problem solving courts are the willingness of the defendant to participate and the organization of other court actors—judge, prosecutor, defense, probation, and treatment officers—into a team that closely monitors offender progress and collaborates to find solutions that support recovery and rehabilitation.

Conclusion

The Washington court system reflects both continuity and change and is characterized by a combination of decentralization, responsiveness, and independence. The basic structure of the state's judicial system has remained the same, with two levels of trial courts at the bottom of the hierarchy and two levels of appellate courts at the top. Additionally, the state has maintained a nonpartisan system for selecting judges. While there have been some shifts in the caseloads of different courts, those changes have been modest for the most part.

Although much has remained the same, the past decade has witnessed some important changes in the Washington judiciary as well. First, reflecting trends in other parts of the country, judicial elections seem to be more competitive, and campaign contributions and expenditures for judicial candidates are on the rise. The influence of money and the involvement of special interest groups and political parties have caused concern over the independence of the judiciary and the nonpartisan nature of judicial elections in the state. Washington is not alone in trying to deal with these issues, however. A vigorous debate among scholars, activists, and practitioners is being waged nationally over the relationship between judicial elections and campaign expenditures on the one hand, and judicial independence on the other. In Washington, some specific judicial campaigns, such as the Alexander and Johnson campaigns for the Supreme Court of Washington discussed earlier in the chapter, seem to suggest that the nature of judicial elections have become more high profile and conflict ridden in recent years, involving greater amounts of money and partisan activity.

Although there are some unifying features of the state's court system, it remains relatively decentralized. The Supreme Court of Washington and administrative units, such as Administrative Office of the Courts and the Office of Civil Legal Aid, provide some degree of centralization and unification. However, a loose group of court associations around the state are also responsible for developing policies for the judiciary. Moreover, as we noted above, funding and day-to-day operations of most individual courts around the state—especially trial courts—are administered locally. Only 17 percent of judicial funding comes from the state's general fund, which is much less than in other states.

Although the administration of the court system is uniquely decentralized, this hasn't prevented the judiciary, even at the local level, from innovating and responding to problems. Courts around the state have adopted reforms in pretrial procedures and various matters related to juvenile justice, and a range of problem-solving courts have been developed and instituted to help the courts better address specific problems within the justice system, such as finding ways to help drug offenders and reduce the harm of drugs in society.

The state's judiciary appears to have maintained a significant degree of judicial independence. As mentioned above, the example of Justice Sanders' disciplinary action by the Commission on Judicial Conduct indicates that the judiciary takes seriously the ethical conduct of its judges. Moreover, Washington has not been plagued, unlike some other states, by high profile examples of judicial decisions that seem to favor parties who have supported judicial election campaigns and call into question the independence of the judges. Nevertheless, the changing nature of judicial elections and the local administration of courts without statewide oversight will require continued vigilance by Washington lawyers, journalists, activists, and scholars.

Endnotes

1. The Supreme Court of Washington's rulings may be appealed to the United States Supreme Court if they involve an issue of federal law, such as a conflict between a state law and the U.S. Constitution. But the state's high court is the final arbiter of Washington State law.
2. Clemmons evaded law enforcement for two days after the shooting before being shot and killed by a Seattle police officer.
3. For graphics, maps, and additional information, see www.courts.wa.gov/court_dir/?fa=court_dir.psc.

References

American Judicature Society. 1991. "Judicial Nominating Commissions—the Need for Demographic Diversity." Editorial. *Judicature* 74 (February-March): 236.

Archer, Dennis W. February 17, 2004. "Anonymous Money Mars Judicial Elections." *ABA Now*. abanow.org/2004/02/op-ed-anonymous-money-mars-judicial-elections.

Bonneau, Chris W. 2007. "The Effects of Campaign Spending in State Supreme Court Elections." *Political Research Quarterly* 60(3): 489–99.

Brace, Paul, and Melinda Gann Hall. 1990. "Neo-Institutionalism and Dissent in State Supreme Courts." *Journal of Politics* 52(1): 54–70.

Champagne, Anthony. 2003. "The Politics of Judicial Selection." *Policy Studies Journal* 31(3): 413–19.

Curriden, Mark. 2010. "Tipping the Scales: In the South, Women Have Made Huge Strides in the State Judiciaries." ABA Journal 96(7): 37.

Elazar, Daniel J. 1984. *American Federalism: A View from the States*. New York: Harper & Row.

Geyh, Charles. 2003. "Why Judicial Elections Stink." *Ohio State Law Journal* 64(1): 43–80.

Hall, Melinda Gann. 1995. "Justices as Representatives: Elections and Judicial Politics in the American States." *American Politics Quarterly* 23: 485–503.

_____. 2001. "State Supreme Courts in American Democracy: Probing the Myths of Judicial Reform." *American Political Science Review* 95(2): 315–30.

Hall, Melinda Gann, and Chris Bonneau. 2008. "Mobilizing Interest: The Effects of Money on Citizen Participation in State Supreme Court Elections." *American Journal of Political Science* 52(3): 457–70.

Justice at Stake Campaign. 2010a. "Washington." justiceatstake.org/state/washington.

_____. 2010b. "'Your State' National Map." justiceatstake.org/state.

Klein, David, and Lawrence Baum. 2001. "Ballot Information and Voting Decisions in Judicial Elections." *Political Research Quarterly* 54(4): 709–28.

Kyckelhahn, Tracey. 2010. "Justice Expenditure and Employment Extracts, 2007." Bureau of Justice Statistics. bjs.ojp.usdoj.gov/index.cfm?ty=pbdetail&iid=2315.

May, David. 2004. "The Washington State Court System." In *Washington State Government and Politics*, edited by Cornell W. Clayton, Lance T. LeLoup, and Nicholas P. Lovrich, 113–29. Pullman: Washington State University Press.

Modie, Neil. September 17, 2002. "Justice Johnson Trailing Opponent in Early Tally." *Seattle PI*. seattlepi.com/default/article/Justice-Johnson-trailing-opponent-in-early-tally-1096329.php.

O'Connor, Sandra Day. May 22, 2010. "Take Justice Off the Ballot." *New York Times*. nytimes.com/2010/05/23/opinion/23oconnor.html?scp=1&sq=Take%20Justice%20Off%20the%20Ballot&st=cse.

Shannon, Brad. September 17, 2006. "This Isn't Your Usual Race for Supreme Court: Attack Ads Raise Campaign Stakes." *The Olympian* Section A.

Skolnik, Sam. September 14, 2004. "Incumbent Judges, Becker Lead in Races." *Seattle PI* seattlepi.com/default/article/Incumbent-justices-Becker-lead-in-races-1154155.php.

Tobin, Robert W. 1999. *Creating the Judicial Branch: The Unfinished Reform.* Williamsburg, VA: National Center for State Courts.

Wallace, Lisa, Christopher Hayes, Lisa McAllister, Sarah Veele-Brice, Eric Trupin, and Nancy Fairbanks. 2011. *Evidence Based Programs, Effective Practices.* Olympia: Washington State Community Justice Accountability Act Committee and Washington State Quality Assurance Committee. dshs.wa.gov/pdf/ojj/resources/EvidenceBasedPrograms&Effective Practices.pdf.

CHAPTER NINE

The Executive Branch in Washington State Government

Steven D. Stehr and Michael J. Gaffney

T HE DELIVERY OF public goods and services would not be possible without
the cadre of professional women and men who occupy positions in the
state executive branch. As of 2010, the state of Washington employed
approximately 112,000 full-time and about 35,000 part-time workers in the
various departments and agencies of state government.[1] According to a common refrain, the primary role of state government is to "educate, medicate,
and incarcerate." An examination of the distribution of Washington State
government employees by function shows that approximately 71.5 percent of
public servants work in the areas of education (with 43% of total state workers
employed in higher education), public welfare and hospitals, and corrections
and police protection, which is slightly higher than the national average for all
state governments (Council of State Governments 2010, 476).

Administrative arrangements in state governments are a reflection of the
cumulative political, social, and economic forces—national, regional, and
local—that shape the scope and functions of contemporary bureaucracy. Paint-
ing with broad strokes, the development of the executive branch in Washington
can be viewed as a product of two oftentimes contradictory forces. The first is
a long-standing ambivalence on the part of citizens regarding the proper scope
of government authority and the belief that the authority possessed by state
government should be highly constrained. These sentiments are reflected in
institutional arrangements such as the use of the long ballot to elect statewide
executive branch officials, a reliance on boards and commissions to oversee
the activities of many state agencies, the use of the initiative process to make
statewide policy, and long-running resistance to establishing a state income tax.
At the same time, Washington's social and economic development has been
closely tied to active (and typically welcomed) intervention in state affairs by
both federal and state agencies. Washington as we know it today would look
much different were it not for the influx of federal dollars made possible by

the growth of the national defense industry, the construction of the Hanford nuclear facility, the network of federally-funded dams on the Columbia and Snake rivers that provide abundant hydroelectric power, and the Columbia Basin Irrigation and Reclamation Project that made eastern Washington both habitable and economically viable. In addition, citizens of Washington have come to expect that their state and local governments will provide necessary goods and services in areas such as transportation, education, health care, fire and police protection, parks, and environmental protection, and that, collectively, state and local governmental agencies engage in many other activities that enhance the quality of life in the state.

Washington State government ranks above national averages in the provision of many publicly provided goods and services directed toward maintaining a high quality of life for its citizens. Thus, the story of the administrative state in Washington is rooted in a mixture of ambivalence toward government coupled with a heavy reliance on the services it provides. In their centennial history of the state, Robert Ficken and Charles LeWarne point out what is, for some, a rather uncomfortable truth about the relationship between Washingtonians and the public sector: "Government has always been a vital presence in Washington. Settlers and their entrepreneurial progeny might think of themselves as self-reliant and independent from public assistance, but the reality was otherwise" (Ficken and LeWarne 1988, 106).

The Great Recession that began in 2007 has once again brought to the surface questions related to the appropriate size and functions of state government. Like nearly every other state, Washington has suffered through a prolonged period of fiscal stress that has caused a series of budgetary reductions, decreases in the number of state government employees, and a systematic reexamination of the role of state government and, by extension, the scope of the state's administrative apparatus. Adding further complications is the fact that approximately 60 percent of the state budget is protected from cuts either by constitutional provisions (in the case of kindergarten through grade 12 education) or mandatory federal requirements in health programs such as Medicaid. This means that the remaining functions of state government—higher education, corrections, transportation, protection of natural resources, and basic needs-based programs—must absorb the lion's share of the budget reductions. The state Department of Personnel oversees all departments and agencies led by governor-appointed executives (for a list of these agencies, see Organizational Chart on page 174). These organizations employ roughly half of all state government personnel. Between 2008 and 2010 these agencies saw their number of employees decrease by 4.3 percent (DOP 2010).

This chapter proceeds as follows. First, we briefly discuss the historical roots of the modern administrative state in Washington. This review highlights the intersection of national and local trends and reveals some perennial thematic currents that have shaped the institutional structures of state government. Second, we examine the contemporary structure and activities of the executive branch in Washington, focusing on personnel and budgets. Third, we look at the administration in Washington from a comparative perspective focusing on how Washington compares to other states in the scope and content of government activities, evidence of trends in the provision of government services over the past two decades, and the extent that state government priorities have changed and how the executive branch has been impacted by these changes. Next, we examine various proposals germane to the executive branch (i.e., reorganizations, efforts aimed at performance enhancement) that have been brought forth to deal with budgetary shortfalls. Finally, we briefly discuss the near-term challenges facing state administrative agencies.

The Development of the Administrative State in Washington

Like many Western states, the structure of government in Washington was highly influenced by national reform movements that took place near the turn of the 20th century. Populism and Progressivism were reform movements that began in response to the corruption and inefficiencies of the powerful legislatures and political machines that dominated 19th century government administration and to the emerging social problems that accompanied a shift from a rural agrarian to an urban industrial economy (Knott and Miller 1987).

The essence of the Populist movement, which was largely a rural Western, Midwestern, and Southern phenomenon, was a deep-seated concern about America's economic, social, and political development and sought to wrestle political and economic power from the "urban oriented oligarchy" (e.g., banks, trusts, monopolies, railroads) and return it to the common people. Progressivism, on the other hand, was urban, middle class, and national in character. The Progressive movement sought to dismantle an emerging plutocracy while addressing the needs of an increasing number of poor people. As a result, reforms favored efforts directed at controlling monopolies and trusts and restoring economic competition, aiding farmers and small-business owners, protecting labor and enhancing its rewards, conserving the nation's resources and protecting the environment, and protecting consumers through governmental regulation. Lastly, Progressive political ideology favored replacing the "politics of administration" with "administrative expertise" by employing merit-based rather than patronage-based personnel systems (Francis and Thomas 1991, 39).

Territories admitted to statehood between the late 1880s and early 1900s often ratified constitutions imbued with the ideals and values of the Progressive and Populist movements. In 1889, the people of Washington voted to accept such a constitution by a ratio of almost four to one (Avery 1973). As adopted, the constitution contained administrative arrangements that attempted to institutionalize the Progressive and Populist ideals. Later, in 1912, the constitution was amended, introducing instruments of direct democracy—initiative, referendum, and recall—to increase popular control of government.

In reaction to legislatures that often abused their relative strength, coupled with the deep-seated distrust of centralized authority, institutional arrangements were adopted by the framers of Washington's constitution that fragmented government authority and moved important policy decision making areas under the purview of independent expert boards and/or commissions (Cox 1991). In fact, distrust of concentrating authority ran so high that the framers of Washington State's constitution protected seven executive branch officers from executive control with the shield of the ballot box—the Superintendent of Public Instruction, Commissioner of Public Lands, Auditor, Attorney General, Secretary of State, Treasurer, and Lieutenant Governor. Later, in 1907, an eighth elected executive officer position, Insurance Commissioner, was created by legislative statute.

The fragmentation of government authority has also been achieved through institutional arrangements within the administrative state that ultimately shape the power bases and agendas of Washington's bureaucracies. As is the case with the federal government, most Washington executive branch functions are carried out by administrative departments, agencies, boards, and commissions, a structure that restricts the amount of formal power the governor is able to exercise over the state bureaucracy. This arrangement of authority limits the governor's influence for two reasons. First, many non-elected officials are under the formal authority and control of elected executive officials other than the governor. Secondly, many bureaucratic entities are under the control of boards, commissions, and councils that act independently of the governor and over which the governor possesses only appointive powers. As a demonstration of this point, in fiscal year 2010 there were roughly 122,000 full time employees working for the state of Washington. Approximately 50 percent of those state employees worked in agencies or organizations that did not report directly to the governor (DOP 2010).

An example of the fragmentation of authority in the state executive branch is the peculiar administrative arrangements of the Department of Natural Resources. The DNR was first authorized by the legislature in 1957 to bring together seven existing boards and agencies and is managed by the independently elected Commissioner of Public Lands. Today, the commissioner manages the Department of Natural Resources and also serves on the six-member Board of Natural Resources, which consists of the governor, Superintendent of Public Instruction, a county commissioner from a county with Forest Board trust land, dean of the University of Washington College of Forest Resources, and dean of the Washington State University College of Agricultural, Human, and Natural Resource Sciences. The members of the eight remaining boards, councils, and committees within the Department of Natural Resources are similarly selected (some are appointed by the governor, others serve as designees for agency heads or are citizens appointed by the commissioner). Bureaucratic influence by the governor within the DNR is circumscribed as a result of the authority of these boards, committees, and councils that often have divergent values, incentives, and distinct power bases.

The shape and form of the modern administrative branch did not develop solely due to factors peculiar to the state. The federal government became an important factor in the delivery of public goods and services in Washington during World War I as military installations were erected and the modern military-industrial complex (which greatly benefited industries in the state) was born. This federal presence would grow dramatically during the era of Franklin D. Roosevelt and the New Deal. Between 1933 and 1939, Washington ranked first among all states in per capita federal spending (Reading 1973). The construction of the Grand Coulee and other dams, the Columbia Basin Irrigation Project, the creation of the Bonneville Power Authority, the establishment of numerous national parks, and hundreds of other projects under the WPA and other New Deal programs cemented the close relationship between state and federal administration. The state was a large contributor to and beneficiary of World War II, the Korean conflict, and the Cold War. For example, the availability of cheap hydroelectric power (made possible by the network of federally-funded dams) allowed for the development of power-dependent aluminum production plants that were needed to provide materials for the production of airplanes at Boeing and ships in Bremerton. The Manhattan Project was responsible for the creation of a nuclear weapon production facility in Richland; Cold War fears of a confrontation with the Soviet Union made the Hanford nuclear warhead production plant important well into the 1980s. As in other states, the Great Society Programs of the Johnson administration greatly increased the responsibilities of state government in Washington, as did the shift toward decentralizing the responsibility for program management through various "new federalism" initiatives (Denhardt 1993). The champions of decentralization expected increased state and local control over the design and implementation of federally funded programs, and an increase in the institutional capacity of states to assume these responsibilities (Weber and Brace 1999). Thus, state governments became increasingly responsible for funding government initiatives and for increasing their respective capacities to administer both state and federally funded programs (Barrilleaux 1999).

As the data displayed in Table 1 show, for most of the last 40 years Washington has depended upon the federal government for 20 to 25 percent of its total revenues. This is significant as it demonstrates the extent to which the delivery of public services in Washington has been linked to national economic and political trends. It also speaks to the benefits flowing from considerable influence exercised by the state's congressional delegation during this time period, in

Table 1

Total State Revenues and Percentage of Revenue from Federal Sources,
Fiscal Biennium 1963–65 to 2007–09

Fiscal Biennium	Total Revenue ($ in Millions)	Percent from Federal Sources
1963–65	$1,818	21.0%
1965–67	2,305	21.5
1967–69	2,998	20.2
1969–71	3,663	22.0
1971–73	4,392	25.6
1973–75	5,137	24.7
1975–77	6,730	24.4
1977–79	8,321	23.1
1979–81	10,319	25.7
1981–83	12,805	20.6
1983–85	18,710	16.2
1985–87	17,865	19.7
1987–89	21,763	19.2
1989–91	25,200	21.1
1991–93	28,758	23.6
1993–95	35,887	22.0
1995–97	38,705	21.3
1997–99	43,598	20.5
1999–01	47,312	22.5
2001–03	49,472	19.7
2003–05	53,463	20.2
2005–07	60,517	18.3
2007–09	68,493	19.4

Source: OFM 1995; OFM 2001; author's calculations from OFM 2010, 30, Table GT02.

particular Senators Warren Magnuson and Henry "Scoop" Jackson, and Speaker of the House Tom Foley.

During the late 1970s and early 1980s, the political legacy of the Progressive and Populist eras resurfaced and converged with growing conservatism to incite a taxpayer revolt that led to attempts to limit government revenues and expenditures (Schwantes 1996, 475). The "taxpayer revolt," in conjunction with the national social and political forces that led to a significant devolution of responsibility for program implementation to state governments, set the foundation upon which Washington's administrative state now operates. Indeed, the current environment is characterized by the now familiar dichotomy of citizenry calls for increased government services while circumscribing state and local government's abilities to generate revenues to fund such services. To address these challenges, the state searched for alternative sources of revenue (for example, the State Lottery was established in 1982) while administrative agencies attempted to satisfy the demands of an increasingly larger and more diverse population. The economic boom of the mid-to-late 1990s (and the tax revenues that resulted) enabled state agencies to provide necessary services despite the growth in key demographic groups such as the K-12 and college-age populations and the elderly, dramatic increases in the size of the prison population, and other factors that drive government spending. However, beginning in 2000 (and again in 2007) economic downturns forced policy makers to make difficult choices regarding the scope and level of government services.

The Contemporary Executive Branch

State administrators are responsible for carrying out a wide range of public functions.[3] They are responsible for maintaining a network of over 8,000 miles of highways and roads and a ferry system (the largest of any state) that carries about 20 million passengers annually. They monitor and partially finance the education of over 1 million grade and high school students and are directly responsible for the education of over 300,000 students in colleges and universities. State agencies also oversee the care and rehabilitation of more than 18,000 prison inmates, manage income assistance for about 60,000 individuals, and provide state-subsidized childcare to over 64,000 children under the age of 12. The state is responsible for managing the natural resources, parks, fish and wildlife, public lands, clean air and water programs, and the use of its over 2,300 miles of shoreline. The state also regulates a wide variety of economic enterprises. Public administrators set rates for telephone and electric service, enforce health and safety standards for businesses, and license many occupations and professions.

Depending on how they are counted, there are approximately 100 statutory departments and agencies charged with interpreting and implementing policies and programs in Washington (see Organization Chart). Twenty-one are cabinet agencies headed by executives who serve at the pleasure of the governor. These include major departmental units such as ecology, agriculture, social and health services, labor and industries, employment security, and corrections. Another dozen or so agencies serve under separately elected statewide office holders, including the Superintendent of Public Instruction. Approximately 50 agencies are under the authority of a board (see Organizational Chart) and an additional 450 or so commissions and committees are charged with responsibilities in a wide variety of specialized areas. At least three dozen boards license and monitor the conduct of individual professions and occupations. There are commissions to regulate boxing, gambling (and a separate one for horse racing), and to over-

2011 Organization Chart
Washington State Government

Legislative Branch

Senate

House of Representatives

Joint Legislative Audit and Review Committee
Joint Legislative Systems Committee
Joint Transportation Committee
Legislative Ethics Board

Legislative Evaluation and Accountability Program Committee
Office of the State Actuary
Redistricting Commission *(activated decennially)*
Statute Law Committee *(Code Reviser)*

Executive Branch

Agencies Managed by Statewide Elected Officials

Commissioner of Public Lands	Insurance Commissioner	Treasurer	Lieutenant Governor	Governor	Attorney General	Superintendent of Public Instruction	Auditor	Secretary of State

| | | | | Office of the Governor | | | | |

Department of Natural Resources
Forest Practices Board

Public Deposit Protection Commission
State Finance Committee

Executive Ethics Board

Board of Education
Professional Educator Standards Board

Productivity Board
State Library

Governor's Office of Indian Affairs
Office of the Family and Children's Ombudsman

Office of the Education Ombudsman

Agencies Led by Governor-Appointed Executives

Environment and Natural Resources

Dept. of Agriculture *(commodity commissions)*
Dept. of Ecology
Pollution Liability Insurance Program
Puget Sound Partnership
Recreation and Conservation Office
 - *Salmon Recovery Funding Board*

General Government

Board of Accountancy
Office of Administrative Hearings
Dept. of Archaeology and Historic Preservation
Dept. of Financial Institutions
Office of Financial Management
Dept. of General Administration
 - *Building Code Council*
Dept. of Information Systems
 - *Integrated Justice Information Board*
Lottery Commission
Military Department
Dept. of Personnel
 - *Personnel Resources Board*
Public Printer
Dept. of Retirement Systems
Dept. of Revenue

Transportation

Dept. of Licensing *(occupational regulatory boards)*
State Patrol
Traffic Safety Commission
Dept. of Transportation

Health and Human Services

Dept. of Corrections
Dept. of Employment Security
Dept. of Health *(occupational regulatory boards)*
Health Care Authority
 - *Public Employees Benefits Board*
Dept. of Labor and Industries
Council for Children and Families
Dept. of Services for the Blind
Dept. of Social and Health Services
Dept. of Veterans Affairs

Education

Center for Childhood Deafness and Hearing Loss
 - *Board of Trustees*
Dept. of Early Learning
School for the Blind
Workforce Training and Education Coordinating Board

Community and Economic Development

Commission on African-American Affairs
Arts Commission
Commission on Asian Pacific American Affairs
Dept. of Commerce
 - *Economic Development Commission*
 - *Energy Facility Site Evaluation Council*
 - *Public Works Board*
Commission on Hispanic Affairs
Office of Minority and Women's Business Enterprises

Judicial Branch

Supreme Court

Administrative Office of the Courts
Office of Civil Legal Aid
Court of Appeals
Commission on Judicial Conduct
District Courts

Law Library
Municipal Courts
Office of Public Defense
Superior Courts
Supreme Court

Agencies Under Authority of a Board

Columbia River Gorge Commission
Conservation Commission
Environmental Hearings Office
- *Pollution Control Hearings Board*
- *Shorelines Hearings Board*

Fish and Wildlife Commission
Growth Management Hearings Board
Board of Natural Resources
Parks and Recreation Commission
Washington Materials Management and Financing Authority

Caseload Forecast Council
Citizens' Commission on Salaries for Elected Officials
Economic and Revenue Forecast Council
Gambling Commission
Horse Racing Commission
Investment Board
Law Enforcement Officers' and Fire Fighters' Plan 2 Retirement System Board
Liquor Control Board
Pension Funding Council
Public Disclosure Commission
Public Employment Relations Commission
Board of Tax Appeals
Utilities and Transportation Commission
Board for Volunteer Firefighters and Reserve Officers

County Road Administration Board
Freight Mobility Strategic Investment Board
Marine Employees' Commission
Board of Pilotage Commissioners
Transportation Improvement Board
Transportation Commission

Criminal Justice Training Commission
Board of Health
Health Care Facilities Authority
Human Rights Commission
Indeterminate Sentence Review Board
Board of Industrial Insurance Appeals
Sentencing Guidelines Commission
Tobacco Settlement Authority

State Board for Community and Technical Colleges
Eastern Washington State Historical Society
Governing Boards of Four-Year Institutions of Higher Education
- *University of Washington*
- *Washington State University*
- *Central Washington University*
- *Eastern Washington University*
- *Western Washington University*
- *The Evergreen State College*

Higher Education Coordinating Board
Higher Education Facilities Authority
Spokane Intercollegiate Research and Technology Institute
Boards of Trustees
- *Community Colleges*
- *Technical Colleges*

Washington State Historical Society

Convention and Trade Center
Economic Development Finance Authority
Housing Finance Commission
Life Sciences Discovery Fund Authority

PREPARED BY THE
OFFICE OF FINANCIAL
MANAGEMENT
APRIL 2011

see the state's sale and distribution of liquor and lottery tickets. The governor appoints all or some of the members of three-fourths of the commissions to overlapping terms. However, once in office, gubernatorial control is typically quite limited over these commissioners as program clients and interest groups take an active interest in their ongoing decision making.

Two major indices of the size and scope of state administration are its personnel and budgets. More than 112,000 people are currently employed full time by the state of Washington (see Table 2). This represents a doubling of the workforce since the mid-1970s and an increase of about 15 percent over the last decade. When the number of employees is adjusted to reflect changes in state population over time, this growth appears more moderate. In 2009, there were 16.9 executive branch employees for every 1,000 persons in the state population (see Table 2), a ratio that has changed relatively little since the late 1980s. For comparison purposes, the average state employed approximately 15 people per 1,000 in population in the mid-1990s (Barrilleaux 1999).

About three-fourths of all state employees work in the fields of human services (broadly defined) or higher education. Approximately 43 percent of state employees currently work for universities, colleges, or community colleges, and another 17 percent work in the Department of Social and Health Services. An additional 14 percent work in various "human services" agencies such as the Department of Labor and Industries, the Department of Corrections, and the Department of Employment Security (see Table 3). Nearly all of the remaining employees work in the areas of transportation (10.1%), natural resources (5.8%), and governmental operations (7.5%). Taking a longer-term view, there has been remarkably little change in the distribution of employees by functional area in the state since the mid-1970s (transportation is a notable exception). The distribution of employees by category in 1975 was as follows: 42 percent education; 30 percent human resources; 14 percent transportation; 8 percent government operations; and 6 percent natural resources (Mullen and Swanson 1985). The largest individual units of state government measured by number of employees in 2010 (excluding colleges and universities) were the Department of Social and Health Services (18,182), the Department of Corrections (8,693), and the Department of Transportation (7,713). Excluding colleges and universities, these three departments account for 54 percent of state employees. The other units in the top ten in terms of number of employees are: Department of Labor and Industry (2,722), Department of Employment Security (2,650), State Patrol (2,288), Department of Health (1,772), Department of Fish and Wildlife (1,760), Department of Natural Resources (1,684), and Department of Ecology (1,609) (see DOP 2010).

The expansion of the activities of state government is graphically illustrated by the increase in state expenditures over time. Over the last four decades, total expenditures of the state executive branch increased by nearly 25 times

Table 2

Full-Time Equivalent Executive Branch State Employees
per 1,000 Population, 1984 to 2009

State Fiscal Year	FTE Executive Branch Branch Employees	Population	FTE Executive State Fiscal Employees per 1,000
1984	64,393.7	4,354,067	14.8
1985	68,837.0	4,415,785	15.6
1986	69,086.3	4,462,212	15.5
1987	70,910.7	4,527,098	15.7
1988	72,819.9	4,616,886	15.8
1989	75,717.6	4,728,077	16.0
1990	78,968.3	4,866,669	16.2
1991	83,103.4	5,021,335	16.6
1992	86,291.3	5,141,177	16.8
1993	88,793.1	5,265,688	16.9
1994	88,344.6	5,364,338	16.5
1995	90,591.9	5,470,104	16.6
1996	90,585.8	5,567,764	16.3
1997	92,375.9	5,663,763	16.3
1998	93,746.4	5,750,033	16.3
1999	96,564.1	5,830,835	16.6
2000	98,560.8	5,894,121	16.7
2001	100,618.8	5,974,900	16.8
2002	102,402.8	6,041,700	16.9
2003	104,262.7	6,098,300	17.1
2004	105,077.5	6,167,800	17.0
2005	106,768.5	6,256,400	17.1
2006	106,641.0	6,375,600	16.7
2007	108,692.5	6,488,000	16.8
2008	111,419.5	6,587,600	16.9
2009	112,545.0	6,668,200	16.9

Source: OFM 2010, 45, Table GT16.

(see Table 4). State budget expenditures for the 2007–2009 biennium were approximately $68.5 billion, more than double the budget of 15 years earlier. One commonly used method to examine state budget spending over time is to express expenditures as a percent of total personal income. As the last column in Table 4 shows, state spending over the past ten years has been relatively stable using this index. This stability is largely the result of increasing personal income,

Table 3

Percentage of State Employees by Function, Selected Fiscal Years 1989–2009

	1989–91	1995–97	2001–03	2007–09
Governmental Operations[1]	7.8%	7.4%	7.1%	7.5%
Human Services[2]	12.8	14.2	14.5	14.3
Social and Health Services	19.3	18.2	17.2	16.8
Natural Resources[3]	7.1	6.5	6.1	5.8
Transportation[4]	11.1	10.6	10.1	10.1
Higher Education	39.4	41.0	43.0	43.4
Other	2.6	2.1	2.0	2.1
Total	100.0%	100.0%	100.0%	100.0%

[1] Includes Department of Revenue, Department of Personnel, Attorney General, State Auditor, Office of the Governor, and Liquor Control Board.
[2] Includes Departments of Labor and Industries, Corrections, and Employment Security.
[3] Includes the Departments of Natural Resources, Ecology, Fish and Wildlife, and Agriculture.
[4] Includes Department of Transportation, Department of Licensing, and State Patrol.

Source: OFM 2011b and OFM 2002.

which went up approximately 70 percent between 1999 and 2009, keeping with increases in state spending.

As previously noted, the majority of state administrative spending is done in the areas of education and social and human services. Nearly 41 percent of the 2007–2009 budget was devoted to education (this figure includes higher education spending and relatively small amounts transferred to elementary and secondary schools); another 36 percent of the budget was expended through the Department of Social and Health Services (DSHS) and human services agencies such as the Department of Corrections (see Table 5). A decade earlier these three broad functional areas accounted for nearly the same percentage of total state expenditures. Of course, the total amount of state spending has increased. For example, between 1999–2001 and 2007–2009 the DSHS budget increased by a little more than 50 percent. This budgetary growth has been fueled by increased spending on medical assistance payments, developmental disabilities programs, and long-term care services. It is apparent that from the early 1990s until the early 2000s a combination of increasing demands for social and health services, a growing prison population, and federal reforms that placed more responsibility on state governments for implementing social welfare programs led to a definite shift in level of state spending (see columns one and three in Table 5). The fiscal stresses brought on by the declining economy beginning in 2007 have frozen these earlier distributions more or less in place.

The federal role in the changing distribution of state-delivered goods and services should not be overlooked. As Barrilleaux points out, developments in

Table 4

State Budgeted Expenditures as a Percent of Total Personal Income
($ in Billions)

Biennium	Total Personal Income	Total Expenditures	Expenditures as a Percent of Total Personal Income
1963–65	$16.279	$1.796	11.0%
1965–67	19.786	2.147	10.9
1967–69	24.296	2.831	11.7
1969–71	28.536	3.841	13.5
1971–73	32.510	4.305	13.2
1973–75	41.315	4.986	12.1
1975–77	51.941	6.433	12.4
1977–79	67.889	8.028	11.8
1979–81	89.255	10.858	12.2
1981–83	104.537	12.388	11.9
1983–85	121.595	15.463	12.7
1985–87	140.200	17.928	12.8
1987–89	164.100	19.789	12.1
1989–91	197.500	24.691	12.5
1991–93	226.000	29.432	13.0
1993–95	250.100	32.854	13.1
1995–97	284.400	36.001	12.7
1997–99	332.000	39.394	11.9
1999–01	378.700	44.548	11.8
2001–03	397.500	49.472	12.4
2003–05	437.600	53.463	12.2
2005–07	501.900	60.517	12.1
2007–09	549.500	68.493	12.5

Sources: OFM 1995; OFM 2001; OFM 2010, 46, Table GT17.

state administrative arrangements are often closely linked to changes in federal policy initiatives. For example, during the 1970s and later in the mid-1990s, the federal government provided incentives to build state social service capacity, and during the 1980s and 1990s to build and staff correctional facilities (Barrilleaux 1999). In both cases, the states—including Washington—responded as expected.

Given the foregoing discussion, a listing of the units of state government that had the largest budgets in fiscal years 2007–2009 should come as no surprise (OFM 2010):

- DSHS: $19.397 billion
- University of Washington and Washington State University: $6.590 billion

- Community/Technical College System: $2.420 billion
- Department of Transportation: $1.473 billion;
- State Regional Universities: $0.980 billion

These units combined accounted for just over 45 percent of state spending during the 2007–2009 biennium.

Table 5

Percent of State Operating and Capital Expenditures by Function,
Selected Fiscal Years, 1989–2009
($ in millions)

	1989–91	1995–97	1999–01	2007–09
Governmental Operations[1]	6.6%	6.7%	6.7%	6.4%
Human Services[2]	5.6	7.1	7.6	7.6
Social and Health Services	23.6	27.5	29.1	28.4
Natural Resources[3]	4.6	3.2	3.2	3.3
Transportation[4]	9.1	9.1	7.3	8.6
Total Education	42.3	41.6	40.7	40.9
Other	8.2	4.8	5.4	4.8
Total	100.0%	100.0%	100.0%	100.0%
Total Expenditures	$24,691	$36,010	$44,548	$68,493

[1] Includes Department of Revenue, Department of Personnel, Attorney General, State Auditor, Office of the Governor, and Liquor Control Board.
[2] Includes Departments of Labor and Industries, Corrections, and Employment Security.
[3] Includes the Departments of Natural Resources, Ecology, Fish and Wildlife, and Agriculture.
[4] Includes Department of Transportation, Department of Licensing, and State Patrol.

Source: OFM 2010, 35, Table GT06.

Washington's Executive Branch in Comparative Perspective

Despite their ambivalence toward government, citizens in Washington are provided with relatively high levels of public services when compared to national averages. Indeed, Washington is a leader among the states in providing a variety of goods and services.[3] As the data set forth in Table 6 show, state government in Washington expended $5,741 per capita in 2007, which ranked 20th among all states. It is significant to note that in 2001 state expenditures per capita in Washington were ranked 5th among all states (Washington Research Council 2001). At various points in time during the period from 2004–2008, Washington ranked in the top 20 among the states in expenditures per capita in the following functional categories: environmental programs (ranked 6), health and hospitals (6), corrections (12), and higher education (17). Among the major expenditure categories where Washington ranked in the bottom half of the states when measured by per capita spending was public welfare programs.

Table 6

State Expenditures on Selected Functions per Capita and Rank
of Washington Compared to All States, Selected Years

	Washington per Capita Spending	Washington Rank	All States
Total State Expenditures (2007)[1]	$5,741	20	$5,434
Environmental Programs (2004)[2]	382	6	270
Health and Hospitals (2004)[2]	766	6	544
Corrections (2008)[3]	264	12	245
Higher Education (2008)[3]	848	17	678
Highways (2004)[2]	428	24	402
Public Welfare Programs (2007)[1]	1,098	33	1,275

[1] Morgan and O'Leary Morgan 2010.
[2] Governing Magazine 2006.
[3] OFM 2011.

These higher than average expenditures are partly explained by social and demographic changes (e.g., increases in school-age children), and by political decisions (e.g., implementation of mandatory sentencing laws), which have forced state agencies to provide higher levels of goods and services. Some of the key factors driving the higher levels of service provision in Washington compared to other states over the past decade include:

- Larger enrollments in institutions of higher education. Between 2001 and 2008, enrollments in Washington's colleges and universities increased by 16 percent. Per capita spending (adjusted to year 2008 dollars) on higher education increased from $564 to $899 during this period (OFM 2011).
- Increasing numbers of people receiving state social services. For example, between 2001 and 2010 the number of monthly average caseloads for food assistance programs increased by 68 percent, medical assistance caseloads increased by 23 percent, and caseloads for the Temporary Assistance for Needy Family program increased by 15 percent (OFM 2011). It should be noted that a large portion of these increases took place in the last five years as the economic downturn took hold.
- Increasing numbers of prison inmates. The number of people incarcerated in Washington increased by nearly 20 percent between 2001 and 2010. Correctional expenditures per capita increased from $216 to $264 (adjusted to 2008 dollars) between 2001 and 2008 (OFM 2011).

These particular cost trends are forecasted to continue. According to the Office of Financial Management, those populations that receive a high proportion of state government services are projected to continue to grow over the next five to ten years. For example, they forecast that the numbers of those seeking state-assisted long-term care will increase by over 10 percent and demand for higher education is projected to increase by over 8 percent during this time period (OFM 2011).

Executive Branch Responses to the Budget Crisis

The state of Washington has been hit at least as hard as the rest of the nation by the budget impacts attendant with the current recession. In some respects the impacts have been even more significant in Washington because of the existing state tax structure and a recent history of citizen and legislative resistance to any efforts to enhance revenue collection at the state level. This combination of tax aversion and economic decline, when coupled with the constitutional requirement of a balanced state biennial budget, has required the application of both draconian responses and innovation to manage the impact on the executive branch.

The reliance solely on budget cutting efforts to respond to budget short-falls and achieve balanced budgets is the end result of a lengthy progression of limitations on the power to tax. Beginning in 1999 with Initiative 695, a series of "tax revolt" initiatives that significantly limit the ability of the state to collect taxes have been proposed. Although not all have been successful, and some have been struck down by the courts or have been superseded by subsequent legislation, several have been passed and sustained. The cumulative effect of these revenue limitations has coincided with the national growth in anti-tax politics to effectively remove increased taxes as a policy option for state government.

In this general fiscal climate, the executive branch has responded to a series of budget shortfalls with a combination of structural reforms, cuts in agencies and personnel, and an increased emphasis on performance and efficiency. The Government Management Accountability and Performance (GMAP) process—an effort to improve agency efficiency and responsiveness by requiring deliberate monitoring and operational transparency— was adopted in 2008 in Washington. This award-winning program produces an annual report to citizens. These reports, and more information on Washington reform efforts focused on efficiency and effectiveness, can be found at accountability.wa.gov. Despite improvements in efficiency and effectiveness, however, Washington has also had to make cuts and more substantial structural adjustments to the executive branch as the economic constraints on government have been exacerbated by the continued economic slump.

Beginning in 2009, reform efforts by the governor and the legislature systematically reduced the number of independent boards and commissions by about one third, eliminating such diverse bodies as the Board for Law Enforcement Training, Board for Standards and Education, and the Midwifery Advisory

Committee. Nearly a score of these eliminations occurred through executive order, but the balance were the result of legislative action. The long-term impact of this reduction on agency autonomy remains to be seen. During the same time frame, the Department of Community Trade and Economic Development (CTED) was transformed into a new Department of Commerce; some 25 functions that had been under the purview of CTED simultaneously devolved to other agencies. Efforts were also begun to reform healthcare and the state pension system, and to create a "shared service" model whereby smaller agencies could share public service capacity to enhance "one stop shopping" for some state services (Executive Directive 09-25). Coupled with the search for efficiencies and structural reforms have been a series of more straightforward budget cuts as well. Over the past two biennia the revenue shortfalls have been significant enough (more than $2.8 billion in 2010, for example) that most agencies have seen their operating budgets cut—some substantially. Among the cost-cutting strategies adopted at the state level has been the mandatory furlough of many state employees (14 days off without pay over as many months). As this chapter is being finalized, more cuts are being implemented, and discussions continue about additional ways that state government might be reduced, restructured, or reformed to allow the continuation of needed services and the provision of public goods in the face of further reductions in funding. Whether the various efforts to continue essential services with reduced budgets will be successful is not yet known.

Conclusion

The agencies of Washington State government face enormous challenges in the near to intermediate term. Like the early portions of the decades of the 1980s and the 2000s, declines in economic growth in the latter stages of the 2000s have prompted new rounds of severe budget cuts in state government. In addition, citizen-supported initiatives passed in the 1990s make it difficult for state officials to raise taxes or find new sources of revenue. This occurs at a time when demands for essential government services such as education, transportation, social services, and public safety continue to grow. Indeed, state and local governments are expected to take on increasing responsibilities in the areas of medical care, income security, and homeland security. The federal government, facing its own challenges, may be unable to provide the same budgetary support for state programs as it has in the past. These new challenges will likely prompt an ongoing reexamination of the size, scope, and content of state government programs. What further changes will occur in the state's executive branch as a consequence remains to be seen.

Endnotes

1. These state government employees are supplemented by an additional 227,000 local government employees working for city and county governments, and for school and special districts.
2. The data reported in this paragraph can be found in "Washington Trends: Budget Drivers" at ofm.wa.gov/trends. These data are updated regularly.
3. The comparative data discussed in this section must, by necessity, be reported for selected years using several source materials. In earlier years, the Washington Research Council produced a document named *How Washington Compares*. This document is no longer published.

References

Avery, Mary Williamson. 1973. *Government of Washington State*. 6th ed. Seattle: University of Washington Press.

Barrilleaux, Charles. 1999. "Statehouse Bureaucracy: Institutional Consistency in a Changing Environment." In *American State and Local Politics: Directions for the 21st Century*, edited by Ronald E. Weber and Paul R. Brace. New York: Chatham House Publishers, Seven Bridges Press.

Council of State Governments. 2010. *The Book of the States, 2010*. Lexington, KY: Council of State Governments.

Cox, Raymond W., III. 1991. "Gubernatorial Politics." In *Politics and Public Policy in the Contemporary American West*, edited by Clive S. Thomas. Albuquerque: University of New Mexico Press.

Denhardt, Robert B. 1993. *Theories of Public Organization*. 2nd ed. Belmont, CA: Wadsworth.

DOP (Department of Personnel). 2010. *2010 Washington State Workforce Report*. Olympia: Washington Department of Personnel.

Executive Directive 09-25, Washington State, December 2, 2009. governor.wa.gov/directives/dir_09-25.pdf.

Ficken, Robert E., and Charles P. LeWarne. 1988. *Washington: A Centennial History*. Seattle: University of Washington Press.

Francis, John G., and Clive S. Thomas. 1991. "Influences on Western Political Culture." In *Politics and Public Policy in the Contemporary American West*, edited by Clive S. Thomas. Albuquerque: University of New Mexico Press.

Governing Magazine. 2006. *State and Local Sourcebook, 2006*. Washington, D.C.: Congressional Quarterly Press.

Knott, Jack H., and Gary J. Miller. 1987. *Reforming Bureaucracy: The Politics of Institutional Choice*. Englewood Cliffs, NJ: Prentice Hall.

Morgan, Scott, and Kathleen O'Leary Morgan. 2010. *State Rankings 2010: A Statistical View of America*. Washington, D.C.: Congressional Quarterly Press.

Mullen, William, and Swanson, Thor. 1985. "The Executives and Administration." In *Political Life in Washington: Governing the Evergreen State*, edited by Thor Swanson, William F. Mullen, John C. Pierce, and Charles H. Sheldon, 55–94. Pullman: Washington State University Press.

OFM (Office of Financial Management). 2010. "Washington State Data Book." ofm.wa.gov/databook.

———. 2011. "Washington Trends." ofm.wa.gov/trends.

Reading, Don C. 1973. "New Deal Activity and the States, 1933 to 1939." *Journal of Economic History* 33(4): 792–810.

Schwantes, Carlos A. 1996. *The Pacific Northwest: An Interpretive History*. Lincoln: University of Nebraska Press.

Washington Research Council. 2001. *How Washington Compares 2001*. Seattle: Washington Research Council.

Weber, Ronald E., and Paul Brace. 1999. "States and Localities Transformed." In *American State and Local Politics: Directions for the 21st Century*, edited by Ronald E. Weber and Paul Brace. New York: Chatham House.

CHAPTER TEN

The Governor and Other Statewide Officials

David Nice and Jacob Day

G OVERNORS OCCUPY an important and highly visible position in state politics and their efforts in policy development may have far reaching impact on citizens of their state. This prominence often projects governors into higher office, as many go on to become members of Congress, judges, and presidents. With higher goals frequently in mind, governors must skillfully attend to the needs of their state while also preparing for a future national presence.

This chapter will examine the numerous aspects of the Washington State governor's office that require the governor to take on various roles and responsibilities. After discussing the historical evolution of the office, we then explore the challenges facing the governor and the multiple roles that the office includes. The third section will explore the trajectory of Washington State governors and explore how the experience they bring to the job contributes to their performance and affects their political future after gubernatorial service. Finally, this chapter will provide a brief overview of the other eight executive branch officials who are elected statewide in Washington and discuss their job descriptions, duties, and interactions with the governor.[1]

Evolution of the Office of Governor

Washington State has had its own governmental structures since the 1853 separation from the Oregon Territory, long before its 1889 admission to the Union. Isaac I. Stevens, the first territorial governor, is known for his settlements of Native American land claims and his efforts to boost economic development in the young territory. Stevens and the territorial governors that succeeded him were presidential appointees and were thus influenced in the kind of leadership they practiced and the policies they pursued. Mostly serving short terms, they were often seen as political operatives for the president who appointed them.

This image of political dependency often undermined their credibility and raised doubts about their legitimacy with residents of the territory (Nice and Otte 2004).

Governors in Washington gained more autonomy after the state was admitted to the Union in 1889. No longer appointed by the president, Washington governors were usually allowed to pursue their own policy agendas without interference from federal actors. The Progressive reform movements of the late-19th and early-20th century led to new demands for accountability in politics at the state, local, and national levels; those demands led to efforts to strengthen the once weak executive branch. Consequently, Washington's governors asserted greater leadership and began taking on a larger role in state politics. This increased influence was partly based on the governor's new powers to call extra legislative sessions, propose and veto legislation, and shape the state's agenda by helping to create the budget (Nice and Otte 2004).

The Washington State constitution, ratified in 1889, illustrates the Progressive era concern for accountability. Like other state constitutions and the U.S. Constitution, it emphasizes the separation of powers and the checks and balances that are needed to prevent one branch of government from becoming too strong. The direct primary for nominating many candidates and the power of initiative, referendum, and recall all reflect Progressive thinking. The executive, legislative, and judicial branches all share overlapping responsibilities but are also able to exercise power to prevent one branch from intruding on another's duties. The early days of Washington State politics were also characterized by part-time citizen-legislators who received meager compensation for their service, a practice that continues today in many states (Nice and Otte 2004).

A period of state corruption and misappropriation of funds led to less faith in state government in the period of cooperative federalism, with its greater use of federal aid to state and local governments and state aid to local governments. State governments often were not trusted and governors were constrained as federal programs funneled funds directly to local governments and required most grants to be spent for narrowly defined purposes, bypassing state governments and hindering governors' abilities to achieve policy objectives. In response, state legislatures and governors began efforts to restore trust in their offices and reduce corruption and pork in state politics (Nice and Otte 2004). The 1950s featured reform in funds allocations by creating formulas for the distribution of government spending programs rather than relying on promises made to legislators in exchange for their support for gubernatorial proposals. Also, the capital budget began going through a more careful prioritization process prior to being submitted to the legislature. That prioritization process included extensive reviews of individual projects in order to assess how urgently they were needed and the probable benefits and costs of each project.

Throughout much of the post-war period, divided government, in which neither political party controls both the executive and legislative branch, has been the norm in Washington. Democrat Christine Gregoire has had the luxury of serving under unified partisan control of government since first being elected in 2005, but many of her predecessors did not. Divided government can cause difficulties in passing legislation as more careful deliberation and negotiation is required to reach agreement among the two parties. In some cases, agreement cannot be reached, and deadlocks result. In order to protect their preferences during such periods, governors may have to resort more often to the line-item veto power, in which a governor can delete selected language from a bill that significantly affects the bill's meaning. This practice led to a 1974 constitutional amendment that allows the governor to delete individual spending items, but limits the governor's ability to veto substantive language to whole sections of legislation unless a section contains multiple spending items (Council of State Governments 2011).

Even as the governor's office has become increasingly professionalized, it faces a public that is often skeptical of its political leaders. Still, the Washington governor's office is afforded greater respect and compensation than in many other states. For example, in 2010, Washington's governor received an annual salary of $166,891, among the highest of all U.S. governors. In comparison, Oregon's governor received $93,600 and Idaho's earned $115,348. The highest paid governor was in New York with an annual salary of $179,000 and the lowest paid governor was that of Maine at $70,000. Additional perks to the Washington governor's office include a personal staff of 36 individuals, access to state automobile and airplane transportation, and the official residence of the Governor's Mansion at the state capitol campus in Olympia. The Washington State Patrol also offers protection for the governor statewide (Council of State Governments 2011; Washington Governor's Mansion Foundation 2011).

Governors in the modern era must serve as the representative of their state regionally, nationally, and globally. They are among the chief advocates for their state's interests and must use their office as a platform for promoting those needs. The creation of the National Governor's Association and its increasing clout illustrate the growing power of governors on the national political scene. In addition to state representatives and senators in Congress, governors now more than ever are lobbying the federal government and mobilizing with other governors to further their interests both collectively and individually.

The Roles of the Governor

The duties of a state governor are complex and multifaceted. The governor must serve a variety of roles, not only as the head of state for all citizens but also as a party leader, legislative leader, and chief executive. Frequently these roles conflict and successfully performing all of them is an arduous task fraught with complications and conflicts of interest that only the most politically savvy governor can successfully execute.

Political Leader and Party Leader

Perhaps the most vital role to a governor's success is that of a politician. Without first gaining office through a carefully crafted campaign and successful election, a candidate will not have a mandate to govern. The Washington governor's office is one of only 12 in the country that does not impose term limits. Washington governors may serve unlimited four-year terms. This breadth and flexibility may impact their behavior, but governors in Washington are still subject to close public scrutiny and must usually endure tight races with very narrow margins of victory.

One major challenge that governors face in Washington is the geopolitical divide. The Cascade Mountain Range represents not only a formidable geological blockade but also a cultural, economic, and political dividing line in the state. The western side of the state features large metropolitan areas such as Seattle and Tacoma that depend on economies driven by industry and business. To the east are smaller, rural populations that rely on agriculture. This distinction is reflected in the political preferences of each side's inhabitants. In recent years the west side has tended to vote Democratic while the east has voted Republican (Nice and Otte 2004).

Governors may face a number of difficulties in trying to be party leaders. Other major officials in the same party may have different political values, and some of them may want to be governor. Some Americans strongly identify with a political party and are hostile to other parties. Many people believe that the parties cause more problems than they solve. Many party leaders and elected officials are chosen locally or by state legislative district; the political climate in some communities may lead some of the governor's fellow partisans to distance themselves from the governor and his or her proposals. Successful party leadership, however, can make passage of legislative proposals a good deal easier.

Chief Legislator

Washington governors also play a vital role in the formation of legislation; their specific policy goals often dominate legislative sessions. Governors can use their state-wide prominence, visibility, and persuasive power to influence popular opinion and lobby the legislature. The governor's office is required to introduce a biennial budget and exercises special influence in this area. Governors can also call extra legislative sessions when budgetary or legislative changes are needed.[2]

Governor Gregoire has had to use her special session powers frequently in order to address the state's budget problems in challenging economic times.

The special session she called for in late 2010 reached a bipartisan agreement cutting close to $584 million from state expenditures. As recently as March 2011, the governor exercised her special session power to hold a seven-day legislative period specifically to address budget issues (Washington State Office of the Governor 2011).

The governor's legislative role, though powerful, is limited by both institutional and political dynamics. Until recently, at least one house of the legislature has often been controlled by a party other than that of the governor, creating a more difficult environment in which to govern. Since 2005 Governor Gregoire has had the luxury of operating under unified government and the number of fellow Democrats in the senate has increased during her two terms, from 26 in 2005 to 31 in 2009–2010 (an increase of 10% of the seats in the senate). The house also has seen an increase in the number of Democrats, from 55 in 2005 when Gregoire came into office, to 61 today (a gain of 6%). This, however, is a very different political environment than that of Gregoire's predecessor, Gary Locke, whose entire service as governor was characterized by divided control of the state legislature (see Table 1).

Despite unified party control in recent years, the ability of Governor Gregoire to pursue her policy agenda has been constrained by the economic downturn and severe revenue shortfalls. One major concern of governors nationally is recovering from the crumbling national economy that has crippled state budgets since 2008. Determining the absolutely essential state resources to deliver to the people and finding the most effective way to deliver services has been no less a challenge in Washington State, which has faced a $2.6 billion budget shortfall, an 8.6 percent unemployment rate, and a 6.2 percent decline in tax revenue in 2010 (Pew Center on the States 2010; McNichol, Oliff, and Johnson 2011). In addition, unlike many states which have state income taxes, Washington State only has three major revenue sources: sales taxes, federal aid, and fees. The reliance on these revenue sources has become especially problematic as the economy has worsened. Nevertheless, a ballot initiative in 2010 to create an income tax on wealthy residents (individuals making over $200,000 annually and couples making more than $400,000 annually), was soundly rejected by a two-thirds margin.

The recession and revenue shortfall forced Governor Gregoire to furlough certain agency employees and to order across the board spending cuts on state agencies (a step many other governors also had to take). In comparison to other states, Washington ranks 13th highest overall in the nation in terms of deficit as a percent of spending at 16.2 percent, according to projected estimates for 2012 (Combs 2011; see chapter 12 on budgeting.)

Another major constraint on the governor's power to deal with the fiscal crisis is a constitutional limit on how much debt the state may incur to fund its programs. The debt limit is 9 percent of general state revenues and this

Table 1

Percentage of Seats Held by Governor's Party

Governor	Year	Senate	House
Langlie (R)	1949	59%	32%
	1951	46%	45%
	1953	54%	58%
	1955	52%	49%
Rosellini (D)	1957	67%	56%
	1959	71%	66%
	1961	73%	59%
	1963	65%	51%
Evans (R)	1965	35%	39%
	1967	41%	55%
	1969	45%	56%
	1971	41%	51%
	1973	39%	41%
	1975	39%	36%
Ray (D)	1977	61%	62%
	1979	61%	50%
Spellman (R)	1981	49%	56%
	1983	47%	44%
Gardner (D)	1985	55%	53%
	1987	51%	61%
	1989	49%	64%
	1991	49%	58%
Lowry (D)	1993	57%	65%
	1995	51%	38%
Locke (D)	1997	47%	42%
	1999	55%	50%
	2001	51%	50%
	2003	49%	52%
Gregoire (D)	2005	53%	55%
	2007	65%	62%
	2009	65%	62%
	2011	55%	56%

Source: Washington State Legislature 2011. Percentages of seats held are based on the first month of the new legislative term.

constraint is factored into budget proposals. The governor plays an integral role in this process as he or she must recommend a budget to the legislature and also maintains the power to veto appropriations bills. Once a budget is enacted, the governor must monitor agency expenditures to assure that they are congruent with legislative policy goals. Budgetary leadership is an important but constrained job for the governor, especially in times of extreme economic uncertainty (Office of Financial Management 2011).

When governors try to influence the legislature they have both veto and line-item veto power, but they are not given free rein in using those powers. The governor must veto entire paragraphs of legislation at a time (instead of being able to delete select language), except in the case of spending bills in which individual items may be vetoed. The threat of this power can be a strong weapon when negotiating with the legislature and can be used often to further gubernatorial policy goals. This power must be used cautiously, though, if a governor does not want to alienate their legislative supporters or appear abusive of their power. The governor of South Carolina ran afoul of this problem recently when she vetoed a number of spending items; the state legislature promptly overrode most of the vetoes.

The Washington State Supreme Court can also play an important role in constraining the governor's influence over the budget. For example, several of the court's rulings have emphasized the importance of primary and secondary (but not higher) education in Washington State. Article IX of the state constitution states that public education is a "paramount duty" of the state; that language is not used for any other state responsibility. The court has used this provision to essentially give education a higher priority in state budget proposals. By consistently ruling for strong enforcement of this provision, the Washington State Supreme Court has helped shape budget decisions by reinforcing the state's commitment to educating its youth. The provision has not prevented significant budget cuts for education in the current recession, however. Social issues are another major legislative area of concern for governors. Governor Gregoire, for example, has made combating discrimination based on sexual orientation a major legislative priority. Under her leadership Washington passed a same-sex civil rights bill in 2006 which added "sexual orientation" as a protected class to state anti-discrimination laws. Then in 2007, the governor signed into law a bill giving legal rights to domestic partners. The law gave same-sex couples rights and responsibilities similar to those of heterosexual couples on issues regarding health care, incapacity, and death (Washington State Office of the Governor 2011). Currently, though, Washington, like most states, defines marriage as being between a man and a woman after the State Supreme Court upheld the state's Defense of Marriage Act in *Andersen v. King County*, 138 P.3d 963 (Wash. 2006). The governor's website indicates a continuing emphasis on combating discrimination based on sexual orientation (see "News Releases for Diversity,"

Washington State Office of the Governor 2011). Another major legislative priority for Governor Gregoire has been affordable health care for Washington residents. Since taking office, she has increased the number of children in the Apple Health for Kids program by 140,000. This program provides health insurance to low-income families and is part of Gregoire's mission to increase health care and prescription drug access for the poor (another area she continues to highlight on her website). A 2005 program she developed has helped more than 132,000 under- and uninsured Washingtonians save almost $10.4 million on prescription drug costs. Her health care initiatives have also focused on decreasing tobacco use, encouraging preventive care, and promoting exercise and healthy lifestyle practices (Washington State Office of the Governor 2011).

Administrator and Chief Executive

The governor also must ensure that laws are properly executed and must direct the many bureaucratic agencies that are responsible for administering state programs. Governors can influence the bureaucracy by directing state agencies on how to implement laws and by requiring them to meet certain reporting schedules. While it is unrealistic for the governor to micromanage every single state employee, his or her influence over them can be significant. Professional staff and assistants are provided, under the Washington Administrative Code (WAC), to assist the governor in these efforts. The governor also meets with her cabinet on a regular basis and WAC requires that commissions, task forces, and similar bodies must report to the chief executive, giving the governor power in this area.

As in any executive branch, Washington's governor cannot personally oversee the many agencies and bureaucrats tasked with implementing policy. The governor cannot ensure that all agents are faithfully executing the law, so the job of an administrator is especially challenging as the many daily activities of various administrative bodies cannot easily be monitored for compliance. Washington State relies heavily on task forces and citizen boards to shape policy and their sheer volume makes it difficult for the governor to adequately attend to all of them. Moreover, most state programs are at least partially carried out by local governments and/or private contractors. With the many demands placed on the governor's office, there is little time to sufficiently deal with all of these agencies and participants.

The governor must also staff many of these positions through gubernatorial appointment, a time-consuming process that requires great vetting and care. While the governor has a network of people to aid in this process, individuals must be carefully screened for public service to assure not only competence but also to avoid future public embarrassment and negative political consequences. Beyond this, the governor may face political pressure from one of the other eight independently elected executive branch offices. Since members of different parties may occupy the same branch, there is a strong possibility that political tension may occur. It is the governor's job to carefully mitigate this and present a unified executive front in Washington State without creating unnecessary political battles.

In the wake of the terrorist attacks of September 11, 2001, governors have taken on increased emergency management responsibilities and power. The governor has the authority to issue executive orders to handle civil defense problems, natural disasters, and other emergencies. Washington's governors can also mobilize the National Guard, force evacuations from dangerous areas, direct funds to emergency relief efforts, and enter into emergency aid agreements with other states. Having a single leader capable of swift action during a calamity can calm public nerves and allows for action to be taken without going through a lengthy political process. States have also focused more energy on emergency preparedness and recovery as governors take on an increasing role in emergency management.

Under Washington State law, after a governor declares an emergency, statutory powers enable the governor to institute a curfew, prevent groups from assembling in specified public areas, restrict personal access to firearms outside one's residence, and restrict any other activity that "he or she reasonably believes should be prohibited to help preserve and maintain life, health, property or the public peace."[3] These broad powers could be necessary for a governor to maintain law and order in the face of natural disaster, terrorist attack, or civil unrest. While these powers often lay dormant, they are robust and strong when called into action. During the 1999 World Trade Organization protests in Seattle, for example, Governor Gary Locke declared a state of emergency, which enabled him to exercise enhanced powers to control rioting downtown. The federal government has also given Washington State more than $400 million since the September 11th attacks for terrorism prevention and first-responder training, which has allowed state and local police agencies to upgrade their bomb vehicles, SWAT units, and emergency operations centers (Mulick 2011).

Governor Gregoire has used the office's emergency powers mainly to deal with natural disasters. Winter storms in early 2008 led to emergencies being declared in several counties, thus affording local agencies greater discretion and expediency in contracting with private sector companies to help with snow removal. More wintry conditions in late 2010 led to a declaration of emergency in 17 counties and ushered in federal assistance for snow removal and to repair damaged homes. Even periods of heavy rain in 2006 led to a declaration of emergency by Governor Gregoire when 26 days of consecutive rain caused heavy flooding and mudflows around the state (Washington State Office of the Governor 2011). Weather conditions are usually the cause for a state of emergency, but Washington governors have substantial authority to declare a state of emergency under other circumstances as well.

Ceremonial Leader

As the leader of the state, the governor plays a symbolic role as the ceremonial figure and official representative of the state in many formal settings. Whether meeting with national or international leaders, the governor is a symbol of both leadership and strength. In an increasingly globalized world, the governor is often involved in international trade delegations and facilitating global trade deals for the state. In late 2010, for example, Governor Gregoire embarked on a travel mission through Asia to promote Washington State products and was able to secure Chinese investment in two Washington biomedical companies. She also attended a state dinner at the White House given in honor of visiting Chinese President Hu Jintao in early 2011, along with former Washington Governor Gary Locke who was serving as Commerce Secretary for President Obama, and other dignitaries. In 2011 she attended the Paris Air Show in order to promote sales of Boeing airplanes and Boeing-made components (Washington State Office of the Governor 2011).

Governor Gregoire is also a leader around the nation in promoting climate change policies and initiatives. Her leadership at the 2010 Governor's Global Climate Summit at the University of California, Davis, highlights her commitment to promoting a green global economy. As co-host of the event, Governor Gregoire helped facilitate the exchange of ideas, programs, and best practices among international leaders who came together to showcase new solutions to climate and energy related issues. Washington State is also a member of the R20, a global organization dedicated to enacting climate change policies at the sub-national level (Governors' Global Climate Summit 3 2010).

In late 2010, Governor Gregoire was selected by her peers to be the chair of the National Governor's Association, a position held by only four other Washington State governors since the NGA's inception in 1908. This role gave her an opportunity to lead America's governors and to carry out the "Complete to Compete" initiative started by her NGA chair predecessor, Jim Douglas of Vermont. This effort focuses on increasing the number of students in the United States who complete college degrees and certificates and encourages the development of America's higher education system. Improving higher education is a theme Christine Gregoire highlighted in Washington as well, where, until the 2008 recession undercut her efforts, she had worked to improve access to colleges and universities and to develop plans for long-term funding of higher education (National Governors Association 2010).

The governor's ceremonial role also includes appearances at many different public and semi-public events: dedications of new bridges and state buildings, openings of new parks, showing sympathy for victims of disasters, and countless other occasions and situations. The governor's visibility can help to raise the profile of almost any event or issue. However, the danger with visibility is that it can also attract blame. As a result, governors generally have lower reelection rates that other elected statewide executives.

Gubernatorial Selection

Washington governors have become increasingly professional and politically skilled as the demands of the office have grown. As the office has assumed more complex fiscal, social, and political tasks, governors must be able to navigate the political landscape and be seen as a legitimate political actor, unlike the presidential appointees of early territorial governments. With such skill comes great responsibility and demands by a diverse constituency who look to the governor to address statewide problems and represent the state nationally and globally.

Today's governors tend to be younger and more educated than their predecessors. Washington's two most recent governors, Governors Locke and Gregoire, both hold law degrees and had prior political experience before reaching the governor's office. Governor Locke attended Boston University School of Law and served in the Washington State House of Representatives for 11 years, while Governor Gregoire received her law degree from Gonzaga Law School and served as the Washington State Attorney General for 12 years prior to reaching the governor's office (Washington State Office of the Governor 2011).

Prior legislative experience is not a requirement for entering into the governor's office, but it certainly facilitates elevation to the position. Most American governors have served in a legislative position, whether at the local, state, or national level. For example, Idaho's governor, C.L. "Butch" Otter, represented Idaho in the U.S. House of Representatives from 2001 to 2007 before becoming governor (Idaho State Office of the Governor 2011). Oregon Governor John Kitzhaber served as president of the Oregon senate from 1985 to 1992 before being elected governor (Oregon State Office of the Governor 2011). The experience these chief executives gained in previous public offices helped them understand the issues and challenges that were important to their states, and doubtless contributed to their successful rise to the governorship. Although Americans tend to be suspicious about politicians, they generally prefer gubernatorial candidates who have some experience in public office.

Increasing diversity in the governor's office is another trend that continues across the country. Washington Governor Gary Locke is the son of immigrant parents and was the first Chinese-American elected governor of any state. In 2011 there were at least five governors with African American, Hispanic, Asian, or Native American ancestry. Christine Gregoire was one of seven female governors in office in 2011 as women assume a more active role in state politics. While in the past many women were elected governor after their husbands died in office, Washington elected Dixy Lee Ray (1977–1981) as one of the first female governors in the nation elected on her own merit (Washington State Office of the Governor 2011). Christine Gregoire is the first female governor of Washington since Ray and her two terms as governor have allowed her to serve as a powerful leader for women.

Ideally the political leadership of a state should reflect the diverse population that it serves. The role of minorities in state-level politics has expanded considerably since the 1950s, and some observers hope that this development will help increase civic trust once underrepresented classes gain a sense of belonging and a feeling of competence in the political arena.

Unfortunately, the increasing cost of running for governor may hinder access to the office. The 2004 and 2008 Washington State election campaigns were among the most costly on record. Christine Gregoire and Republican challenger Dino Rossi spent a combined $12.3 million on their campaigns in 2004, and the same pair spent a combined $25.3 million in the 2008 governor's race. This growth (more than 100% in four years) is a dramatic contrast with the total campaign costs for all 11 gubernatorial races held in 2004 and 2008; those costs went from $112.6 million to $118.9 million (an increase of less than 6%; Beyle and Jensen 2011). National trends indicate that campaign costs have reached staggering amounts, especially as candidates spend money on television advertising and travel to campaign across the entire state. Candidates who hope to win the governorship must make themselves agreeable to people and groups that give money (or be personally wealthy and willing to finance their own campaigns).

The governor's office often is a springboard for politicians seeking higher office in the federal government or sometimes lucrative careers in the media. The 112th Congress has many former governors. In the past, 17 governors have become presidents, including former President Bill Clinton, who served two non-consecutive terms as the governor of Arkansas, and former President George W. Bush, who was the governor of Texas from 1995 to 2000. Sarah Palin served as the governor of Alaska from 2006 to 2009 and resigned abruptly in the middle of her term (amid ethics charges against her) to pursue other avenues of political punditry after losing as John McCain's running mate for vice president in the 2008 election. Governor Eliot Spitzer of New York also resigned amid scandal in 2008 and has made recent forays into the world of broadcast television, co-hosting a political roundtable on CNN. Former Governor Mike Huckabee of Arkansas sought the White House in 2008 and lost, but he then built a successful career as a media commentator and author. Governors sometimes become national personalities known well beyond the confines of their state, although other governors maintain a lower profile.

Governors have entered other positions in the federal government as well. Former governor of Pennsylvania Tom Ridge became the first U.S. Homeland Security Secretary in 2003; former New Jersey Governor Christine Todd Whitman was the administrator of the Environmental Protection Agency from 2001 to 2003. Other notable governors who in recent years have served in the federal government include Nebraska Governor Mike Johanns (2005–2007

Secretary of Agriculture), Mike Leavitt of Utah (2005–2009 Secretary of Health and Human Services), Gary Locke from Washington (2009–2011 Commerce Secretary), and John Huntsman (2009–2011 Ambassador to China). Two governors, both from New Hampshire, rose to White House chief of staff: Sherman Adams for Dwight Eisenhower and John Sununu for George H.W. Bush. Several other chiefs of staff have unsuccessfully run for governor.

Bear in mind that these men and women may or may not enter the governor's race with the goal of moving up the political ladder, but the intense demands of the governor's office leave little room for ignoring the needs of the state and focusing on grander aspirations. Sitting governors must first focus on the many jobs required of them as governor and put long-term career aspirations on the back burner. It is also true that many governors do not seek further public offices but rather return to the private sector, in part because major private sector leadership positions usually pay much more than do public sector leadership posts. In addition, many former governors appreciate that private sector positions tend to give them greater privacy and increased time to spend with families and friends.

Other Statewide-Elected Officials

In addition to the governor, Washington State has eight other elected officials in the executive branch. Their responsibilities are essential to the overall operation of the executive branch and vary a great deal in their primary functions and duties. Overseeing the legislature, defending the legal interests of the state, and managing state-owned public lands are some of these functions. In addition to these eight constitutionally mandated offices, there is an insurance commissioner who is elected by a statewide constituency. His or her primary purpose is to oversee insurance companies, making sure they follow Washington laws and rules governing the insurance industry. These elected officials each serve four-year terms and, like the governor, must balance their own interests against those of the general public, especially as they rely on approval from voters to get and maintain their jobs.

Lieutenant Governor

The lieutenant governor is the second-highest ranking official in the executive branch. The office is independently elected and does not run on the same ticket as the governor like a vice president does with a presidential candidate. He or she may act on behalf of the governor in the event that a governor is out of state or incapacitated. The primary responsibility of the lieutenant governor is to act as state senate president and oversee that body. They also serve as an appointed member and chair of the Senate Rules Committee. Occasionally, lieutenant governors have the responsibility of appointing individuals to statewide commissions or task forces. Current Lieutenant Governor Brad Owen (D) has been serving

Washington since 2000 and has been especially active in protecting the state's children through programs designed to make communities safer. International trade and developing goodwill with foreign countries is another area of focus for Owen and he frequently speaks to trade organizations and community events involving people of diverse nationalities.

Secretary of State

The secretary of state has many responsibilities in Washington. He or she is required by the state constitution to keep records of the legislative and executive branches and to possess and regulate use of the state seal. The office is charged with the responsibility of supervising elections and verifying signatures on the filing of initiatives. After Florida's voting problems in the 2000 presidential election, Secretary of State Sam Reed was particularly active in updating Washington's voting technology. He also engineered projects to digitize the state archives and institute a legacies project to document the oral histories of past members of state government. The office is also charged with redistricting efforts after each decennial census. Secretary Reed also oversaw the movement of state elections to a vote-by-mail system and worked to improve Washington's voting procedures following the tightly contested 2004 gubernatorial race, the closest governor's race in U.S. history. In the course of a few months during that dispute, Reed was the target of lawsuits filed by each of the major parties. Each party accused him, in effect, of unfairly favoring the other party (Heffernan 2010).

Besides the Election Division, the office also includes the state Archives, including the Digital Archives and regional branches; Corporations and Charities Division; the state Library; including Washington Talking Book & Braille Library; Combined Fund Drive; Address Confidentiality Program; Legacy Project; and the Domestic Partner Registry.

Attorney General

The attorney general is the primary legal counselor for the state. The office represents the state's interests in any supreme or appeals court proceedings and issues opinions on constitutional or legal questions when requested by state executive officials or the legislature on matters pertaining to their official capacity. The attorney general is responsible for the oversight of deputy attorneys and has the authority to initiate or intervene in local prosecutions at their own discretion or by request of the governor, and may also commence civil or criminal proceedings on a limited basis. The office administers consumer protection programs and handles consumer complaints and may also review legislation prior to passage or before it is signed into law.

The attorney general's authority to litigate on behalf of state interests can have enormous policy ramifications. For example, when Christine Gregoire served in the office before becoming governor, she headed a multi-state group of attorneys general who won the largest civil settlement in history. They sued the tobacco industry for smoking-related healthcare costs imposed on state Medicaid and Medicare budgets (Derthick 2011). In 2010, Attorney General Rob McKenna joined a multistate lawsuit challenging the constitutionality of the Obama administration's health care overhaul that had passed Congress. The suit, which was largely supported by Republican state attorneys general but resulted in failed legal action by the city of Seattle to prevent McKenna's participation,[4] charged that the law violated the 10th Amendment and exceeded congressional authority under the Commerce Clause.[5]

McKenna also argued on behalf of Washington State before the U.S. Supreme Court in a 2007 case dealing with political speech and a Washington law allowing public sector labor unions to collect fees from non-members (though it required permission by the non-members before those fees could used for political purposes). In *Davenport v. Washington Education Association*, 551 U.S. 177 (2007), the U.S. Supreme Court unanimously upheld the constitutionality of the law. He also personally argued and won U.S. Supreme Court cases defending the voter-approved Top 2 Primary (see chapters 2 and 3 in this volume) and the state's practice of releasing initiative petition signatures under the state Public Records Act. He also prevailed in the U.S. 9th Circuit Court of Appeals in a case involving the state's right to deny voting rights to incarcerated felons.

Because the attorney general is responsible for implementing and defending the entire spectrum of laws and policy interests, the office is prominent in state politics and often serves as a spring-board for those seeking the governor's office. Rob McKenna, for example, has already announced he will run to replace Governor Gregoire in 2012, while Gregoire herself served as attorney general before her election in 2004.

State Treasurer

The state treasurer has the primary responsibility for managing state finances and serves as the state's representative in any financial contract into which the state may enter. The treasurer's office manages all state financial accounts and trust funds and provides annual updates of those accounts to the legislature and governor. The treasurer's office also oversees local government investments. James McIntire has held this position since his election in 2008.

Although the work of state treasurers often attracts limited attention, it sometimes becomes more visible. For example, McIntire has called attention to some state pension programs that are inadequately financed, along with noting that most are in sound condition (Grygiel 2010). He has called attention to the possible financial problems that could result from climate change and has also supported greater use of toll charges for financing transportation improvements (Dickie 2009; *Olympian* 2010).

State Auditor

The state auditor oversees the public accounts of over 2,400 government units in Washington. The auditor must monitor these public resources to prevent misappropriation or misuse and ensure that offices throughout the state adhere to financial laws and regulations. The office is also responsible for setting forth accounting and budgeting standards and provides training and advice on implementing those standards. When needed, the auditor can also launch investigations of financial irregularities. Any financial accounting problems that arise under the supervision of the state auditor must be reported to the governor and the legislature. The current state auditor is Brian Sonntag and he has served since 1992.

Sonntag has earned the reputation of being a political maverick by sometimes endorsing candidates from the Republican Party (Sonntag is a Democrat). When the state legislature considered cutting his department's budget, he sought and won the protection of Governor Gregoire. She used the item veto to strike down a provision reducing the funding of the auditor's office in 2009 (Shannon 2009).

Superintendent of Public Instruction

The superintendent of public instruction is in charge of public instruction throughout the state. The office works with the 295 school districts in the state to facilitate basic education programs and implement education reforms. With a budget of $13.63 billion (2007–2009), the duties of this office impact all 1.04 million K-12 students and over 53,000 teachers. The superintendent also serves as a liaison between public schools and the governor and legislature on various matters, especially management and policy issues. The superintendent must also manage education records and keep track of all teaching certificates in the state.

Superintendent Randy Dorn has been especially active in trying to maintain school budgets in the wake of the 2008 economic recession. Among his many legislative priorities have been ensuring that funds are available for school facility projects, modifying math and science requirements, and expanding career and technical education opportunities to students. Dorn criticized Governor Gregoire's 2011 plan to consolidate K-12 and higher education oversight into one large department of education, effectively eliminating his office in an effort to save money and give colleges in the state more discretion and flexibility in tuition hikes.

Commissioner of Public Lands

The commissioner of public lands has a primary responsibility to manage the more than five million acres of state-owned public land. This includes forests, farms, state parks, commercial properties, and underwater areas in addition to agricultural and grazing lands. Part of the mandate of this office includes overseeing these lands so they are profitable and sustainable in the long term. Funds from the sale of such products as timber and wheat can be used by the state to fund public schools and universities. The commissioner is also responsible for overseeing fire protection and prevention measures during the annual summer fire season, protecting 12.7 million acres of non-federal land including private, state-owned, and tribal land.

Current commissioner Peter Goldmark was elected in 2008. He has repeatedly struggled to provide funding for state parks, an issue that has been sensitive during the recession. The latest effort to improve park funding is an access fee. An earlier experiment with an access fee yielded more criticism than the system could sustain. Whether the newer fee system will survive remains to be seen.

Insurance Commissioner

The insurance commissioner is the only non-constitutionally mandated officeholder selected by a state-wide election. Established in 1907 to enforce the state's insurance rules and regulations, the insurance commissioner investigates and, when necessary, brings charges or fines against insurance companies acting in violation. The commissioner is authorized to revoke licenses or issue fines to insurance agents, brokers, solicitors, or insurance adjusters acting unethically. This office is also responsible for ensuring that the rights and privileges promised to Washingtonians by insurance companies are duly provided and that they are abiding by Washington State laws pertaining to insurance policies. Former U.S. Congressman Mike Kreidler is the current insurance commissioner. One of his most important recent efforts has explored the use of insurance programs to manage the risks associated with climate change.

Conclusion

The office of the governor of Washington State has evolved over time from a small office with little power and questionable legitimacy to a large, multi-faceted office with many responsibilities and powers. The office has state, regional, and national importance, and when governors work together they can become extremely influential in the national political process. No longer seen as parochial state figures, governors across the country often use their prominence and visibility as state chief executives to launch national political careers.

Along with the other branches of state government, the governor is expected to pursue the policy goals of the state and represent Washington in its many public endeavors. As both a ceremonial leader and a powerful political actor, the governor must carefully navigate complex political issues and encourage negotiation and compromise, especially in partisan times. The successful governor is the one who can stay true to his or her campaign promises by creating unity and cooperation in both state government and among the citizenry.

The state's other elected executives also play important roles in shaping state policies and programs. Although their activities are often less visible than the governor's efforts, the other elected executives wield significant influence over the lives of many Washingtonians.

Endnotes

1. See Nice and Otte (2004) for a previous version of this chapter and Scott (1992) for an excellent resource on the office of the governor and other statewide officials.
2. Washington State Constitution, Article III, Section 7: Extra Legislative Sessions.
3. Revised Code of Washington 43.06.220, Section 1(i). State of Emergency: Powers of Governor Pursuant to Proclamation.
4. *City of Seattle v. Robert McKenna*, 2011. No. 84483-6, Supreme Court of the State of Washington.
5. *State of Florida, et al. v. U.S. Department of Health and Human Services, et al.*, 2011. U.S. Dist. LEXIS 8822, U.S. District Court for the Northern District of Florida, Pensacola Division.

References

Beyle, Thad, and Jennifer M. Jensen. 2011. *The Gubernatorial Campaign Finance Database*. unc.edu/~beyle/guber.html.

Combs, David. March 15, 2011. "State Budget Gaps: How Does Your State Rank?" stateline.org/live/ViewPage.action?siteNodeId=136&languageId=1&contentId=15158.

Council of State Governments. 2011. *The Book of the States* 43. Lexington, KY: Council of State Governments.

Derthick, Martha A. 2011. *Up in Smoke: From Legislation to Litigation in Tobacco Politics*, 3rd ed. Washington, D.C.: CQ Press.

Dickie, Lance. October 15, 2009. "Real-World Problems Turn Climate-Change Debate Pragmatic." *Seattle Times*. seattletimes.com/html/opinion/2010073031_lance16.html.

Governors' Global Climate Summit 3. 2010. University of California, Davis. ces.ucdavis.edu/ggcs3.

Grygiel, Chris. January 21, 2010. "Billion Dollar Headache: Looming Pension Liability Worries State Officials." *Seattle PI*. seattlepi.com/default/article/Billion-dollar-headache-Looming-pension-887699.php.

Heffernan, Trova. 2010. *An Election for the Ages: Rossi vs. Gregoire, 2004*. Pullman: Washington State University Press.

Idaho State Office of the Governor. 2011. gov.idaho.gov.

McNichol, Elizabeth, Phil Oliff, and Nicholas Johnson. June 17, 2011. "States Continue to Feel Recession's Impact." *Center on Budget and Policy Priorities*. www.cbpp.org/cms/?fa=view&id=711.

Mulick, Stacey. September 6, 2011. "Washington State Ready If Terrorists Strike." *Tacoma News Tribune*. thenewstribune.com/2011/09/06/1811173/a-decade-of-war-state-ready-if.html.

National Governors Association. November 17, 2010. "Washington Gov. Chris Gregoire Elected Chair of National Governors Association." www.nga.org/cms/home/news-room/news-releases/page_2010/col2-content/main-content-list/title_washington-gov-chris-gregoire-elected-chair-of-national-governors-association.html.

Nice, David, and Erin Otte. 2004. "The Office of the Governor." In *Washington State Government and Politics*, edited by Cornell W. Clayton, Lance T. LeLoup, and Nicholas P. Lovrich. Pullman: Washington State University Press.

Office of Financial Management. 2011. *Washington State Budget Process*. ofm.wa.gov/reports/budgetprocess.pdf.

Olympian. January 22, 2010. "Panel Backs Toll Increase on Tacoma Narrows Bridge." theolympian.com/2010/01/22/1110687/olympia-panel-backs-toll-increase.html.

Oregon State Office of the Governor. 2011. governor.oregon.gov.

Pew Center on the States. 2010. *The State of the States 2010*. pewcenteronthestates.org/uploadedFiles/State_of_the_States_2010.pdf.

Scott, George W. 1992. "The Office of Governor and Elected Statewide Officials." In *Government and Politics in the Evergreen State*, edited by David C. Nice, John C. Pierce, and Charles H. Sheldon, 117–31. Pullman: Washington State University Press.

Shannon, Brad. May 20, 2009. "Gregoire Vetoes Cuts to Auditor." *The Olympian*. theolympian.com/2009/05/20/856112/gregoire-vetoes-cuts-to-auditor.html.

Washington Governor's Mansion Foundation. 2011. wagovmansion.org.

Washington State Legislature. 2011. *History of the State Legislature: Senate and House Political Division*. leg.wa.gov/History/Legislative/Pages/factsandbilldata.aspx.

Washington State Office of the Governor. 2011. governor.wa.gov.

CHAPTER ELEVEN

The State Legislature

Francis Benjamin and Nicholas Lovrich

*The legislative authority of the state of Washington shall be vested in the legislature...
but the people reserve to themselves the power to propose bills, laws, and to enact or
reject the same at the polls, independent of the legislature, and also reserve power,
at their own option, to approve or reject at the polls any act, item, section, or part
of any bill, act, or law passed by the legislature.*

Washington State Constitution Article II, Section 1

WASHINGTON STATE CITIZENS, historically rather reserved in their
judgment regarding state representative government, are becoming
undeniably cynical toward state government writ large—and in
particular with respect to their state legislature. This is ironic given the high
regard in which the Washington legislature is held by other states, and in light of
the well-deserved praise it receives for its public accessibility through TVW, its
maintenance of highly skilled and experienced nonpartisan committee staff, its
highly envied page and internship programs involving hundreds of high school,
college, and law school students, and its pioneering use of nonpartisan policy
research on evidence-based practices and outcome-oriented policy studies carried out by the Washington State Institute for Public Policy. The frequency with
which the public reverses policies developed by the legislature in the initiative
process—in many areas of legislation, including public finance—bespeaks of the
low regard in which the public holds its legislative branch and its inclination to
provide voter support for initiative challenges to legislative plans and enactments.

The ambivalence seen in surveys over the past several decades has given way
to widespread disapproval in more recent years. For example, through 2010 and
into 2011, a monthly survey of adult citizens consistently shows two out of three
citizens expressing disapproval of the job being done by the state legislature.
Rather consistently, only one in five citizens in these monthly surveys indicate
that they approve of the work of the state legislature (see Figure 1).

What might account for this disjuncture between what the Washington State
legislature is known to be like outside of the state and how it is seen by its own

Figure 1. Washington State Legislature Approval Rating

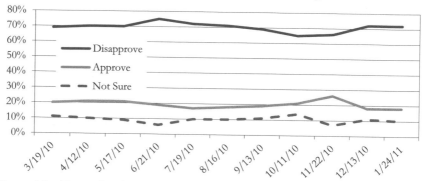

Source: Monthly samples of 600 randomly selected adults. Telephone surveys were conducted by SurveyUSA 2010–2011.

citizens? In this chapter we try to explain the disconnect between the putative quality of legislative practices and products and the unfavorable impression held by Washingtonians of the state legislature. In seeking to provide this explanation, we rely on the presentation of information on the legislative process, the discussion of the major elements of that process, and the identification of the principal problems to be faced in maintaining a productive legislative branch of state government. In the course of making our argument we rely in part on recent surveys conducted among current and past state legislators, legislative staff, legislative interns, and lobbyists who work in the state legislative setting (Benjamin, Lovrich, and Parks 2011). In the results derived from this set of surveys, referred to as the Legislative Service Project in this chapter (Benjamin and Lovrich 2010a), it is clear that one major problem is a decline in the civil discourse and conduct that characterizes a respected legislative assembly. In the view of one of the state's most well-known political figures, former Speaker of the U.S. House of Representatives Thomas S. Foley, civility in the legislative chamber begets the public respect required of a well-functioning democratic order. Speaker Foley offered some telling observations in a National Dialogue on Civility and Democracy held simultaneously March 3–5, 2011, in four locations across the country. The National Endowment for the Humanities sponsored major conferences in Chicago (hosted by the American Bar Association), Los Angeles (hosted by the California Council for the Humanities), Philadelphia (hosted by the National Constitution Center), and Spokane (hosted by Washington State University Spokane) where the decline in civility in American politics was addressed in depth. In offering opening remarks for the Spokane session, Speaker Foley offered the following cogent observations:

> This conference—and related events elsewhere in the country—could not come at a more appropriate time. One of my goals when I was Speaker was to promote

an atmosphere of civility and respect among Members regardless of party or policy. Today our politics has become more confrontational and antagonistic, which is one of the reasons the Congress [and perhaps the Washington State legislature by inference] is so unpopular with the public. I believe there is a need for the Leadership of both parties to work to maintain civility. When I was in Congress, although Members often held strong divergent views on policy issues, there were many warm, personal friendships across party lines. For example, one of my good friends in Congress was Bob Michel, who was then the Minority Leader. These personal friendships were not unusual then; they are today.

In the following pages of this chapter you will learn how the state legislative process is organized and how two of the principal actors in that process—the legislators and the lobbyists who attempt to influence legislative outcomes—assess past and current levels of civility of the legislative process.

The Nature of Washington's Legislative Districts: Diversity Abounds

The Washington State legislature is comprised of two chambers, the House of Representatives and the Senate. Since 1973 the house has maintained 98 members, and since 1959 the senate has had 49 members. Washington is apportioned into 49 state legislative districts with each district electing three legislators—two representatives to the house and one to the senate. The entire house membership is elected in even-numbered years to two-year terms. Half of the senate membership is elected each even-numbered year to four-year terms. At the time of the last reapportionment (done every ten years following the U.S. census), each legislative district, based on the 2010 census, is supposed to contain about 137,230 people. In the 2010 general election about 52,358 voters cast ballots in each legislative district.

One result of differential population growth and the shifting of population centers in the state is the redrawing of legislative district boundaries after each decennial census. In many states the re-crafting of boundaries is controlled by the legislature and governor, and the process tends to be highly partisan. This often means that the party in control of government during the redistricting process can take advantage of their control and maximize the number of seats that are "safe" for its party and thereby protect incumbents. In Washington, in stark contrast, a five-member bipartisan commission draws district boundaries. The four legislative party caucus organizations each appoint one citizen member to the commission. While closely tied to the party caucuses, commissioners cannot have held elected office within two years of serving. These four commissioners appoint a fifth non-voting commissioner to serve as chair. The commission then draws up the redistricting plan. The redistricting plan must be approved by at least three of the four voting members. The commission's plan is then sent to the state legislature for review. The legislature may only make minor amendments which affect no more than 2 percent of a legislative district's population; these amendments must be approved by two-thirds supermajorities of both the house and the senate. The governor cannot veto the plan.

One major objective of the redistricting commission is to create a process wherein no one party exercises total control over the process, and direct pressure from legislators wishing to protect their seats is held to a minimum. Additionally, there is a desire to create a higher percentage of districts where neither party holds the loyalties of an overwhelming majority of voters. The ultimate outcome associated with this process is intended to be more competitive elections and legislators being elected based on statewide swings of voter sentiment (Washington State Redistricting Commission 2011).

While legislative districts are redrawn every ten years to maintain equivalent total population, the factors of geographical location, population density, and legislative turnover are not uniform across legislative districts. Legislative districts based on the 2000 census ranged from a low of 15 to a high of over 11,000 square miles in size, with population density ranging from a low of 11 to a high of 10,517 people per square land mile. Based on the 2000 census, 12 legislative districts had population densities of fewer than 100 persons per square mile, and thereby met the criteria of the Office of Financial Management for designation as a rural area. These districts are predominantly in the central to eastern geographical regions of the state. The highest density districts are located in Seattle, Spokane, and Tacoma. The Cascade Range provides a natural divide that separates Washington into east and west regions. There are 11 eastside and 38 westside legislative districts. Legislation is sometimes discussed in the context of being an eastern Washington matter or a western Washington issue (OFM 2011).

Another noteworthy variation in legislative districts is that of turnover, a characteristic based on how many legislators over a certain period have served in the district. District turnover rates over the last 20-year period have ranged from a low of 6 to a high of 14. The average number of unique legislators serving in a district during the period 1990 to 2009 was 9.49. A district with low turnover has longer-serving legislators who are more likely to be in positions of leadership and influence in the legislature. Legislators in districts with higher turnover tend to spend more money in their electoral campaigns than legislators coming from districts with lower turnover where candidate name recognition is more firmly established.

The Partisan, Longevity, and Gender Composition of the Legislature

Democratic legislators have experienced three bienniums of majority control of both houses. The margin has at times been over 20% and has provided Democrats with control over the legislative agenda (see Figure 2). At the end

Figure 2. Partisan Composition of the Washington State Legislature, 1974–2011

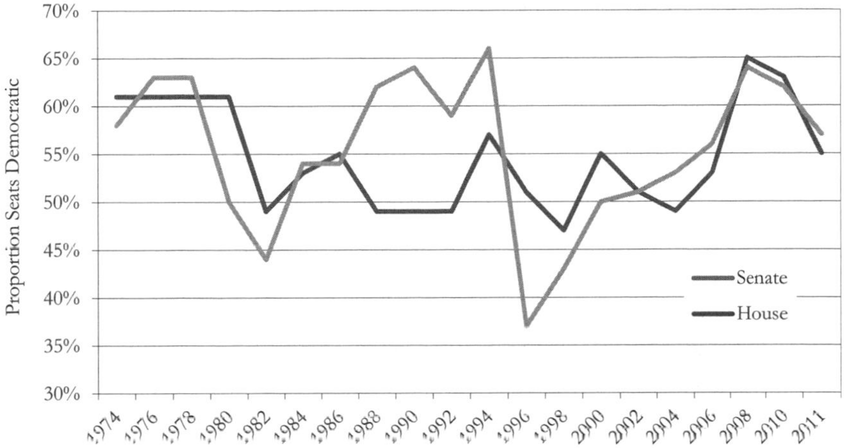

Source: WSL 2010.

of the 20th century this imbalance in favor of Democratic legislators was not present. Instead, the legislature was so closely balanced that the house was deadlocked in a 49-49 tie for three consecutive sessions (1999, 2000, and 2001). During this time, the senate Democratic majority had only a single seat advantage. When commenting on the differences between a partisanship-balanced legislature and one-party control, legislators in the Legislative Service Project surveys underscore the fact that during times of a partisanship-balanced legislature, legislators have to be more civil in speech and conduct, and work more closely together to accomplish their goals.

During Washington State's existence, legislators have ranged in age from 22 to 84, and have served a range of 3 days to 52 years. Over the period 1990–2009 there have been 458 individual legislators. While there is a common misperception that most legislators serve in the house prior to becoming a senator, 60% of senators have never served in the house. The average length of service for those who serve in the house is 5.29 years, in the senate is 6.38 years, and in both houses is 6.36 years. During this time period almost 25% of legislators served only one term, while over 25% served longer than nine years. Of the legislators serving during these 20 years, over half served in a legislative district where the legislators where all from the same party. Approximately 20% of the legislators commuted daily from home during session. The picture that emerges is that in each legislative session there is a wide variety of actors—seasoned veterans, new politicos seeking to make a name for themselves, legislators far from home, and others commuting daily from cities on the I-5 corridor (WSL 2009; WSL 2011a).

In regard to gender equity concerns, Washington State has always led in women's political involvement. In fact, Washington State accorded women the right to vote ten years prior to women's suffrage becoming the law of the land. In 1913, two women were elected to the state house. In 1992, Washington led all states in the proportion of women in the legislature. By 2000, women held 40% of all seats. Currently (2011) there are 48 state women legislators; this represents 33% of legislative seats. The average of all states is 24% (WSL 2010).

In the Legislative Service Project, legislators who served during the 1990–2009 sessions were surveyed in 2009 concerning their own experiences as legislators. Based on these surveys involving 145 current and past state legislators, individuals tended to feel that their legislative experience was highly worthwhile. When asked if they had the opportunity to go back in time and decide anew on whether to go into legislative service, they were overwhelmingly of the opinion that they would choose to serve in the Washington State legislature again. Legislators noted many benefits: they were able to represent and help constituents, learn the legislative process in-depth, influence the crafting of legislation, have access to important policy influencers, and grow personally and professionally. At the same time, state legislators found a number of challenges associated with being a state legislator; these challenges and disliked aspects of the job included periods of prolonged separation from family, the short election cycle requiring much attention to campaigning and fundraising, the tight schedule leading to high stress and fatigue, the high degree of partisanship, the frequent experience of disrespect and incivility, and being part of public policy outcomes that are poorer than they might be because of the lack of bipartisan collaboration and civility.

In regard to the importance of civility to the legislative process, Washington's legislators were in strong agreement with Speaker Foley's observations on the subject. Just as he noted the importance of this legislative norm with respect to the U.S. Congress, Washington's legislators accord the same level of importance of civility to the operation of the Washington State legislature. On a ten-point scale with one representing unimportant and 10 signifying very important, overwhelming percentages of legislators indicate that civility is quite important to both bipartisanship and achieving good public policy outcomes (see Figure 3).

The importance of civility norms in legislative bodies is perhaps a universal aspect of parliamentary governance, in the United States and its state governments as well in other democratic countries (Brooks and Geer 2007). Given this ubiquitous importance, these same Washington State legislators were also asked to give their opinion of the degree to which they witnessed change in civility norms during the course of their legislative service; the results are set forth in Figure 4.

Legislators surveyed for the Legislative Service Project differed a good deal on the level of civility they experienced during their own period of service, and on whether the level of civility was increasing, remaining constant, or declining during that period. As a group, however, few were inclined to opine that civil-

Figure 3. Importance of Civility for the Promotion of Bipartisanship and Achieving Good Public Policy Outcomes for the State

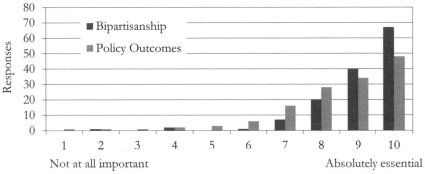

Figure 4. Change Observed in Legislative Civility While a Legislator

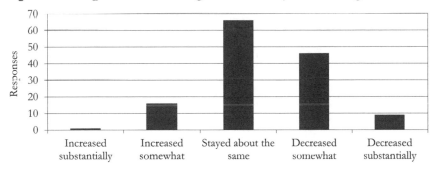

ity was on the increase during their period of service; most were inclined to say that it stayed about the same and a substantial proportion were of the view that civility was in decline during their period of service. Another noteworthy finding of the survey was that virtually all (94.8%) of the legislators taking part felt that bipartisan collaboration improves the effectiveness of the legislative process. These same legislators also felt that since they became involved in the Washington State legislature, the legislative process had become substantially more partisan and that less bipartisan collaboration is taking place than was the case in the past.

While the views of legislators themselves are important to record, perhaps even more important to assess are the views of veteran observers of the legislative process. In the Legislative Service Project, registered lobbyists were asked about their perceptions of the Washington State legislature over the course of the past 20 years. Many of these veteran observers were once legislators themselves, and virtually all are highly experienced professional representatives of established interests in the state and know "the hill" extremely well. What are their views

Figure 5. Change Observed in Legislative Civility by Registered Lobbyists

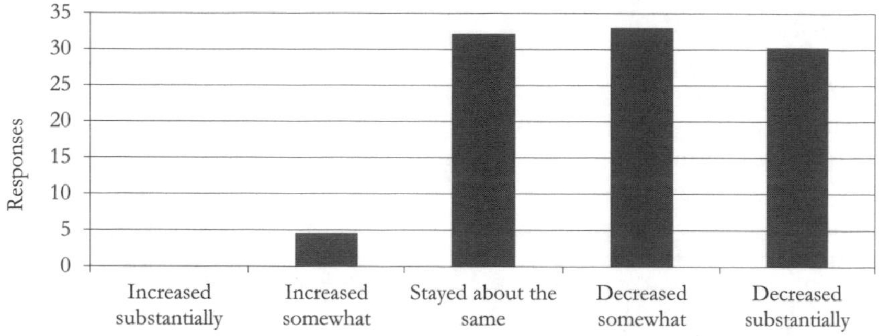

of the state of civility in the contemporary Washington State legislature? The collective assessment of the state of civility in the contemporary Washington State legislature by 112 registered lobbyists is set forth in Figure 5.

While legislators are rather mixed in their assessment of trends in civility, the registered lobbyists are far more united in their collective judgment that civility norms are in decline in the legislative bodies in which they carry out their work.

Legislators and Their Legislative Experience

The Washington State legislature is officially characterized as a citizen legislature composed of persons from diverse backgrounds whose primary occupation is not that of a professional politician. These "part-time" legislators are tasked with reaching consensus on a wide range of issues affecting citizens and the future of the state. Many legislators responding to the legislative service survey indicated that they had prior experience with the legislative process before becoming a state legislator. In this regard, 9% had previously served as a student intern while in school, 33% worked as legislative or state agency staffer, 32% had held a previous elected office (city, county, special purpose district), and 9% had been a lobbyist advocating for an interest group.

In regard to high school and college student involvement with the Washington State legislature, it should be noted that the tradition of pages and interns serving in Olympia during legislative sessions is a deep and respected one. Seven in ten of the legislators responding to the survey had experience with student interns, and over 85% of the current legislators in 2009 who had worked with interns wanted one again. Student interns responding to the survey found the intern experience to be of great benefit. The main reasons given for participation in an internship were to gain political/legislative experience, enhance résumés, expand networking contacts, supplement classroom experience, and "for the challenge." The intern experience not only increased the interns' understanding of the legislature, but also provided an opportunity for them to contribute to the legislative process. The internship provided networking opportunities, enhanced job skills, and gave students the opportunity to assist constituents and people in need of the state's attention (Benjamin and Lovrich 2010b).

A number of technology changes (televising the process, instant access to email, electronic messaging, and laptop computers) have changed how the legislature does business today. These changes include televising most important proceedings so that citizens throughout the state can watch the process from the comfort of their homes, or can see proceedings of interest captured by TVW in an online video archive. Washington was among the first states to permit TV access to all public proceedings, and it provides by far the most comprehensive range of coverage of legislative sessions, committee hearings, and virtually every other public meeting held during legislative sessions. In this regard, the Washington State legislature is given high marks as a progressive institution vis-à-vis public access to the public's business. Likewise, the Washington State legislature was among the first state legislatures to issue laptops to legislators, providing the opportunity for legislative committees to work in a paperless network for the processing of bills and amendments.

The televising of legislative proceedings means that legislators are talking both to the people present and to the televised audience when they speak in public forums in Olympia. Legislators taking part in the Legislative Service Project tended to feel that televising legislative proceedings had increased the openness and public awareness of the process and slightly increased the ethical conduct of legislators. At the same time, they tended to feel that it had slightly decreased the candidness of legislators and their willingness to work in a bipartisan fashion, and that the televising of proceedings had resulted in legislators relating to each other in a somewhat more formal fashion. It is clear that changes made in the use of communication and information technology have affected the work of the legislators. Legislators admit that use of computer-assisted technology has reduced legislators' attention and increased distractions in public and private legislative meetings alike. This bad side effect of the fracturing of attention, however, is offset for most legislators by increases in legislator and legislative staff work efficiency, constituent access to legislators, legislators' interaction with other legislators, and the legislators' timely access to bill information.

The Legislature Lives Under the Shadow of Initiatives

Washington State citizens, historically rather ambivalent regarding state representative government, in recent years are taking a more proactive role in the governmental process. As noted at the start of this chapter, the constitutional provision for the establishment of a legislative branch accords citizens a major continuing role in state politics. As part of the state's Progressive era legacy it was decided that the article of the state constitution relating to the legislature should be amended to read:

> The people reserve to themselves the power to propose bills, laws, and to enact or reject the same at the polls, independent of the legislature, and also reserve power, at their own option, to approve or reject at the polls any act, item, section, or part of any bill, act, or law passed by the legislature. (WSL 2011d)

In recent decades the citizens have frequently disapproved of the work of their legislators and are taking advantage of the constitutionally established initiative process, often with dramatic effects. The relatively easy access to the state ballot for interest groups wishing to challenge legislative actions has had major consequences for the state's politics, both in terms of legislative mandates overturned and in terms of issues being addressed "with one eye on the initiative process" by state legislators.

There are two types of initiatives under state constitutional provisions: initiatives to the people and initiatives to the legislature. Initiatives to the people, if certified through the request (signature) of a certain number of registered voters, are submitted for a vote of the people at the next state general election. Initiatives to the legislature follow a similar signature certification process. If certified, these initiatives are submitted to the legislature for a vote. The legislature can adopt the initiative as proposed, reject or refuse to act on the initiative, or approve an alternate initiative. If the original initiative sent to the legislature isn't passed, it goes to a vote of the people.

Washington State became one of the first states to adopt the initiative and referendum process in 1912. The first initiatives were filed in 1914, with seven being certified to ballot and the voters approving two of those initiatives. From 1914 to 2010, some 1,139 initiatives to the people were filed, 139 were certified, and voters approved 69 of them. This represents a 12% certification rate of filed initiatives and a 50% approval rate of certified initiatives. There has lately been a considerable growth in initiative filing with 50% (571) of the initiatives having been filed in the last 20 years (1991–2010) and 33% (376) of the initiatives having been filed in the last 10 years (2001–2010). Similarly, there has been an increase in the number of initiatives approved, with 39% (27) of the voter approved initiatives having been filed in the last 20 years (1991–2010) and 22% (15) of the voter approved initiatives having been filed in the last 10 years (2001–2010) (Washington Secretary of State 2010).

When asked in 1999, "Who do you think are better at making public policy, elected representatives, or the voting public?" a clear majority of voters (57%) replied that the public is just as good as the legislature; another 21% indicated that the public is better at making policy than legislators, and fewer than one in five voters (18%) felt that the legislature was better suited for the task. This same finding is likely to be true today, and this low esteem held for the legislature is most likely the driving force underlying an increased use of citizen initiatives in Washington politics in recent decades. In recent years initiatives approved by citizens have included reducing car licensing fees (I-695), increasing teacher pay (I-732), limiting property tax increases (I-747), requiring performance audits of government entities (I-900), prohibiting smoking in public buildings and vehicles (I-901), allowing those who are terminally ill to self-administer lethal medication (I-1000), requiring a two-thirds legislative vote on new or increased fees or taxes (I-1053), and overturning certain taxes on candy and beverages previously established by the legislature (I-1107).

Once passed, an initiative becomes a law subject to court rulings and subsequent legislative action. A small number of initiatives have been overturned by the courts, and almost half have been suspended or changed by the legislature. To change, repeal, or suspend an initiative requires a two-thirds vote of both houses during the first two years after passage. After two years, however, only a simple majority of both houses is required to alter a law established through the initiative process.

For some, the state's initiative process is viewed as a good thing—permitting citizens to set the political agenda in Washington. To others, it is viewed as a liability whereby often thoughtful and well-considered legislative mandates are too easily dismissed in a process subject to shameful misrepresentation of facts and the politicization of issues best dealt with in a bipartisan and compromise-oriented process of legislative deliberation. The reality is, however, that the prerogatives for long-term leadership by the state legislature are greatly diminished in good measure because of the frequent use of the initiative process to nullify legislative enactments.

Professionalization

Most Washington State legislators either have limited staff assistance or share staff with other legislators. They normally have no personal research budgets, and there is very little time during the session for legislators to conduct their own research. Their annual salary of $42,106 requires many to keep their "regular" job and greatly limits the amount of time they are able to spend in Olympia between sessions of the legislature. When compared to the 40 states that pay state legislators an annual salary (the other ten states pay by the day, week, or session) Washington State ranks 13th (WCCSEO 2010).

State legislatures are ranked as full-time, greater than two-thirds of a full-time commitment, and greater than half of a full-time position. Washington's legislators are considered to be in the greater than two-thirds of a full-time category (National Conference of State Legislatures 2011). While the Washington State legislature is not seen as being a full-time professional legislature, it is most clearly moving in this direction with frequent inter-session meetings and committee hearings. Legislators participating in the Legislative Service Project indicated that outside of the sessions they devoted an average of 28 hours per week to their legislative duties.

Observers of state legislatures view non-professional legislatures as ineffective and as leaving a disproportionate amount of power in the hands of the governor. The movement toward creating a professionalized legislature is seen as a way to build institutional capacity and enhance the effectiveness of state governments. In Washington that professionalization process is clearly in evidence. The state receives high marks from students of state legislatures for its ample use of inter-session hearings and its investment in a strong nonpartisan staff of permanent employees who provide outstanding service to the standing committees of both chambers. Newly elected legislators are uniformly grateful for the help of the professional staff and the work they do to prepare legislators for taking part in the legislative process. It was clear from the survey of veteran legislators that legislative committee staff services are highly regarded and deeply appreciated.

Turnover and Competitiveness of Legislative Elections

Legislative careers increase in attractiveness as legislatures become more profes-sionalized. At the same time, a more professionalized legislature tends to have fewer competitive elections as legislators are able to accomplish more and receive more public recognition for their work. This development can insulate repre-sentatives from the citizens and lessen the pressure of elections. To some extent this is the case in Washington (see Table 1). Even in high turnover years, the Washington State legislature still retains a very healthy proportion of veterans. Since 1989, even during the highest turnover years of 1993–1995, the house retained a majority (53%) of its legislators. This is compared to its best retention years (2005–2007) when the house retained 87% of its veterans.

While Table 1 identifies turnover rates between odd-year sessions, it does not provide the full picture of changeover in legislators. While the table statis-tics indicate when there is a new legislator in a legislative position, they do not indicate how many times the position changed hands between the two sessions. A single position may turnover one, two, or even three times during the course of two years. Turnover is the result of incumbents losing elections, resigning, being called to active military duty, dying, or a process of redistricting. The next table looks at turnover based on this broadened range of events.

Table 2 shows that a greater number of legislative seats change hands due to an incumbent choosing not to run than from an incumbent losing an election to a challenger. It is also clear that there are a large number of incumbents who run unopposed. Since 1990, on average, only 22.5 house seats turnover during even-year elections. Since 1990, on average, only 30.5 house and senate seats turnover during even-year elections.

Table 1

Turnover Across Odd-year Sessions of the House of Representatives:
1989–2011

Year	New Members	Percent Turnover[1]
1989–1991	23	23%
1991–1993	43	44%
1993–1995	46	47%
1995–1997	30	31%
1997–1999	24	24%
1999–2001	18	18%
2001–2003	27	28%
2003–2005	22	22%
2005–2007	13	13%
2007–2009	22	22%
2009–2011	23	23%

[1] How many legislators at the start of the session were not legislators in the previous session.
Source: Authors' calculations from election data maintained by the Washington Secretary of State (2011).

Another area of concern that arises from the professionalization of a state legislature is the phenomenon of "safe seats"—that is, legislative districts in which the election for state representative is seldom in doubt and the legislator is relatively free from the accountability pressures of public sentiment in the home district in deciding what measures to propose and to oppose, and what matters to pursue and what matters to avoid in the course of their legislative service. Table 3 sets forth data on this aspect of the Washington State legislature.

In the literature on competitiveness in elections (Salka 2009), a legislative seat is considered "safe" if the incumbent gets 60+% of the vote, and thereby wins by at least 20 percentage points. A seat may be safe due to the legislator's popularity or due to the legislator's party designation with respect to the district voters' party preference. Since 1990, incumbents have won 91% of their contested races and over 50% of these races would be considered safe. Of note in this regard is the election of 2010, where incumbents won only 38% of their races with at least 60% of the vote. The general pattern is clear, however. There are many legislators who are relatively immune from the pressures of competitive elections, and who increasingly see their legislative job as their "real" occupation, particularly as they become committee chairs and assume leadership positions within their respective parties.

Table 2

Turnover Based on Even-year Elections of the House of Representatives:
1990–2010

Election	Incumbent Unopposed	Incumbent Won	Challenger Won	Incumbent Didn't Run	% Turnover[1]
1990	15	62	7	14	21%
1992	7	48	5	38	43%
1994	18	44	19	17	36%
1996	14	62	5	17	22%
1998	25	51	7	15	21%
2000	9	73	3	13	16%
2002	22	55	3	18	21%
2004	16	64	3	15	18%
2006	27	58	4	9	13%
2008	17	65	3	13	16%
2010	18	59	5	16	21%

[1] Turnover is the number of challengers who beat incumbents plus the number of incumbents who didn't run, divided by the total number of seats.
Source: Authors' calculations from data maintained by the Washington Secretary of State (2011).

Organization of the Legislature

Regular sessions of the Washington State legislature begin the second Monday in January of each year. The biennial cycle starts on odd years, with a 105-day regular session. During this "long session," work is done on bills and the biennial budget, which begins July 1 of that year. This session is followed during even-numbered years with a 60-day regular session ("short session"). During even-year sessions, work is done on bills and a supplemental budget is passed to finish out the biennial budget. Special sessions are called by either a governor's proclamation or by a two-thirds vote of the legislature. The major activities taking place during the legislative sessions entail working on bills. During odd years since 1983, on average there are 2,489 bills introduced and 481 (19.3%) are passed into law. During even years since 1984, on average there are 1,501 bills introduced and 323 (21.5%) are passed into law. Over the period 1983–2010, the legislature passed 20.2% of the bills introduced (Washington Secretary of State 2010).

The constitution specifies two ways to establish a law in Washington. Either a bill is passed by the legislature and not vetoed by the governor, or a law is established directly by the people through the initiative process. For the

Table 3

Incumbent Safe Seats in Even-year Elections of the House of Representatives: 1990–2010

Year	Incumbent Didn't Run	Incumbent Unopposed	Incumbent Won	Challenger Won	% Incumbent Won[1]	Incumbent Won >60%	% Safe Seat Incumbent[2]
1990	14	15	62	7	90%	44	64%
1992	38	7	48	5	91%	26	49%
1994	17	18	44	19	70%	27	43%
1996	17	14	62	5	93%	34	51%
1998	15	25	51	7	88%	23	40%
2000	13	9	73	3	96%	46	61%
2002	18	22	55	3	95%	30	52%
2004	15	16	64	3	96%	33	49%
2006	9	27	58	4	94%	35	56%
2008	13	17	65	3	96%	41	60%
2010	16	18	59	5	92%	24	38%

[1] Percentage of seats won by the incumbent when they are challenged by an opponent.
[2] Percentage of seats won by the incumbent by 60+% of the votes when challenged by an opponent.
Source: Authors' calculations from data maintained by the Washington Secretary of State (2011).

legislature, all bills can originate in either chamber, but they must be sponsored by a sitting legislator. By tradition, the house and senate rotate which year they are the originators of the state budget. The actual legislative process is a mixture of formal procedures and informal practices. The formal process is defined by the state constitution, house rules, senate rules, joint rules, and Reed's Parliamentary Rules. The informal process is one born of consensus, what legislators can agree upon, and what priorities legislators decide to address. The legislative process is open to the public, except for party caucus meetings. The legislative process is designed so that the majority party makes the decisions and the minority gets to be heard. The intent is for any bill to get a thorough review by legislators, staff, lobbyists, and citizens (WSL 2011b).

The political party with a majority of seats in a legislative chamber controls how that chamber is organized and what bills move forward. Washington's legislative process is organized around committees. With hundreds of bills introduced each legislative session there is no way for every legislator to have full understanding of each bill. It is within the committee structure that bills are reviewed prior to reaching the floor of its chamber of origin. Committee members are generally specialized and become experts in their respective policy areas. Bills are then usually assigned to the committee having jurisdiction over the policy area included in the bill. It is in the committees where much of the legislative work is done: research, hearings, investigations, and bargaining. The committee chairs also have significant influence concerning the fate of a bill, since chairs control meeting agendas and determine whether a bill will receive a hearing and whether to put the bill to a committee vote (WSL 2011e).

For a bill to become a law, it must be approved in both houses. This is generally a long and complicated process where bills can easily be delayed or derailed. There is also a specific process that a bill must go through by specific deadlines, outlined in the legislative calendar, or it can no longer move forward. Even with a slot on the legislative calendar, there is still a crush of business on the floor of each house at the end of session and the session generally adjourns before all the bills that cleared their respective committees and received clearance from the rules committee are brought to a vote. Most bills dropped during a session die in their chamber of origin, and only the bills that pass both houses go to the governor for signature or veto. It is important to know that in some sense no bill submitted during a session is completely dead if not passed out of committee. Any bill can be brought to the floor and be acted upon whatever its prior fate—and such "resurrections" have been witnessed by veteran legislators frequently enough so that a common refrain heard in Olympia during legislative sessions is that "no bill is really dead until sine die" (Seeberger 1997).

Parties and the Legislature

Even though Washington's voters are not required to register by party, the state legislature is organized by party caucuses. It is the legislative party caucuses that set the legislative agenda, assign leadership positions, and determine the rules of legislative deliberation. Each party's caucus elects leaders for their respective chamber. These leaders set the party's goals and strategies, and they work to maintain party unity throughout the legislative session. The leadership maintains influence by controlling partisan staff and committee assignments, including committee chair assignments, as well as managing the purse strings of campaign resources. Because of these assets, party affiliation is generally the principal determinant of how a representative votes on many bills.

The central leadership position in the house is that of the Speaker, who assigns committee members and chairs the powerful Rules Committee, which makes decisions on which bills proceed to the floor for debate and determines what limits are placed on that debate. Other house leaders include the majority leader, majority party caucus chair, majority floor leader, and majority whip. The minority party maintains a corresponding leadership structure. The senate leadership structure is similar to that of the house, except that there is no comparable senate leader with as much influence as the Speaker has in the house. Given that the senate is a smaller body by half, the influence of each individual senator is far greater than that of a member of the house where the leadership is much more in command. The most powerful committee positions are associated with the Rules Committee in both chambers. Also highly esteemed are positions on the Ways and Means (budget), Transportation (public works projects), and Judiciary (law and order issues) committees. The caucus leaders work to coordinate the pace and substance of legislation as it moves through each body. The party that controls a majority in a chamber chairs every committee and holds a majority of each committee's seats. The majority party has control over the progress of all bills in its chamber.

Parties, Political Contributions, and Legislative Campaigns

The political parties actively work to maintain or establish party control by winning campaigns. Washington parties are recruiters of legislative candidates and represent a major source of campaign funds for state legislators. Party leaders' control over campaign finances also helps to maintain caucus discipline. In 2010, political parties constituted the top nine contributors to state legislative campaigns. Of the top 50 contributors to legislative races in 2010, 19 were associated with the political parties and contributed $2,873,132. The remaining 31 top contributors were not associated with a political party, and combined contributed $1,736,180 (see Table 4).

Given the gathering of such funds by the parties and the contributions made by interested groups, what can be said about the amount of money being spent by legislative candidates to gain their elective offices? Fortunately, Washington has quite robust laws regarding campaign contributions and expenditures, and these transactions are duly reported to the state's Public Disclosure Commission. Table 5 displays this information for the 2008 election.

In 2008, the legislative race winner's average spending was about $120,000. On average, candidates spent about $97,000 each in 2008. Clearly, running for the state legislature requires a substantial campaign war chest, and the political parties are willing to support most candidates who subscribe to the party's platform and priorities. What can be said of the total amount of money being invested in legislative races over time? Is that amount increasing in recent decades? Table 6 displays information on that specific question.

It is clear that the amount of money being spent on legislative races is increasing at a substantial rate. In some cases the expenditures are unprecedented. In 2010, for example, two candidates spent almost $1 million on a contested senate seat in Spokane. Also in 2010, 14 legislative districts had candidates whose combined expenditures were over $500,000. Interestingly, four of these legislative districts were jurisdictions listed among the top six districts for legislative turnover. Overall, districts with higher legislative turnover rates attracted candidates who spent more money on their campaigns than did districts with a lower legislative turnover rate, as might be expected.

Table 4

Top Contributors to Washington State Legislative Races, 2010

Top Eight Contributors Associated with a Political Party

Senate Republican Campaign Committee	$356,933
House Democratic Campaign Committee	$349,757
Washington State Republican Party	$345,419
Senate Democratic Campaign Committee	$258,221
House Republican Organization Committee	$253,635
Washington State Democratic Central Committee	$196,859
House Democratic Campaign Committee II	$185,891
House Republican Organization Committee II	$157,425

Top Eight Contributors Not Associated with a Political Party

WA State Dental PAC	$108,900
Premera Blue Cross	$107,650
Puget Sound Energy	$101,200
Muckleshoot Indian Tribe	$86,900
Puget Sound Pilots	$75,600
Physicians Insurance	$69,600
Victims Advocates	$61,400
Credit Union Legislative Action Fund	$59,200

Source: WSPDC 2011b.

Lobbying the Legislature

Interest groups seek to influence the legislative process both through their contributions to campaigns and through expenditures made to support professional spokespeople who offer testimony in public hearings, propose amendments to pending legislation, negotiate with the spokespeople of other interests in search of collaborative proposals to make to legislators, and speak directly with legislators concerning their group's positions on pending legislation. Lobbyists are in constant search for ways to connect with legislators and communicate their message, during legislative sessions and between sessions alike. Lobbyists use face-to-face meetings, send emails, provide drafts of sample bills, testify at committee hearings, mobilize grassroots supporters, and in a variety of other ways take an active part in the legislative process. A key role is providing information requested by legislators and legislative staff.

The better-funded interest groups maintain a permanent presence in Olympia, with office space, full-time staff, and contracted professional lobbyists who

Table 5

Average Election Campaign Expenditures, 2008
(General election candidates only)

Senate		
Winners	26	$166,627
Losers	17	$87,998
Incumbents in contested seats	16	$182,049
Challengers in contested seats	16	$101,267
House of Representatives		
Winners	97	$107,124
Losers	68	$58,282
Incumbents in contested seats	54	$84,239
Challengers in contested seats	54	$36,653

Source: WSPDC 2008.

Table 6

Cost of Legislative Races 1992–2008, Primary and General Election

Year	Total spending	# of candidates
1992	$13,465,718	343
1994	$10,516,508	316
1996	$13,064,270	313
1998	$12,994,043	267
2000	$16,257,511	303
2002	$15,847,338	258
2004	$18,904,376	257
2006	$18,850,341	216
2008	$21,306,132	244

Source: WSPDC 2008.

interact with legislators on an ongoing basis. Washington requires paid lobbyists to register with the state's Public Disclosure Commission and to report their expenditures. The most active lobbying is done for interests that are directly affected by state laws and regulations. Interests such as healthcare providers, public utilities, the insurance industry, builders and the construction trades, real estate brokers, and the banking industry are dramatically affected by state policies and regulations. The amount spent on lobbying activities by these interests has increased from slightly more than $30 million in 2001 to over $50 million during the latter part of the decade; lobbyists reported expenditures for 2010 exceeding $55 million. Figure 6 and Table 7 display lobbyists' reported expenditures for the past decade and list the major interests involved in lobbying the state legislature.

Concluding Observations and Concerns

A question was posed early in this chapter regarding the ironic disconnect between the objective quality of the Washington State legislature and its undeniably poor standing among the public. The state of Washington gets high marks in comparison to other states for its legislative commitment to managing for results and support for public management training (Ingraham, Joyce, and Donahue 2003); its legislative track record is exemplary with respect to avoidance of particularistic bills (Gamm and Kousser 2010); its legislative page and internship programs are widely considered among the best managed and most well organized in the country (WSL 2011c); its nonpartisan committee staff is broadly viewed as the envy of most other state legislatures (Lundin 2007); its provision of access to TVW for the creation of a video archive of virtually all significant committee hearings is considered most exemplary (TVW 2011); and its creation of the Washington State Institute for Public Policy in 1983 as a nonpartisan research unit for the provision of well-researched and timely information to the legislature (Maki and Lieb 2009) is broadly considered best practice behavior for state legislatures. Why, then, do the citizens of Washington have little knowledge of these hard-earned distinctions and maintain such low regard for their state legislature?

Figure 6. Annual Registered Lobbyists' Expenses

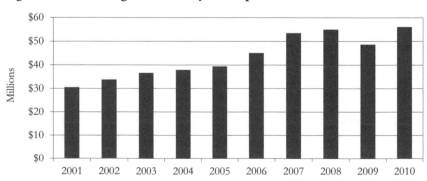

Source: WSPDC 2011a.

Table 7

Most Active Interest Groups' Lobbying Expenditures in 2010

Unions (teachers, public employees, trade)	$8,320,928
Healthcare industry (providers, practitioners, products)	$7,930,403
Business (general)	$5,350,993
Local governments (and tribes)	$4,291,465
Utilities (electric, telephone, water, waste)	$4,133,881
Construction industry	$3,379,897
Insurance industry	$2,894,189
Transportation (air, land, marine)	$2,054,423
Food, beverage, and lodging industry	$1,851,860
Education	$1,572,947
Financial industry	$1,562,326
Manufacturing firms	$1,272,598
Real estate and development interests	$1,230,904
Agriculture	$1,182,148
Law and justice (lawyers, prosecutors, judges)	$1,119,331
Social Services	$1,109,715
Environment	$895,272

Source: WSPDC 2011b.

We have argued here that at least part of the reason for the clear disconnect between the quality of state legislative practice and public perceptions is that public perceptions are mediated through an expectation of civility filter (Loomis 2000; Fiorina and Abrams 2009). As Speaker Foley has noted with regard to the U.S. Congress, the civility practiced in the legislative setting is critical to maintaining the respect of citizens for their elected officials. Incivility and hyper-partisanship among legislators begets loss of trust in legislators and the chambers in which they serve (Mutz and Reeves 2005; Ahuja 2008). It is quite likely that the same dynamics of citizen opinion and attitude formation noted by Speaker Foley with regard to Congress are at play with respect to the Washington State legislature. The fact that legislators who have served over the course of the past 20 years and registered lobbyists with long service in legislative advocacy sense that civil norms are in decline in the Washington State legislature suggests that this decline may be coloring public perceptions to a far greater extent than are the positive things being done in the legislature to promote the public interest. The fact that legislative campaigns are attracting so much political contribution funding, and the fact that interest groups are spending so much money to influence legislation, raises understandable suspicions about special interests exercising undue influence in the state legislature (Salka 2009).

Early warnings issued to Washington State legislators by former state sena-tor Eugene Prince deserve particular mention here. An agricultural engineering graduate of Washington State University in 1952, his political career in Olympia began in 1959 when he was invited to work as a bill clerk during the legislative session. He rose to the rank of assistant chief clerk of the house in 1963 and committee clerk on redistricting in 1965. Members of the house elected him sergeant-at-arms in 1967, and he served on the house staff until elected to the chamber from the 9th legislative district in 1980. He served in the house for 12 years, the last six as Republican caucus chair. In 1992 he was elected to the senate, where he served until he decided to leave office in 1999. When that decision was announced, the *Seattle Times* (1999) editorialized on January 10 in a column entitled "A Prince of a Guy" the following: "The Senate as an institution will lose something precious and increasingly rare. The gentleman from Thornton in eastern Washington is a moderate Republican, a throwback in the best sense of the term. The part-time lawmaker, farmer, and philosopher always understood public service is more important than rabid partisanship." The *Seattle Times* went on to observe in its editorial: "Prince believes passionately in principled debate, bipartisan lawmaking and talking—always talking—with disparate sides on an issue…Lawmakers of both parties admire Prince for his collegial style… People who care about smart government and civility in lawmaking will miss Gene Prince, a genuine class act."

In an interview done with Chris Peck (1999), then-editor of the *Spokesman-Review*, shortly after announcing his decision to step down from his senate seat, Prince placed a special focus on the norm of civility. Peck wrote the following in this regard in the January 10 editorial: "Prince recalls with most regret the lost rules on civility." He observed that when he came to the legislature in 1959 every freshman legislator attended a basic course in political civility at the invitation of the "old pros" in the chamber. Prince is quoted as saying, "New freshmen legislators learned two rules, right off. First, if you don't respect the other person's opinion, he won't respect yours. Second, what goes around comes around." Prince added, "That's all gone by the wayside. Everybody wants to be a dictator, just tell other people what to do. I don't know how you hold a free society together if you can't keep people civil to one another and working together." Prince favored a return to open debate in caucus, legislative rules that ensured a meaningful role for minority party legislators, and the practice of having genuine respect for one's fellow legislators in both parties.

Sadly, Prince's admonishments were not heeded. A decade later a similar column written in the *Vancouver Columbian* in April 2010 by Don Brunell, then-president of the Association of Washington Business, echoed many of the same themes of loss and concern for the future. In a guest column regarding a veteran Democratic representative stepping down from office entitled "Kessler's Civility Will Be Missed in State Legislature," Brunell (2010) acknowledged her many accomplishments in office, but gave special attention to how Lynn Kessler conducted herself while in office and while exercising influence in legislative leadership roles. He observed the following: "Most of all, we need to continue the civil and respectful way she approached governing, working with the opposition and listening. We don't need, nor do we deserve, the bitterness, political gaming and disrespect so prevalent today…We need more Lynn Kesslers in public service."

In a state with easy access to the ballot, the door is wide open for single-issue advocates, extreme partisans of left and right leanings, populists, and minimal government groups to challenge policies and programs that emerge from the complex but open process of legislative deliberation. The increasingly frequent use of the initiative for just this purpose serves as evidence of the adverse outcomes associated with a public that is unaware of the legislature's qualities and is increasingly suspicious of its motives. The nationwide discourse taking place on civility and democracy has a particular pertinence to our discussion of the Washington State legislature (Hamilton 2005). We might hope that this discourse will affect the behavior of Washington's legislative community in a favorable way, and that the many strengths and assets of the Washington State legislature will be realized by citizens who are currently largely unaware and unimpressed. Perhaps the examples set by Senator Prince and Representative Kessler will once again become the norm of the Washington State legislature and the citizens of the state will accord their legislature greater respect and support as a consequence.

References

Ahuja, Sunil. 2008. *Congress Behaving Badly: The Rise of Partisanship and Incivility and the Death of Public Trust.* Westport, CT: Praeger Publishers.

Benjamin, Francis, and Nicholas Lovrich. 2010a. "Legislative Service Project: Legislators." wsu.edu/psychology/research/labs/politicalinteraction/Legislative%20Service%20 Survey%20Full%20Summary%20Legislator.pdf.

_____. 2010b. *Washington State Legislative Service Project: Legislative Interns, Full Report.* Pullman: Division of Governmental Studies and Services.

Benjamin, Francis, Nicholas Lovrich, and Craig Parks. 2011. "Civility in the Washington State Legislature: Documentation of a Decline over Time." Paper presented at the Annual Meeting of the Western Political Science Association in San Antonio, April 21–23.

Brooks, Deborah J., and John G. Geer. 2007. "Beyond Negativity: The Effects of Incivility on the Electorate." *American Journal of Political Science* 51(1): 1–16.

Brunell, Don. April 20, 2010. "Washington View: Kessler's Civility Will Be Missed in State Legislature." *Vancouver (WA) Columbian.* columbian.com/news/2010/apr/20/kesslers-civility-will-be-missed-in-state-legislat.

Fiorina, Morris P., and Samuel J. Abrams. 2009. *Disconnect: The Breakdown of Representation in American Politics.* Norman: University of Oklahoma Press.

Gamm, Gerald, and Thad Kousser. 2010. "Broad Bills or Particularistic Policy? Historical Patterns in American State Legislatures." *American Political Science Review* 104(1): 151–70.

Hamilton, Lee. 2005. "A Responsibility for Civility." *State Legislatures* 31(1): 19.

Ingraham, Patricia W., Philip G. Joyce, and Amy Kneedler Donahue. 2003. *Government Performance: Why Management Matters.* Baltimore: Johns Hopkins University Press.

Loomis, Burdett A. 2000. "Civility and Deliberation: A Linked Pair?" Chapter 1 in *Esteemed Colleagues: Civility and Deliberation in the U.S. Senate.* Washington, D.C.: Brookings Institution Press, 1–12.

Lundin, Steve. 2007. *The Closest Governments to the People: A Complete Reference Guide to Local Government in Washington State.* Pullman: Washington State University Division of Governmental Studies and Services.

Maki, Janie, and Roxanne Leib. 2009. *Washington State Institute for Public Policy: Origins and Governance.* Document No. 09-06-4101. Olympia: Washington State Institute for Public Policy.

Mutz, Diana C., and Byron Reeves. 2005. "The New Videomalaise: Effects of Televised Incivility on Political Trust." *American Political Science Review* 99(1): 1–15.

National Conference of State Legislatures. 2011. ncsl.org.

OFM (Office of Financial Management). 2011. "Legislative District Population 2000." ofm. wa.gov/pop/census2000/sf3/stcopl/LegDensity02_C.xls.

Peck, Chris. January 10, 1999. "This Prince Sees Royal Pain in Legislature." Editorial. *Spokesman-Review* p. B5.

Salka, William M. 2009. *Reforming State Legislative Elections: Creating a New Dynamic.* Boulder, CO: Lynne Rienner Publishers.

Seattle Times. January 10, 1999. "A Prince Of A Guy." Editorial. *Seattle Times.* community. seattletimes.nwsource.com/archive/?date=19990110&slug=2937918.

Seeberger, Edward D. 1997. *Sine Die: A Guide to the Washington State Legislative Process.* Seattle: University of Washington Press.

SurveyUSA. 2010–2011. "Washington Approval Rating State Legislature." Clifton, New Jersey. surveyusa.com/50StateTracking.html.

TVW: Washington State Public Affairs TV Network. 2011. tvw.org.

Washington Secretary of State. 2010. "Elections & Voting: Index to Initiative and Referendum History and Statistics: 1914–2010." sos.wa.gov/elections/initiatives/statistics.aspx.

_____. 2011. "Elections & Voting: Previous Elections." wei.secstate.wa.gov/osos/en/PreviousElections.

WSL (Washington State Legislature). 2009. "Legislative Information Center: Members of the Legislature 1889–2009." leg.wa.gov/History/Legislative/Documents/Members_of_Leg_2009.pdf.

_____. 2010. "Washington State Legislative History Chart Book: A Selected Graphical and Tabular History of the Washington State Legislature." leg.wa.gov/History/Legislative/Documents/ChartBook2010.pdf.

_____. 2011a. "Legislative Information Center: Facts about the Members of the Legislature." leg.wa.gov/LIC/Documents/Statistical%20Reports/FACTS_ABOUT_THE_MEMBERS_OF_THE_LEGISLATURE.pdf.

_____. 2011b. "Legislative Information Center: Guide to Lawmaking: Washington State Senate Civic Education Program." leg.wa.gov/LIC/Documents/EducationAndInformation/Guide%20to%20Lawmaking.pdf

_____. 2011c. "Legislative Intern Program." leg.wa.gov/internships.

_____. 2011d. "Washington State Constitution." leg.wa.gov/LawsAndAgencyRules/Pages/constitution.aspx.

_____. 2011e. "Washington State Legislative Committees." leg.wa.gov/legislature/pages/committeelisting.aspx.

Washington State Redistricting Commission. 2011. redistricting.wa.gov.

WCCSEO (Washington Citizens' Commission on Salaries for Elected Officials). 2010 "Legislator Salaries Nationally." www.salaries.wa.gov/documents/LegSalariesNationally_000.pdf.

WSPDC Washington State Public Disclosure Commission. 2008. "2008 Election Financing Fact Book." www.pdc.wa.gov/home/historical/pdf/FactBook2008.pdf.

_____. 2011a. "Lobbyist Expenditure Summary Reports." www.pdc.wa.gov/public/page2.aspx?c1=0&c2=100.

_____. 2011b. "Public Disclosure Commission Legislative Races." www.pdc.wa.gov/public/legmap/legmap.aspx.

CHAPTER 12

Public Finance and Budgeting in Washington State

Jenny L. Holland and Steve Lundin

Introduction

THE STATE OF WASHINGTON faced numerous economic challenges in the first decade of the new millennium, and 2011 proved to be no different. The state continued to experience a prolonged budget crisis with back-to-back biennial budget shortfalls—no doubt residual effects of the national economic downturn that occurred between December 2007 and June 2009. In 2010, the state legislature closed a $2.8 billion budget shortfall for the 2009–2011 biennium by increasing taxes, reducing funding for statewide programs, and using federal bailout funds. The state faced yet another budget shortfall, this time an estimated $5.1 billion, for the 2011–2013 biennial operating budget that was addressed in the 2011 regular legislative session and subsequent special session.[1] Options were more limited, however. Federal funds were no longer available, and Washington voters passed a statewide initiative that requires a two-thirds vote in the legislature in order to raise taxes—a formidable limitation.

In this chapter we address the recent economic challenges and provide an overview of public financing and budgeting in the state of Washington. This chapter includes discussion of the latest demographic trends and economic conditions, as well as state and local government finances. Discussion will also address Washington State's political environment, initiative and referenda powers, and subsequent influences on the budgeting process. Finally, the chapter concludes with a discussion of overall state budget priorities in an update on budgeting decisions.

Demographic Trends and Economic Challenges in Washington

Over the past two decades, Washington State has experienced one of the fastest population growth rates in the country. In 2000, Washington was ranked 15th nationwide in terms of population growth; the latest trends reported in 2009 indicate the state moved up two spots to 13th (U.S. Census Bureau 2011b). This rapid growth rate is similar to projections earlier in the decade predicting an estimated population of over 6.5 million people by 2010 (LeLoup and Herzog 2004); the latest statistics indicate the population is above 6.7 million people as of the 2010 decennial census (U.S. Census Bureau 2011a). Washington State will receive an additional U.S. congressional seat based on these numbers. Consistent with trends in 2000, the number of young persons under age 18 and adults over age 65 continue to increase in the state. As of 2009, children under 18 comprised 23.6 percent of the state's population, while adults over 65 increased to 12.1 percent.[2] These two age cohorts are of particular importance to state finances and budgetary allocations, as are college students (ages 17-22) and the most elderly population (ages 85 and over) because an increase in any of these age groups presents new demands on the economy through education and social services. Interestingly, the number of live births in Washington increased between 2000 and 2010, an increase from approximately 80,000 per year to 90,000 per year, translating into increased demand on the K-12 educational system by 2012 (OFM 2010).

Along with nearly every other state, Washington experienced serious economic challenges as a result of the national economic recession that occurred between December 2007 and June 2009 (National Bureau of Economic Research 2010) and the ensuing slow economic recovery. In fact, Washington was among 46 states that faced budget shortfalls in 2010. Of those, Washington was among the top 14 facing the largest shortfall as a percent of the FY 2011 budget, an estimated 22.5 percent gap. These developments were clearly residuals from the state recession that occurred between February 2008 and July 2009 (WSERFC 2010), and largely paralleled national trends. To deal with these shortfalls, the legislature made difficult decisions in 2010, including raising taxes to generate more revenue. However, the tax increases were eliminated by state voter initiative action in the November 2010 general election. Despite the recession's official end, the state economy was still not fully recovered as of 2011. The economy instead made a modest turnaround following 2009 and began to grow slowly only in some sectors.

Additionally, Washington was one of 18 states to cut services in each of the following five categories to help close its budget gap: public health, elderly and disabled, K-12 and early education, higher education, and the state workforce (Johnson, Oliff, and Williams 2011). The state, which places K-12 education as a high priority in its constitution, suspended a program to reduce class size and provide professional development for teachers, and reduced a program to maintain 4th grade student-to-staff ratios by $30 million, indicative of the dire need to save money in even the most protected areas. In addition to the effects on elementary and secondary education, the two largest universities in the state, the University of Washington (UW) and Washington State University (WSU) were affected as well. The legislature reduced UW's state funding by 26 percent over the 2009–2011 biennium and WSU increased tuition by nearly 30 percent over the next biennium to offset a similar deep cut in its allocation. In fact, the state cut direct aid to the six public universities and 34 community colleges by 6 percent, which will inevitably lead to additional tuition increases, administrative cuts, layoffs, furloughs, and other cuts (Johnson, Oliff, and Williams 2011).

In addition to the operating budget, the 2009–2011 transportation budget was not free from challenges. The transportation department experienced a budget reduction of nearly $23 million, though many essential projects were still funded. This included continuation of regional projects including the Alaskan Way Viaduct Replacement project, Tacoma I-5 HOV project, State Route 520 Bridge Replacement, and the I-90 Snoqualmie Pass project, among others (Washington State Department of Transportation 2011). Several other highlights included maintenance of existing tolling operations and rail operating levels, and the building of several new ferry boats. Additionally, 2010 capital budget highlights included new state projects (such as affordable housing for low income residents) that will cost an estimated $450 million in total (La Corte and Woodward 2010). However, in the November 2010 general election Washingtonians voted down $500 million in bonds that would have created energy-efficient renovations for public schools (Secretary of State 2010).

Washington State has typically experienced low unemployment rates compared to the rest of the country. Throughout the 1990s and early 2000s, unemployment hovered at or around 4.0 percent. But unemployment was on the increase in mid-2007 and consistently remained in the range of 8.0 to slightly above 9.0, indicating that the state is not immune to trends in the national economy. During this time period, the state government implemented policies to help slow the effects of the recession. In August 2008, Governor Gregoire implemented a hiring freeze, which caused a decrease in the state workforce of 1,400. Then in January 2009, the state replaced the hiring freeze with a cap on the number of budgeted positions in each state agency, which is expected to result in 2,600 additional public jobs lost.

The health of the state economy is largely impacted by Boeing and Microsoft, Washington's top two private sector employers. Despite significant job losses in both the aerospace and software industries throughout the state, both experienced an upswing after Washington's recession. The airline industry recovered relatively quickly, which positively impacted Boeing's future outlook—in 2010 alone the company received orders for 530 aircraft, more than three times the number of orders in 2009 (WSERFC 2011a). In 2010, Boeing added production projects to its growing list of future projects, and by early 2011, the backlog grew to more than seven years worth of production, a favorable development for both Boeing and the state. The software industry lost over 2,500 jobs in 2009, many of them at Microsoft. However, nearly half of those positions have been gained back and the overall outlook of the software industry is expected to continue to improve in the next few years (WSERFC 2010). These latest developments in both industries greatly impact the health of finances in the state and subsequent budgeting decisions.

State Finances

A description of Washington State's finances necessarily involves discussion of the relationship between two broad classes of revenues—general state revenues and other revenues constitutionally restricted to funding highway purposes—and the three different budgets—operating, transportation, and capital.

State Revenues

Taxes

Washington is one of several states that does not impose net income taxes on people or businesses. However, taxes generate the largest portion of revenue for the state and are divided into two classes: a variety of different excise taxes and property taxes.

Excise taxes comprise the majority of tax revenue for the state, which include sales and use taxes and business taxes, and also a number of minor excise taxes.

Washington State imposes a retail sales tax at a rate of 6.5 percent on the selling price of most tangible personal property and some services sold in the state, and a use tax of 6.5 percent on the value of personal property acquired out of state but used in state (Revised Code of Washington 82.08.020 and 82.12.020). Sales and use tax receipts are general revenues and are the largest source of state tax revenues. See Figure 1 for a comparison of Washington's state and local taxes compared to national averages.

In an effort to raise more revenue, the legislature passed sales tax increases on convenience items such as bottled water and canned soda in early 2010; however, in November 2010 voters passed Initiative 1107[3] which repealed the tax increases and also passed Initiative 1053, which states that taxes may only be increased if approved by a two-thirds vote of both chambers, or if a ballot proposition authorizing the increase is approved by a simple majority of state voters (RCW 43.135.034). The measure also established that fees may only be imposed or increased by a simple majority in both chambers (RCW 43.135.055).

Washington State also imposes a business and occupation (B&O) tax on most non-utility business activities in the state and a utility tax on most utility business activities in the state (RCW 82.04 and 82.16). B&O taxes are imposed on the gross receipts of the business operations in the state at rates varying from 0.138 percent to 1.8 percent, depending on the type of business. Utility taxes

Figure 1. FY 2008 Per Capita State and Local Taxes

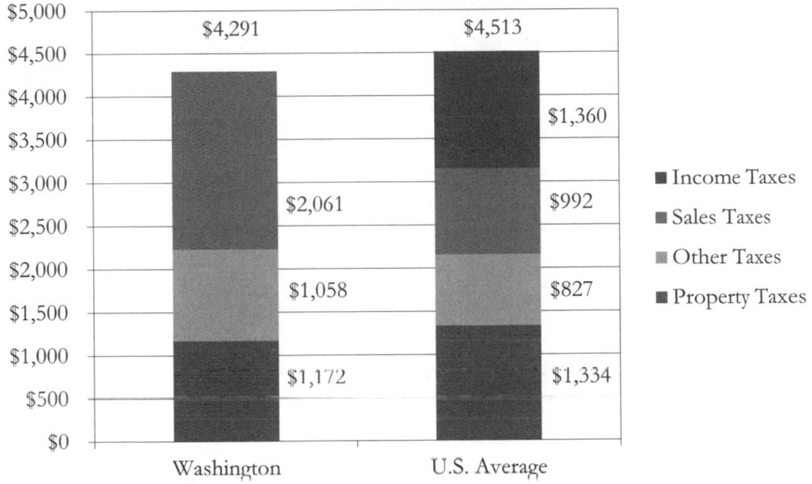

		Income Taxes
		Sales Taxes
		Other Taxes
		Property Taxes

Source: SWMC 2011b, 17.

are imposed on the gross receipts of the utility business operations in the state at rates varying from 0.642 percent to 5.029 percent, depending on the type of utility business. B&O taxes and utility taxes are general state tax revenues and are the second largest source of state tax revenue.

In addition, Washington State imposes a variety of other excise taxes, generating less significant amounts of revenue than the two primary sources of tax revenue. This includes various liquor taxes, tobacco taxes, real estate excise taxes, and insurance premium taxes, which are general state tax revenues. Washington State also imposes excise taxes on motor vehicle fuels, but Article II, Section 40 (Amendment 18), of the Washington State constitution restricts the use of motor vehicle fuel taxes to "highway purposes." The fuel tax is imposed at a rate of 37.5 cents per gallon.

The state's property taxes are subject to a variety of constitutional and statutory restrictions.[4] RCW 84.52.043 limits the rate of the state property tax levy to no more than $3.60 per $1000 "of assessed value adjusted to the state equalized value in accordance with the indicated ratio fixed by the state department of revenue." RCW 84.52.043 also restricts receipts from this property tax levy to the support of the common schools. The state distributes its property tax receipts, along with other moneys, to school districts. Article VII, Section 2 of the state constitution established the 1 percent limit on the combined rate of most property tax levies imposed in Washington. Under this limitation, the combined rates of regular property taxes imposed by most taxing districts in any year may not exceed 1 percent of the value of taxable property. This limitation does not restrict voter approved excess property tax levies imposed by any taxing district or non-voter approved property tax levies imposed by port districts and public utility districts. Initiative 747 was approved by state voters in 2001 establishing a similar sounding, but much different, restriction on property tax levies called the 101 percent levy lid. Under this limit, regular property taxes imposed by a taxing district in any year may not exceed 101 percent of the highest amount of regular property taxes imposed by that taxing district in any of the most recent three years (not including regular property taxes imposed on increases in assessed valuation from new construction). This measure has had the effect of reducing property tax rates below the maximum statutory rates.

Other Revenues

The state receives additional revenue from imposing fees on a wide variety of its operations, issuing licenses, and through intergovernmental revenue (essentially money from the federal government).

Indebtedness

Washington State also receives revenue from the sale of bonds, but incurs an obligation to repay both the principal and interest on this debt for the term of the bonds. Basically, state debt is issued to finance capital projects. However, the state is authorized to issue short-term certificates of indebtedness to meet temporary deficiencies in the treasury to provide money for appropriations made by the legislature.

Three Biennial State Budgets

The Washington State legislature enacts three biennial budgets—operating, transportation, and capital—every two years. The total of these three budgets was $74.8 billion for the 2009–2011 biennium, including a $60.6 billion operating budget, $8.7 billion transportation budget, and $5.6 billion capital budget (SWMC 2011b).

Operating Budget

The operating budget is the largest of the three budgets and appropriates moneys for the general, day-by-day, non-transportation operations of the state agencies, public institutions of higher education, and for the support of the common schools (though a small amount is included for capital purposes). The operating budget expends general fund moneys and amounted to approximately $60.6 billion for the 2009–2011 biennium, or 81.0 percent of the total funds appropriated by the legislature for that biennium (SWMC 2011b).

State voters approved Initiative 601 in 1993, which limited in part the state's authority to make expenditures from the general fund during any fiscal year by more than a fiscal growth factor without voter approval (RCW 43.135.025);

Figure 2. State General Fund-State Revenues, 2001–2011 (in thousands of dollars)

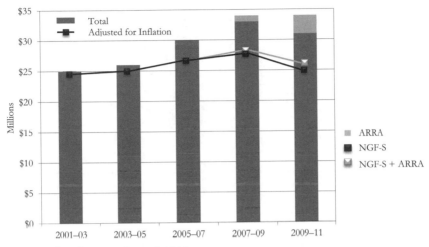

Source: Office of Program Research 2011.

subsequent budgets have not exceeded the fiscal growth factor. State general fund revenues for fiscal year 2009 consisted of taxes ($12,790,799 or 57%), other revenues ($1,340,298 or 6%), and federal grants in aid ($8,325,957 or 37%). State general fund revenues increased for each biennium since 2001, with the exception of the 2009–2011 biennium (see Figure 2).

Transportation Budget

The transportation budget is the second largest budget and appropriates moneys for both operating and capital transportation purposes. Highway purposes are defined as constructing and maintaining state highways, county roads, city and town streets, highway-related activities of the Washington State Patrol, auto ferries, and support facilities such as sidewalks and trails on highways. Non-highway transportation purposes include transit, passenger and freight rail, vanpools, and commute trip reduction programs. Revenues constitutionally dedicated to highways, along with other non-constitutionally-dedicated revenues, are appropriated by the transportation budget. Moneys obtained from the issuance of bonds, payable from revenues dedicated to highways, are appropriated in the transportation budget for capital highway purposes. This budget amounted to approximately $8.6 billion for the 2009–2011 biennium, or 11.8 percent of the total funds appropriated by the legislature for that biennium (SWMC 2011b). State transportation fund revenue sources for the 2009–2011 biennium were as follows:

Figure 3. 2009–2011 Biennial Transportation Budget Fund Sources

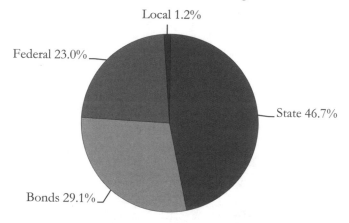

Source: Senate Transportation Committee 2010.

Funds included under "State" in Figure 3 above primarily include fuel taxes, licenses, fees, and tolls, but also include a relatively small amount of local moneys provided to the state to perform and manage construction projects for various local governments. About one third of the state fuel tax collections are distributed to counties, cities, and towns and do not appear in the state transportation budget. State fuel taxes constitute 61.2 percent of the moneys shown as state revenues.

Capital Budget

The capital budget is the smallest of the three budgets and appropriates moneys for the state's non-transportation capital projects, including state office buildings, higher education buildings, prisons and juvenile rehabilitation facilities, parks, public schools, some housing, and other capital facilities and programs. This budget amounted to approximately $3.4 billion for the 2009–2011 biennium, or 4.7 percent of the total budget (SWMC 2011b). About half of the capital budget is financed by the issuance of debt and the other half is financed from dedicated accounts, trust revenue, and federal funding (Washington State Treasurer 2011, A-19). Separate legislation, authorizing bonds to be issued to finance the capital budget, is enacted in concert with the capital budget.

Debts and Obligations

Washington State has various debts it is required to retire and various obligations it must fund. Article VIII, Section 1 of the state constitution includes an indirect limitation on the amount of general indebtedness the state may incur.

This limitation restricts the annual payments of principal and interest on most general indebtedness to no more than 9 percent of the mean of the general state revenues for the three preceding fiscal years. Legislative authorization of general indebtedness retired by principal and interest payments that are subject to this restriction requires a three-fifths vote of both chambers of the legislature.

There are a number of exceptions to the constitutional limitation on expenditures made to retire most forms of general obligation debt. These include expenditures made to retire general indebtedness payable from the state excise tax on motor vehicle fuel or license fees, to retire general indebtedness payable from the permanent common school fund, to retire voter-approved general indebtedness of school districts, and to retire revenue bonds payable solely from revenues derived from the ownership or operation of facilities or projects. In addition, payments made to retire general indebtedness are not subject to the constitutional limitation if a ballot proposition authoring the debt for a distinct work or object is approved by a simple majority of state voters.

As of June 30, 2010, Washington State had a total outstanding indebtedness of approximately $16.6 billion, of which approximately $10.4 billion was payable from general revenues and approximately $6.2 billion was payable from state motor vehicle fuel tax revenues (Washington State Treasurer 2011, A-30). The state may enter into financing contracts on behalf of local governments for the local government to acquire real or personal property, if the local government has taxing powers and pledges its full faith and credit to make required debt payments (RCW 39.94). The state incurs a contingent liability to make debt payments for the local government if the local government is unable to make the debt payments. State moneys that are distributed to the local government are used by the state to make the debt payments if the local government fails to make the payments. It appears from practice rather than declared law that any state payment of these financing contracts are not subject to the constitutional limitation on expenditures made to retire most general obligation debt.

Washington State administers a number of retirement systems for various groups of state and local government employees, and two of these retirement systems have unfunded liabilities (Washington State Treasurer 2011, A-48). The Washington State Supreme Court has held that pension obligations are to be treated as retirement annuities, and payments for these obligations are not subject to the constitutional limitation (*State ex rel. Wittler v. Yelle* 1965).

Washington State operates a number of insurance-type programs for various purposes and has obligations to make certain payments under these programs. These obligations are not general obligations, and payments of these obligations are also not subject to the constitutional limitations. The programs include a worker's compensation program, a self-insurance program for the state's tort liability, and various public employee benefit programs such as a medical, dental, and life insurance plans.

Washington's most significant obligation is found in Article IX of the state constitution, which says that the state's paramount responsibility is to "make ample provision for the education of all children," an obligation that has been treated very seriously by state leadership in recent years. The mandate to prioritize K-12 public education in Washington likely comes from the well-known Doran Decision handed down by the state supreme court in 1978, a ruling which recognized and established this paramount responsibility (*Seattle School District v. State* 1978).[5] As part of this mission, the state is required to fund basic education but is allowed to define what basic education means. Several recent lawsuits have been filed challenging the adequacy of funding provided by the state under this mandate. King County Superior Court Judge John Erlick ruled on February 4, 2010, that the state is not meeting this responsibility (*McCleary v. State* 2010). The case is on appeal at this writing. It should be noted that this obligation is not a general obligation, and payments made to meet this obligation are also not subject to the constitutional limitation on expenditures made in order to retire most general obligations.

State Voter Action

State voters approved Initiative 601 in 1993 creating a statute that limits annual general fund budget increases, restricts the ability of the legislature to increase taxes, and reinforces a previous voter initiative that precluded the legislature from imposing unfunded mandates on local governments (RCW 43.135). The state general fund budget has never exceeded the limitations established by Initiative 601. The portion of Initiative 601 restricting the ability of the legislature to increase taxes was altered and reapproved by voters a number of times, the most recent of which was Initiative 1053, approved by state voters in 2010. Under these restrictions, the state may increase taxes if approved by a two-thirds vote of both chambers or if a ballot proposition authorizing the increase is approved by a simple majority of voters.

Washington voters approved ballot measures in 1979 and again in 1993 limiting the ability of the state to establish unfunded mandates on local governments.[6] Under these ballot measures the legislature is precluded from imposing the responsibility for new programs on political subdivisions, or increasing the level of service required under existing programs, without fully reimbursing the political subdivisions. The term "political subdivision" is not defined. Initiative 601 also added a new requirement that the cost of any state program transferred to local governments reduces the dollar amount of the program from the state expenditure limit. Literally, these provisions provide for a "double hit" on the state for transferring a state program to local governments since the state is required to fully reimburse local governments for the costs of these programs and the expenditure limitation on the state is reduced by the cost of the program that is transferred.

Local Governments

A large number of local governments exist in Washington State. They are classified as counties, cities and towns, and different types of special purpose districts.
Thirty-nine counties, 281 cities or towns, and about 1,700 special purpose
districts exist in the state.[7] Local government financing authority and budgeting
requirements vary widely across the different types of local government and is
based upon specific statutes that provide for those particular local governments.

Finances

Potential finances for a local government include moneys obtained from imposing taxes, imposing rates and charges for providing services and facilities, imposing special assessments to finance facilities and services, and receiving transfers
or grants of money from other governments. The Washington State constitution
does not grant inherent taxing authority to local governments, though they may
impose taxes if authorized to do so by state law. Statutes grant different types
of local governments the authority to impose various taxes, but not all types of
special purpose districts are authorized to impose taxes.

Cities and towns possess the broadest array of taxing authority among the
local governments in Washington State—they are authorized to impose various
property taxes, sales and use taxes, business license taxes, and a variety of minor
excise taxes. Counties possess the next broadest array of taxing authority. They are
authorized to impose various property taxes, sales and use taxes, and a variety of
minor excise taxes. However, unlike cities and towns, counties are not authorized
to impose business license taxes. A number of different types of special purpose
districts are authorized to impose property taxes, and a few different types of
special purpose districts are authorized to impose voter-approved sales and use
taxes to finance public transportation services and facilities.

Statutes granting local governments the authority to impose taxes normally
(1) define the base upon which the taxes are imposed and (2) establish the
maximum rate of taxes based on the type of tax. The major exception to this
rule is the authority of cities and towns to license businesses and occupations
and to impose business license taxes for both regulatory and revenue generating
purposes; this was authorized by the first state legislature in 1890. Initially, this
authority did not limit the maximum rate of business license taxes that could
be imposed and did not define the base upon which these taxes were imposed.
However, legislation was enacted in 1982 limiting the maximum rate of these
taxes, unless local voters approve a higher rate (RCW 35.21.706, 35.21.710,
35.21.711, and 35.21.870).

Counties, cities and towns, and some types of special purpose districts,
receive grants from the state and federal governments. These grants may be in
the form of regular, on-going distributions of money or one-time distributions

of money for a specific purpose. School districts receive the vast majority of their finances from the state but also receive some federal financing and impose voter-approved property tax levies.

Tax revenues for many local governments decreased during the 2008–2009 recession. This was especially acute for various types of special purpose districts that provide transit services and facilities, and for cities and towns that relied more heavily on sales and use tax revenues than do counties. Sales and use tax receipts tend to vary directly with the economy.

Property tax revenues, however, remained fairly steady during the economic downturn. This was due, in part, from the artificial reduction in property tax rates that has occurred under the 101 percent levy lid.[8] As a result, the rate of regular property taxes imposed by a taxing district is gradually reduced since property values tend to increase by more than 1 percent each year.

Budgeting Requirements

Local government budget requirements vary widely throughout the state. Different requirements exist for local governments to adopt budgets, and those requirements are found in separate statutes. This includes counties, cities and towns, school districts, fire protection districts, port districts, and public utility districts.[9] Statutory requirements do not exist for a few major types of special purpose districts to adopt budgets, including water districts, sewer districts, public transit benefit areas, and metropolitan park districts. However, these special purpose districts typically adopt annual budgets.

Budgeting details differ widely depending on the type of local government. Differences principally include the following:
- Procedural requirements for adopting a budget;
- Details for what must be included in a budget; and
- Whether or not the local government is expressly required to make its expenditures following an adopted budget.

Budget requirements have considerable detail, minimal detail, or no detail depending on the type of local government. Normally, local governments adopt annual budgets for a calendar year; counties, cities, and towns are allowed to adopt either annual or biennial budgets.[10]

There is no constitutional provision that requires local governments to adopt balanced budgets. However, as a practical matter, local governments nearly universally adopt balanced budgets. Article VIII, Section 5 of the state constitution limits the dollar value of general indebtedness that any local government may incur as a percentage of the taxable property within its boundaries. In most instances, statutes reduce these indebtedness limitations below the constitutional levels. Almost all local governmental indebtedness is issued for capital purposes, but it is possible for local governments to issue indebtedness for operating purposes as well.

Washington's Political Environment and Its Influence on State Budgeting

The Democratic Party has dominated most elections for state and federal offices in Washington over the most recent decades. In fact, Washington has become increasingly reliable as a blue state in U.S. presidential elections; the state has voted for the Democratic candidate in all elections of the past two decades, voting for Clinton in 1992 and 1996, Gore in 2000, Kerry in 2004, and Obama in 2008. Interestingly, the gap between the Republican and Democratic vote in the last presidential election was much larger than in previous years; in 2004 the state voted 53 percent for Kerry and 46 percent for Bush, and in 2008 voted 58 percent for Obama to McCain's 41 percent (although turnout must also be considered as a factor in any comparison). One observation is certain—the state was much more solidly Democratic in its statewide vote in 2008.

Despite the remarkably reliable Democratic vote for president, political parties in Washington are more competitive in state-level elections, and thus Democratic dominance has not been absolute. The race for governor in 2004 was the state's closest on record, with Democrat Christine Gregoire and Republican Dino Rossi vying for Washington's highest elected office. The election was so close that a total of three recounts were conducted; in the end, Gregoire won by an extremely close margin of 133 votes. Many Republicans objected to the vote-counting process and argued that votes were cast by illegal immigrants and convicted felons in King County. In a highly anticipated rematch, Gregoire and Rossi faced each other again in the 2008 gubernatorial race. Polls leading up to November pegged the contest as neck-and-neck, but Gregoire was reelected by a comfortable margin of 53 percent to 47 percent (Washington State Elections and Voting 2010). The close gubernatorial races in 2004 and 2008 demonstrate the large base of support for each party, although the Democrats typically enjoy the competitive edge.

Consistent with the close gubernatorial statewide vote, the legislature often experienced a close partisan split in the late 1990s and early 2000s, when the house of representatives had an equal number of Democrats and Republican members in 1999, 2000, and 2001, and the Democrats had a slim two-seat majority in 2002. Since then, Democrats have maintained control of the legislature. Democrats had large majorities in the house (61-37) and senate (30-18) after the 2008 general election, but these majorities were reduced in the house (56-42) and senate (27-21) after the 2010 general election. Retention of control by the Democrats in both houses of the Washington State legislature contrasts with the loss of control by Democrats in the United States House of Representatives in the 2010 general election.

The retention of power by the Democrats in the state legislature proves interesting, especially given the events of the 2010 session in which the legislature was faced with closing a $2.8 billion shortfall in the operating budget for the 2009–2011 biennium. Although the Democrats enjoyed a large majority in both chambers, the legislature was unable to close the gap by the end of the 60-day regular session and subsequently entered into a 30-day special session. Resolving the budget shortfall proved difficult and lasted into the final hours of the special session. The legislature finally closed the gap through a series of program cuts and revenue enhancements that included new taxes, cancelation of some tax incentives, spending cuts, and use of federal aid. Because resolving the budget gap required an extended session, Republicans hoped to capitalize on what they termed the Democrats' inability to get things done and the "irresponsible" tax increases on items such as bottled water and soda pop. Although Democrats maintained control of both houses after the 2010 general election, voters rejected Democratic fiscal efforts by approving Initiative 1107 repealing the tax increases and Initiative 1053 reinstating the requirement that the legislature may only increase taxes by a two-thirds vote of both chambers, which the legislature had suspended.

Initiative and Referendum Powers

State voters obtained the power of initiative and referendum on state matters with the approval of Amendment 7 to the Constitution in 1912. Amendment 7 only applies to state statutes and does not allow voters to initiate constitutional amendments (*Gerberding v. Munro* 1998; *Local 587 v. State* 2000). Amendment 7 only applies to state statutes and does not grant local voters initiative and referendum powers over county, city, or town ordinances.[11]

Initiative Powers

State voters possess two different initiative powers in Washington State. Initiatives to the people are the most common type of initiatives. These measures are submitted directly to state voters for their approval or rejection at a state general election, thus bypassing the legislature.

Initiatives to the legislature are measures that are submitted to the legislature for its consideration. In this case, three options are available to state legislators:
- The legislature may enact the measure as submitted and a ballot proposition is not submitted to state voters.
- The legislature may adopt alternative measures. Both the original measure contained in the initiative and the alternative proposals are submitted to voters at the next state general election. Voters decide which, if any, measure should be adopted.
- The legislature may do nothing with the measure, in which case the measure is submitted to voters at the next state general election.

The initiative petition states whether the measure is an initiative to the people or an initiative to the legislature. An initiative petition must have the valid signatures of state voters equal in number to at least 8 percent of the number of votes cast for governor at the last gubernatorial election prior to submission of the petition. The petition for an initiative to the people must be submitted at least four months before the state general election at which it shall be submitted to voters. The petition for an initiative to the legislature must be submitted at least 10 days before the regular session of the legislature.

State voters approved Amendment 72 to the state constitution in 1981. This amendment allowed the legislature to amend an initiative or referendum measure by a two-thirds vote in both chambers during the two-year period after voters had approved the measure. Prior to this amendment, the legislature was not allowed to amend an initiative or referendum measure during the two-year period after voters had approved the measure. The legislature has always possessed the authority to amend an initiative or referendum measure by a simple majority vote of both chambers two years after voters had approved the measure.

Referendum Powers

Voters in Washington State possess two different referendum powers. First, there are referendum bills that are measures the legislature, by its own action, submits directly to voters for their approval or rejection. Second, there are referendum measures that are initiated by voter petition subjecting a bill, or portion of a bill, enacted by the legislature to voter approval or rejection. Referendum action may not be taken on emergency bills that are necessary for the immediate preservation of the public peace, health or safety, or support of the state government and its existing public institutions. A petition for a referendum must have the valid signatures of state voters equal in number to at least 4 percent of the number of votes cast for governor at the last gubernatorial election prior to submission of the petition. In addition, the petition must be submitted no later than 90 days after the final adjournment of the session in which the bill was enacted. The bill, or portion of the bill, is delayed until considered by voters at the next state general election.

Measures That Have an Impact on State Finances

A number of initiative measures have had significant impacts on state finances in Washington. Among these measures is Initiative 64, passed in 1932, which established the "40 Mill Limit" on the cumulative rate of property taxes imposed in any year, with property valued at 50 percent of its true and fair value.[12] The 40 mill limit was readopted by either initiative or referendum action of state voters every two years until 1940. Voter approval of an initiative or referendum providing for the 40 mill limit precluded the legislature from altering the limitation since, at that time, the legislature could not amend an initiative or referendum for two years after its approval by voters. The 40 mill limit was added to the state constitution with the approval of Amendment 17 in 1944. State voters approved Amendment 55 in 1972 changing the 40 mill limit to a 1 percent limitation, with property valued at 100 percent of its true and fair value.

State voters approved Initiative 601 in 1993 limiting annual general fund budget increases and restricting the ability of the legislature to increase taxes. The portion limiting increased taxes was altered and reapproved by voters a number of times afterward.

State voters approved Initiative 1053 in 2010 reestablishing the limitation on the legislature prohibiting increasing taxes unless approved by a two-thirds vote of both chambers or a simple majority of voters. Some critics of this measure argue that super-majority voting requirements for the legislature may only be established in the state constitution and may not be made by statutory law, including initiative action. Article II, Section 22 of the state constitution provides that legislation is enacted by a simple majority vote of the elected members of both houses approving the measure. However, it should be noted that the constitution includes some express exceptions to this simple majority voting rule, but not a provision requiring a two-thirds vote of both chambers to impose or increase taxes.[13]

The State Budget Process

Washington is one of 20 states (Snell 2011) operating under a biennial or two-year budget schedule. Each biennium has two fiscal years running from July 1 of one year through June 30 of the following year. A biennium is described as, for example, the 2011–2013 biennium, which runs from July 1, 2011 through June 30, 2013. As mentioned, the Washington legislature enacts three biennial budgets—an operating budget, a transportation budget, and a capital budget—as well as periodic supplemental budgets altering the biennial budgets. See Figure 4 for an overview of the budget development process.

Washington operates with balanced budgets—which essentially means that borrowed moneys are not used for operating expenses. However, the state borrows and expends these borrowed moneys for capital purposes. Although the state constitution does not require the state to adopt a balanced budget, statutory law establishes a budget allotment procedure that indirectly provides for "balanced budgets." Under this budget allotment procedure, budgets, expenditures, and projected revenues are closely tracked and the governor is required to make across-the-board reductions in expenditures from a fund or account if a cash deficit in the fund or account is projected (RCW 43.88.110(7)). However, another option exists if a short-term budget shortfall exists where the state may issue short-term "certificates of indebtedness" to meet "temporary deficiencies in

Figure 4. Overview of Washington State Budget Process

	Timeline of Budget Decisions (2011–13 Biennium)		
Formulation of the governor's budget	State agencies prepare budget requests and submit them to the Office of Financial Management. ⬇ The governor reviews the requests and makes decisions about what goes in the governor's proposed budget.		July 2010– December 2010
Legislative action on the budget	⬇ The legislature reviews the governor's budget, develops its own budgets, and approves revenue bills. The budget is signed or vetoed by the governor.		January 2011– April 2011
The Biennium Begins			*July 2011*
	⬇ Agencies execute the enacted budget		July 1, 2011– June 30, 2013
Supplemental budgets	The 2011–13 biennial budget may be adjusted in the 2012 and 2013 legislative sessions.		January 2012– March 2012 January 2013– April 2013

Source: SWMC 2011b.

the state treasury" that are not subject to the indirect constitutional limitation on the extent of state indebtedness (Article VIII Section 1j).

Multiple state entities are involved in the drafting, revising, and implementing stages of the adoption of the biennial budget. The governor, as head of the executive branch, must draft and submit a budget proposal to the legislature for consideration; once floor and committee debate concludes, usually including changes to the governor's budget, the house and senate must pass identical versions of the budget. In addition to these two branches of government, several state agencies that deal with finance and budget issues are involved in the development of the biennial budget and subsequent supplementary budgets. The Office of Financial Management (OFM) is the most involved agency in this process; it works closely with the governor's office in preparing the executive budget proposals, works closely with state agencies to record and justify budget requests, and is also responsible for maintaining Washington's statewide accounting systems (OFM 2011b; OFM 2011a). Additionally, the Economic and Revenue Forecast Council, created in 1984 by the state legislature, is an independent, nonpartisan agency designed to oversee the preparation and approval of the official state economic and revenue forecasts. The governor and OFM then use these forecasts as the basis of the state budget proposals (WSERFC 2011b).

The governor is required by law to propose biennial budgets that the legislature then considers. The governor's budget proposals are released in December of even-numbered years prior to the start of a regular legislative session in January of odd-numbered years. Submission of these budgets is the result of efforts starting earlier in the year. In even-numbered years, the OFM issues budget instructions to state agencies in May, and agencies have several months before they must submit official budget proposals to the governor's office in August. Early that fall, the OFM and governor review the requests, and usually the OFM assists the governor with this process, formulating the expected budget total needed for each agency. In odd-numbered years, mid-way through a given biennium, the OFM assists the governor in processing receipts and budget trends to form a supplemental budget for the following year, the remaining year of the biennium. Budgeting in this way allows the latest economic trends to be taken into account through budget revisions. If needed, the legislature will also adopt additional supplemental budgets within a biennium.

The legislature considers the three budgets submitted by the governor's budget in January, and usually passes these budgets during the regular legislative session (Article III, Section 1, Washington State Constitution). By statute, the budget must be passed and signed by July 1 of the odd-numbered year of the new biennium (RCW 43.88.080). In even-numbered years when supplemental budgets are considered, the negotiation process can be particularly important— and challenging—as was the case for both the 2002 and 2010 supplemental budgets when the state faced significant shortfalls (LeLoup and Herzog 2004). In particular, the 2010 session was especially difficult—by the end of the short session only the supplemental transportation budget had been passed, and the governor had to call a special session that extended the legislative period by 30 days in order to pass the remaining operating and capital budgets. Enacting budgets in 2011 was characterized in much the same way—the legislature passed a transportation budget by the end of the 2011 regular session, but the governor once again had to order a special session to pass the operating and capital budgets.

In the budget formation process in the legislature, the major fiscal committees of both houses (the House Ways and Means Committee and Senate Ways and

Means Committee) are the basic committees that consider the operating budget and the capital budget. The House Transportation Committee and Senate Transportation Committee are the basic committees that consider the transportation budget. The full house or senate considers each budget after it passes out of the respective committee of origin. By tradition, the budgets originate in different houses each biennium. If the house and senate cannot agree on a budget, differences are worked out using an informal process where leaders of both houses resolve the differences or a formal conference committee is convened to resolve the differences. Once a budget is passed by the legislature, the governor has several options. The governor may sign the entire budget bill, or may sign the entire budget bill but veto separate budget items within the bill, or may veto the entire bill. Governors in Washington typically sign the budget bill but veto budget items within the bill (LeLoup and Herzog 2004). However, the use of the gubernatorial veto has specific limitations; the governor cannot eliminate sections of a bill that are smaller than an allocation set by law, and cannot add any funding to programs that have not been approved by the legislature. Of course, the legislature can override a veto by a two-thirds vote of each chamber, but this is not typically a realistic option. The governor can reduce the size of the budget as long as it is across the board (LeLoup and Herzog 2004).

Budget Update

The 2009–2011 total biennial budget was an estimated $74.8 billion, as of the 2010 legislative session. It is comprised of a $60.6 billion operating budget, $8.7 billion transportation budget, and $5.6 billion capital budget (see Figure 5). More than half of the operating budget is composed of the general state fund budget, which usually gets the most attention because it is where the funds for most state programs originate. The revenues to support this budget come from various sources. Taxes were the largest revenue source for the 2009–2011 biennium, comprising 41.0 percent ($30.3 billion) of the revenue used to cover budget expenditures, followed by federal and other grants at 30.6 percent ($22.6 billion), licenses, permits, and charges for services at 17.0 percent ($12.6 billion), borrowing at 8.9 percent ($6.6 billion), and other sources at 2.5 percent ($1.9 billion) (SWMC 2011b).

For the 2009–2011 biennium, the state of Washington faced an operating budget shortfall of $2.8 billion, a gap that was closed in the 2010 legislative session. Potential options included increasing revenues (e.g., increasing taxes) or decreasing budgeted amounts. Another option that could have been used are so-called accounting gimmicks, which artificially increase revenues by counting revenues from the first month of the next biennium as part of the current biennium or artificially reducing budget amounts by not funding a program for the final month of the biennium and pushing the obligation to fund this program

Figure 5. 2009–2011 Biennial Budgets

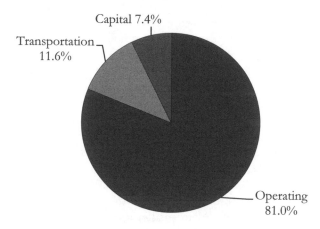

Source: SWMC 2010.

off to the next biennium. The so-called 13th month of revenues within a fiscal year gimmick was used to eliminate a shortfall in a prior budget several years ago.

Revenues may be increased by increasing tax and fee rates, expanding the base on which taxes are imposed, and eliminating tax exemptions. However, as described above, voter initiatives have restricted the ability of the legislature to increase taxes. The budget process became so difficult and heated that a special session was necessary to resolve the budget issues. Consequently, the governor called the legislature into special session to finish the budgets. In the end, the legislature closed the budget gap through a series of new taxes, spending cuts, cancelation of some tax incentives, and the use of federal aid.

The legislature faced an even more difficult task yet again in 2011 for the three biennial budgets, this time to close a forecasted $5.1 billion gap for the 2011–2013 biennial operating budget. Governor Gregoire's proposed operating budget to the legislature, released in December 2010, was a budget characterized by more cuts—this time more severe after the existing cuts that occurred in the previous year (Office of the Governor 2010). In fact, Governor Gregoire's proposed operating budget used the word "terminate" over 80 times, and at the time she admitted that she hated her budget, but emphasized it was a budget "meant for the worst economic downturn in eight decades" (Garber 2010). The general fund proposal for 2011–2013 was particularly unique in that it was smaller than the GSF budget for 2009–2011; since the Great Depression, the Washington State budget has increased each year. For example, the governor's proposed 2011–2013 operating budget is $32.4 billion, a decrease from the $33.6 billion budget for both the 2009–2011 and 2007–2009 biennia.

Closing the budget gap for the latest biennium was a more difficult process the second time around, not only because the proposed budget was smaller but because federal bailout funds used to help states fill their shortfalls in 2010 were not available again, and in the fall midterm elections, Washington voters approved Initiative 1053, sponsored by tax limitation activist Tim Eyman. The initiative requires a two-thirds vote in the legislature for approval to increase taxes, which in practice removes tax increases from among potential options for legislators.

The state makes it very clear that human services and public education (K-12) are its top two spending priorities. In fact, both of these categories comprised just under 60 percent of all funds for the 2009–2011 biennial total operating budget. Much of the money used to finance public education and human services are restricted to those purposes and may not be used for other areas. For example, statutory law restricts receipts from the state's property tax levy to fund public education and other moneys are federal moneys provided to the state for the common schools or various human service purposes and may not be used to fund other purposes. In addition, Article IX, Section 1 of the state constitution states that it is "the paramount duty of the state to provide ample provision for the education of all children." Article II, Section 40 of the state constitution restricts use of the state's motor vehicle fuel taxes to highway purposes. Other expenditures, such as those for higher education and government operations, do not enjoy exclusive claim to particular revenues or enjoy priority status.

To help fill the estimated $5.1 billion shortfall for the 2011–13 biennium, significant budget reductions in the operating budget were achieved from, among others, a $1.2 billion reduction for K-12 education by temporarily suspending two education-related initiatives (I-728 and I-732) for the new biennium, a $535 million reduction for higher education institutions (which in part will be offset by assumed tuition increases), a $344 million reduction from certain public employee pension benefits by eliminating cost of living increases for Plan 1 beneficiaries, a $215 million reduction by eliminating K-4 class size enhancements, a $179 million reduction in K-12 employee salaries, and a $177 million reduction by reducing state employee salaries by 3 percent. These changes were achieved through much debate during a special legislative session, and ultimately the remaining two budgets, both operating and capital, were signed into law by Governor Gregoire on June 15, 2011 (Camden 2011a). The governor vetoed a number of budget items in both the operating and capital budgets, but the dollar values involved in these vetoes were not significant.

Although the 2011–2013 biennial budgets were enacted into law by the end of the 2011 regular and special sessions, the budget numbers are not likely to remain the same for long.[14] At the time of this publication, a special legislative session is being planned due to revenue forecasts of continued budget shortfalls for the 2011–2013 biennium. The September 2011 revenue forecast projected an additional $1.4 billion shortfall and the November 2011 forecast is expected to reflect an even larger shortfall (Camden 2011b). Thus, both the governor and legislature will continue to face considerable economic challenges and difficult budget decisions heading into the January 2012 regular session.

Conclusions

Overall, Washington legislators have had a difficult set of decisions to make since the beginning of the Great Recession several years ago. The main budget priorities of the state, such as K-12 education, have been at the top of the preservation list as budgets have been cut, hiring freezes implemented, and programs eliminated. The substantial role of the voters in the Washington State budgeting process has been evident through the initiative and referendum processes, which has demonstrated not only the strong level of distrust of legislators (see the legislative chapter for evidence of a continuing decline in popular confidence) commonly held by voters throughout the state, but also the significant impact voters have on statewide public policies. For example, voter input continues to shape the tax structure in the state through repeated votes to reject an income tax, thereby reinforcing the heavy reliance on sales taxes as a large source of revenue. Yet voters also overrode the increase in sales taxes passed by legislators, which further highlighted the challenges—and perhaps even the disadvantages—of voter-based initiatives. Only time will indicate what type of long-term impact voter reaction will have on the economy, though in the short-term special sessions certainly seem to be a growing trend.

Endnotes

1. This latest estimated shortfall, $5.1 billion, is current as of March 2011. December 2010 forecasts estimated a $4.6 billion gap, thus a deficit growth of approximately $700 million occurred over the period of several months (Buck 2011).
2. 2010 Population Trends released by the State of Washington Office of Financial Management indicate slightly different estimates with adults over age 65 at 12.4 percent (U.S. Census Bureau 2011a).
3. Initiative 1107 was one of several initiated by Tim Eyman, a well-known political actor in Washington State who has proposed numerous Initiatives to the People in the 2000s (see Brunner 2010).
4. A concise description of property taxation in Washington State is found in Lundin 2007, 617–28.
5. This decision is known as the Doran Decision after Thurston County Superior Court Judge Robert J. Doran who wrote the superior court decision on March 17, 1977, that was appealed to the State Supreme Court.
6. Initiative to the Legislature 62 was presented to the legislature in the 1979 session. The legislature refused to take action on the measure, so the measure was submitted to state voters at the 1979 general election, where voters approved the measure. This measure was amended by the legislature and then revised by voter action as part of Initiative 601 in 1993. These provisions are codified in RCW 43.135.060. A more detailed discussion of unfunded mandates is found in Lundin 2007, 891–94.
7. A comprehensive discussion of local governments in Washington State, including their finances and budgeting requirements, is found in the seminal study of local government in Washington—Lundin 2007.
8. The 101% limitation was established by state voters in 2001 with their approval of Initiative 747. Prior to the approval of I-747, voters had approved a less restrictive limitation on property tax revenue that was known as the 106% limitation. These limitations only apply to what is generally called "regular property tax revenues" and do not restrict the so-called voter approved excess property tax levies. The 101% limitation is codified as RCW 84.55.
9. Counties are required to adopt budgets in RCW 36.40, 36.82.160–36.82.200, 36.56.060, 36.62.180(4), 36.68.060(7), 36.81.130, and 36.92.040. Cities are required to adopt budgets in RCW 35.32A, 35.33, 35.34, 35A.33, and 35A.34. School districts are required to adopt budgets in RCW 28A.505. Fire protection districts are required to adopt budgets in RCW 52.16.030. Port districts are required to adopt budgets in RCW 53.35. PUDs are required to adopt budgets in RCW 54.16.080.
10. Counties are allowed to adopt biennial budgets in RCW 36.40.250. Cities are allowed to adopt biennial budgets in RCW 35.34 and 35A.34.
11. Local voters in Washington State do not possess a constitutional right to general initiative and referendum powers on local matters. However, county voters may obtain the powers of initiative and referendum on county matters by adopting a county charter under Article XI, Section 4 of the state constitution, which includes a provision granting these powers. City voters may obtain the powers of initiative and referendum on city matters in a variety of ways, including adopting a charter under Article XI, Section 10 that includes a provision granting these powers, becoming a code city under Title 35A RCW and providing for initiative and referendum powers, or adopting a commission form of government under RCW 35.17.
12. A *mill* is equal to one-tenth of a cent ($0.001).

13. Article II, Section 1(c), Amendment 72, of the state constitution requires a two-thirds vote of both chambers to amend an initiative or referendum measure for two years after voters approved the measure. Article III, Section 12 of the state constitution provides that the legislature may override the governor's veto of legislation by a two-thirds vote of both chambers. Article VIII, Section 1(h) of the state constitution allows the legislature to contract indebtedness by a three-fifths vote of both houses. Article II, Section 42 of the state constitution provides that a redistricting plan approved by the Redistricting Commission may only be amended by the legislature with a two-thirds vote of both chambers.

14. The following numbers are the latest approximations of the 2011–2013 biennial budget totals at the time of publication. It is important to note that these are not final and are likely to be amended as the budget process continues to move forward. Operating budget $62.1 billion (SWMC 2011a), transportation budget $8.9 billion (Rosbach 2011; Hindery 2011), capital budget $3.8 billion ($1.1 billion in bond funds, $1.7 billion in new appropriation funds, and $1.0 billion in reappropriation funds; House Committee on Capital Budget 2011a and 2011b).

References

Brunner, Jim. April 13, 2010. "Tim Eyman Files Initiatives to Block Tax Increases." *Seattle Times*. seattletimes.com/html/politicsnorthwest/2011596431_tim_eyman_files_initiatives_to.html#loop.

Buck, Howard. March 17, 2011. "Washington State Deficit Grows by Nearly $700 Million." *Vancouver (WA) Columbian*. columbian.com/news/2011/mar/17/washington-state-deficit-grows-by-700-million.

Camden, Jim. June 16, 2011a. "Trying to 'Get Through It,' Gregoire Signs Unpopular Budget." *Spokesman Review*. spokesman.com/stories/2011/jun/16/trying-to-get-through-it-gregoire-signs-unpopular.

———. September 23, 2011b. "Special Session Planned to Cut $2 Billion from State Budget." *Spokesman Review*. spokesman.com/stories/2011/sep/23/special-session-planned-to-cut-2-billion-from.

Garber, Andrew. December 15, 2010. "Gregoire Budget Would Slash Programs, Cut $4 Billion." *Seattle Times*. seattletimes.com/html/localnews/2013685184_budget16m.html.

Hindery, Robin. April 20, 2011. "Wash. Senate Passes $9B Transportation Budget." *Seattle Times*. seattletimes.com/html/localnews/2014830194_apwaxgrtransportationbudget1stldwritethru.html.

House Committee on Capital Budget. 2011a. "Final Bill Report ESHB 1497." apps.leg.wa.gov/documents/billdocs/2011-12/Pdf/Bill%20Reports/House%20Final/1497-S.E%20HBR%20FBR%2011%20E1.pdf.

———. 2011b. "Final Bill Report ESHB 2020." apps.leg.wa.gov/documents/billdocs/2011-12/Pdf/Bill%20Reports/House%20Final/2020-S.E%20HBR%20FBR%2011%20E1.pdf.

Johnson, Nicholas, Phil Oliff, and Erica Williams. February 9, 2011. "An Update on State Budget Cuts: At Least 46 States Have Imposed Cuts That Hurt Vulnerable Residents and Cause Job Loss." Center on Budget and Policy Priorities. cbpp.org/files/3-13-08sfp.pdf.

La Corte, Rachel, and Curt Woodward. April 14, 2010. "Analysis: Scorecard for the 2010 Wash. Legislature," *Seattle Times*. seattletimes.com/html/localnews/2011608406_apwaxgranalysiswinnerslosers.html.

LeLoup, Lance T., and Christina Herzog. 2004. "Budgeting and Public Finance in Washington." In *Washington State Government and Politics*, edited by Cornell W. Clayton, Lance T. LeLoup, and Nicholas P. Lovrich, 189–207. Pullman: Washington State University Press.

Lundin, Steve. 2007. *The Closest Governments to the People: A Complete Guide to Local Government in Washington State.* Pullman: Division of Governmental Studies and Services, Washington State University.

National Bureau of Economic Research. September 20, 2010. Business Cycle Dating Committee. nber.org/cycles/sept2010.html.

Office of Program Research. January 2011. Washington State Operating Budget Briefing Book. leap.leg.wa.gov/leap/budget/WAYS_BriefingBook.pdf.

Office of the Governor. 2010. "Proposed 2011–2013 Budget and Policy Highlights: Transforming Washington's Budget." governor.wa.gov/priorities/budget/press_packet.pdf.

OFM (Office of Financial Management). 2010. "Forecast of the State Population: November 2010 Forecast." ofm.wa.gov/pop/stfc/stfc2010/stfc2010.pdf.

_____. 2011a. "Washington State Budget Process." ofm.wa.gov/reports/budgetprocess.pdf.

_____. 2011b. "What We Do." ofm.wa.gov/about.

Rosbach, Molly. March 25, 2011. "House Approves $8.9 Billion Transportation Budget." *Seattle Times.* seattletimes.com/html/politics/2014602072_transportationbudget26.html.

Secretary of State. 2010. "November 2, 2010 General Election." vote.wa.gov/Elections/WEI/Results.aspx?RaceTypeCode=M&JurisdictionTypeID=-2&ElectionID=37&ViewMode=Results.

Senate Transportation Committee. 2010. "A Citizen's Guide to the Washington State Transportation Budget." leap.leg.wa.gov/leap/budget/citizensguidetranspo2010.pdf.

Snell, Ronald K. April 2011. "State Experiences with Annual and Biennial Budgeting." National Conference of State Legislatures. ncsl.org/documents/fiscal/Biennial Budgeting_May2011.pdf.

SWMC (Senate Ways and Means Committee). 2010. "A Citizen's Guide to the Washington State Budget." leg.wa.gov/Senate/Committees/WM/Documents/Publications/BudgetGuides/2010/CGTB2010Final_3.pdf.

_____. 2011a. "2011–2013 Operating Budget (Including the 2011 Supplemental): Statewide Summary and Agency Detail." leap.leg.wa.gov/leap/Budget/Detail/2011/SOAgencyDetail0603.pdf.

_____. 2011b. "A Citizen's Guide to the Washington State Budget." leg.wa.gov/Senate/Committees/WM/Documents/Publications/BudgetGuides/2011/2011CGTBFinal (rev).pdf.

U.S. Census Bureau. 2011a. "State and County Quickfacts." quickfacts.census.gov/qfd/states/53000.html.

_____. 2011b. "Table 13. State Population—Rank, Percent Change, and Population Density: 1980 to 2009." census.gov/compendia/statab/2011/tables/11s0013.pdf.

Washington State Department of Transportation. 2011. "Washington's Transportation Budget for 2009–2011 Biennium Overview." wsdot.wa.gov/Finance/budget.

Washington State Elections and Voting. 2010. Washington Secretary of State's Office. vote.wa.gov/Elections/WEI/Results.aspx?RaceTypeCode=M&JurisdictionTypeID=-2&ElectionID=37&ViewMode=Results.

Washington State Treasurer. January 19, 2011. "Various Purpose General Obligation Bonds, Series 2011B and General Obligation Bonds, Series 2011T-2 (Taxable)." tre.wa.gov/documents/debt_2011B-2011T-2-POS_FINAL-Complete.pdf.

WSERFC (Washington State Economic and Revenue Forecast Council). 2010. "Economic and Revenue Update." erfc.wa.gov.

_____. January 11, 2011a. "Economic and Revenue Update," www.erfc.wa.gov

_____. 2011b. "About Us." erfc.wa.gov/about.

Court Cases Cited
Gerberding v. Munro, 134 Wn.2d 188, 210 (1998)
Local 587 v. State, 142 Wn.2d 183, 204 (2000).
McCleary v. State, No. 07-2-02323-2 (Wash. Super. Ct. Feb. 4, 2010).
Seattle School District v. State, 90 Wn.2d 476 (1978).
State ex rel. Wittler v. Yelle, 65 Wn.2d 660, 669-671 (1965).

Washington State Statutes Cited
RCW 28A.505
RCW 35.17
RCW 35.21.706
RCW 35.21.710
RCW 35.21.711
RCW 35.21.870
RCW 35.32A
RCW 35.33
RCW 35.34
RCW 35A.33
RCW 35A.34
RCW 36.40
RCW 36.40.250
RCW 36.56.060
RCW 36.62.180(4)
RCW 36.68.060(7)
RCW 36.81.130
RCW 36.82.160–36.82.200
RCW 36.92.040
RCW 39.94
RCW 43.88.080
RCW 43.88.110(7)
RCW 43.135
RCW 43.135.025
RCW 43.135.034
RCW 43.135.055
RCW 43.135.060
RCW 52.16.030
RCW 53.35
RCW 54.16.080
RCW 82.04
RCW 82.08.020
RCW 82.12.020
RCW 82.16
RCW 84.52.043
RCW 84.55

Contributors

David Ammons is the communications director and senior policy advisor to the Office of the Secretary of State and personal advisor to Secretary of State Sam Reed. Previously, he was the longest-serving member of the Capitol Press Corps in Olympia, serving as political writer and statewide columnist for the Associated Press for 37 years, and served as the original host of TVW's *Inside Olympia*.

Andrew Appleton is an associate professor of political science at Washington State University, where he teaches courses in political parties, political participation, and comparative politics. He is currently editor of the international journal *French Politics*.

Francis Benjamin directs the Political Interaction Lab in the Department of Psychology at Washington State University and also serves as a research associate with the Division of Governmental Studies and Services.

María Chávez is an associate professor and chair in the department of political science at Pacific Lutheran University, specializing in American government, public policy, and race and politics. She is author of *Everyday Injustice: Latino Professionals and Racism* (Rowman and Littlefield 2011).

Cornell W. Clayton is the director of the Thomas S. Foley Institute for Public Policy and Public Service and C.O. Johnson Distinguished Professor of Political Science at Washington State University. His research and publications focus on the politics of law and courts. He is currently co-editor of *Political Research Quarterly*.

Jacob Day is a doctoral candidate in the Department of Political Science at Washington State University.

Todd Donovan is a professor of political science at Western Washington University. He has coauthored several books and numerous journal articles on voting, elections, and representation.

Reneé Edwards is a doctoral candidate in the Department of Political Science at Washington State University.

Richard Elgar is the assistant director of the Thomas S. Foley Institute for Public Policy and Public Service and a doctoral candidate in the Department of Political Science at Washington State University.

H. Stuart Elway is president of Elway Research Inc. and has directed research projects for large and small businesses, associations, foundations, public agencies, political candidates, ballot measures, and media outlets. Since 1992 he has published *The Elway Poll*, a nonpartisan, independent analysis of public opinion in the Northwest, and he has been on the adjunct faculty in the graduate public affairs programs at both the University of Washington and The Evergreen State College.

Luis Ricardo Fraga is the associate vice provost for faculty advancement, Russell F. Stark University Professor, director of the Diversity Research Institute, and professor of political science at the University of Washington. His latest coauthored book is *Latino Lives in America: Making It Home* (Temple 2010). His coauthored monograph, *Latinos in the New Millennium: An Almanac of Opinion, Behavior, and Policy Preferences*, is forthcoming with Cambridge University Press in 2012.

Michael J. Gaffney is the acting director of Washington State University's Division of Governmental Studies and Services and the executive director of the Washington State Institute for Criminal Justice. His research interests include negotiation and conflict management, social capital, policing, environmental stewardship, emergency management and disaster response, and governance.

Jenny L. Holland is a doctoral candidate in the Department of Political Science at Washington State University.

Austin Jenkins has been the Olympia-based legislative and politics reporter for the Public Radio Northwest News Network since 2004. He also hosts *Inside Olympia* on TVW and maintains a statehouse blog at waledge.com.

Nicholas Lovrich is Regents Professor Emeritus at Washington State University and Claudius O. and Mary W. Johnson Distinguished Professor of Political Science. He served as director of the Division of Governmental Studies and Services from 1977 to 2010 and was elected by the WSU Faculty Senate to serve as representative to the legislature for six sessions over the period 2002 to 2010.

Steve Lundin is an expert on local government law in Washington State and an amateur historian. He recently retired as senior counsel for the Washington State House of Representatives after nearly 30 years as a career service legislative research staffer.

Carl J. McCurley is the manager of the Washington State Center for Court Research housed in the Administrative Office of the Courts. His research examines various aspects of court and justice administration, including the management of juries, pre-trial practices, assessment and treatment of juvenile offenders, disproportionate minority contact, and outcomes for children and youth in foster care.

Lucas McMillan is a doctoral candidate in the Department of Political Science at Washington State University.

David Nice is a professor of political science at Washington State University. He has conducted extensive research on state and local government. His publications on state public policy in particular are prolific and widely cited. He is the coauthor (with John Harrigan) of multiple editions of *Politics and Policy in States and Communities*.

J. Mitchell Pickerill is an associate professor in the Department of Political Science at Northern Illinois University. Prior to coming to NIU, he was an associate professor of political science at Washington State University. His teaching and research interests include American politics, law and courts, constitutional law and theory, and federalism.

John Pierce is former dean of the College of Liberal Arts at Washington State University and retired executive director of the Oregon Historical Society. He currently is an affiliate research and graduate faculty member in the School of Public Administration and an adjunct faculty member in the museum studies graduate program at the University of Kansas.

Kathleen Searles is an assistant professor at Augusta State University. Her research focuses on American politics, political communication, and political psychology, specifically including campaigns and emotions associated with political communication.

Steven D. Stehr is an associate professor in the Department of Political Science at Washington State University. His primary teaching and research interests are in the areas of public policy and public administration. His research has been supported by the National Science Foundation, the National Research Council, National Academy of Sciences, the Century Foundation, and the Natural Hazards Center at the University of Colorado, Boulder.

Clive S. Thomas is an affiliate professor in the Thomas S. Foley Institute for Public Policy and Public Service at Washington State University. Previously he taught at the University of Alaska in Juneau. He has published extensively on interest groups at the federal, state, and international levels and on political parties and state politics.

Simon Zschirnt is a doctoral candidate in the Department of Political Science at Washington State University.